W9-BXT-651

Ways of Knowing in Science and Mathematics Series

RICHARD DUSCHL, SERIES EDITOR

ADVISORY BOARD: Charles W. Anderson, Raffaella Borasi, Nancy Brickhouse, Marvin Druger, Eleanor Duckworth, Peter Fensham, William Kyle, Roy Pea, Edward Silver, Russell Yeany

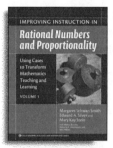

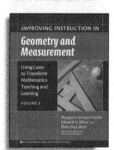

Improving Instruction in Geometry and Measurement

Using Cases to Transform Mathematics Teaching and Learning, Volume 3

Margaret Schwan Smith
Edward A. Silver
Mary Kay Stein

*with Melissa Boston and
Marjorie A. Henningsen*

TEACHERS COLLEGE PRESS

Teachers College, Columbia University
New York and London

The material in this book is based on work supported by
National Science Foundation grant number ESI-9731428 for the
COMET (Cases of Mathematics Instruction to Enhance Teaching)
Project. Any opinions expressed herein are those of the
authors and do not necessarily represent the views of the
National Science Foundation.

Published by Teachers College Press, 1234 Amsterdam Avenue, New York, NY 10027

Library of Congress Cataloging-in-Publication Data

Smith, Margaret Schwan.
    Improving instruction in geometry and measurement / Margaret Schwan Smith,
Edward A. Silver, Mary Kay Stein, with Marjorie A. Henningsen, and Melissa Boston.
        p. cm. — (Using cases to transform mathematics teaching and learning ; v. 3) (Ways of
    knowing in science and mathematics series)
    Includes bibliographical references and index.
        ISBN 0-8077-4531-6 (pbk. : acid-free paper)
        1. Geometry—Study and teaching (Middle school)—United States—Case studies.   I.
Silver, Edward A., 1948–   II. Stein, Mary Kay.   III. Title   IV. Series.

    QA461.S65 2005
    516'.0071'2—dc22   2004055350

    ISBN 0-8077-4531-6 (paper)

    Printed on acid-free paper
    Manufactured in the United States of America

    12   11   10   09   08   07   06   05   8   7   6   5   4   3   2   1

To the teachers in the QUASAR Project—although nearly a decade has passed since our work together ended, we continue to draw inspiration from your work. You were true pioneers in creating instructional environments that promoted mathematics learning for all students. Thank you for sharing your successes and struggles with us. We continue to learn so much from you.

Contents

Acknowledgments

The ideas expressed in this book grew out of our work on the QUASAR Project and have developed over the past decade through our interactions and collaborations with many teachers, teacher educators, and mathematicians. We would like to thank mathematicians and mathematics teacher educators Hyman Bass, John Beem, Nadine Bezuk, Kathleen Cramer, George Bright, Victoria Kouba, John Moyer, John P. Smith III, Judith Roitman, and Orit Zaslavsky, who provided feedback on early versions of the cases. Your thoughtful comments helped ensure that the cases were both sound and compelling.

We are indebted to Victoria Bill whose varied and frequent use of the cases over the past 5 years has helped us recognize the flexibility and power of the cases to promote learning in a range of situations; and to our colleagues Fran Arbaugh, Cathy Brown, Marta Civil, Gilberto Cuevas, Beatrice D'Ambrosio, Skip Fennell, Linda Foreman, Susan Friel, Judith Jacobs, Jeremy Kahan, Rebecca McGraw, Jack Moyer, Kathy Pfaendler, Elizabeth Phillips, and Judith Zawojewski who piloted early versions of the cases, provided helpful feedback, and expanded our view regarding the possible uses of the cases and related materials.

Finally we would like to acknowledge the contributions of Cristina Heffernan who developed the COMET website, provided feedback on early versions of the cases and facilitation materials, and identified tasks in other curricula that corresponded to the cases; Michael Steele who created final versions of the figures and provided technical assistance; Amy Fleeger Hillen who provided feedback on all aspects of the book and assistance in the final stages of writing the facilitation chapters and appendices; and Kathy Day who provided valuable assistance in preparing initial versions of the figures, locating data, and copying materials.

Introduction

There is general agreement that teachers of mathematics in the middle grades face a difficult task. Middle school mathematics teachers may have felt overlooked for many years, as more attention was paid to the secondary school because of demands made by colleges and employers, or to the primary grades because of interesting research-based initiatives related to young children's learning of mathematical ideas. In recent years, however, the spotlight has shown brightly on middle-grades mathematics.

GREAT EXPECTATIONS FOR MIDDLE GRADES MATHEMATICS

Evidence of mediocre U.S. student performance on national and international assessments of mathematical achievement has sparked public and professional demand for better mathematics education in the middle grades. National organizations and state agencies have published guidelines, frameworks, and lists of expectations calling for more and better mathematics in grades K–12. Many of these give specific attention to raising expectations for mathematics teaching and learning in the middle grades. For example, *Principles and Standards for School Mathematics*, published by the National Council of Teachers of Mathematics (NCTM, 2000), calls for curriculum and teaching in the middle grades to be more ambitious. To accomplish the goals of developing conceptual understanding and helping students become capable, flexible problem-solvers, there are new topics to teach and old topics to teach in new ways.

There is some variation across the many policy documents produced in recent years regarding the teaching and learning of mathematics in the middle grades, but the essential message is the same: The mathematics instructional program in the middle grades needs to be more ambitious, setting higher expectations for middle school students and for their teachers. Much attention has been focused on algebra as a component of the middle-grades curriculum that needs to be enhanced; geometry and measurement have received far less attention. Yet, these topic areas are no less important. In fact, geometry and measurement are the topic areas on which U.S. students have exhibited their worst performance on national and international assessments during and since the 1990s.

New Curricular Materials

Some help in meeting higher expectations for mathematics teaching and learning in the middle grades is likely to come from new mathematics curricular materials that reflect more ambitious demands. Some new materials have been developed along the lines suggested by the NCTM standards. In general, these curricular materials provide teachers with carefully sequenced, intellectually challenging instructional tasks that focus on important mathematical ideas and that can be used with students to develop their mathematical proficiency.

New curricular materials with interesting and challenging tasks are undoubtedly crucial to any effort to upgrade the quality of mathematics education, but ambitious materials will be effective only if they are implemented well in classrooms. And good implementation is a nontrivial matter since a more demanding curriculum requires that middle school teachers become effective in supporting student engagement with complex intellectual activity in the classroom. In short, new curricular materials are unlikely to have the desired impact on student learning unless classroom instruction shifts from its current focus on routine skills and instead focuses on developing student understanding of important mathematics concepts and proficiency in solving complex problems.

Improving Teacher Preparation and Continuing Support

The success of efforts to enhance mathematics teaching and learning in the middle grades hinges to a great extent on the success of programs and practices that prepare teachers to do this work and those that continue to support them along the way. Unfortunately, the approaches typically used to prepare and support teachers in the middle grades have well-documented limitations. Many who currently teach mathematics in the middle grades received their initial preparation in programs intended for generalists rather than for mathematics specialists. In such programs too little attention is paid to developing the specific proficiencies needed by mathematics teachers in the middle grades, where the mathematical ideas are complex and difficult for students to learn. Moreover, components of the knowledge needed for effective teaching usually are taught and learned in isolation from one another—mathematics content in a mathematics department, issues of student learning in a psychology (or educational psychology) department, and pedagogical strategies in a teacher education department. Rarely is the knowledge integrated and tied to settings in which it is used by teachers. As a consequence, this fragmented, decontextualized approach often fails to build a solid foundation for effective teaching of mathematics in the middle grades. Compounding the challenge is the fact that most schools and school districts usually are not able to offer the right kinds of assistance to remedy weaknesses in preparation that their teachers may possess.

The current set of challenges facing teachers of mathematics in the middle grades calls for a new approach and new tools to accomplish the work. Just as new curricular materials can assist teachers of mathematics to meet the challenges they face, new resources can assist teacher educators and professional development specialists in their work. What is needed is an effective way to support teachers to increase their knowledge of mathematics content, mathematical pedagogy, and student learning of mathematics in a manner likely to affect classroom actions and interactions in support of improved student learning. The materials in this volume have been designed to help teachers of mathematics and those who prepare and support them in their work to meet the challenges that are implicated in the higher public and professional expectations.

THE MATERIALS IN THIS VOLUME

This volume is divided into two parts. Part I is written primarily for teachers, prospective teachers, or other readers interested in exploring issues related to mathematics teaching and learning. Part I begins with a chapter that describes the use of cases to promote learning (Chapter 1) and includes four chapters (Chapters 2–5) that feature narrative cases of classroom mathematics lessons along with materials intended to engage readers in thinking deeply about the mathematics teaching and learning that occurred in the cases. Part II is written for teacher educators or other professional development providers who work with teachers. Part II begins with a chapter that provides general suggestions for case facilitation (Chapter 6) and includes four chapters (Chapters 7–10) that feature facilitation materials including suggestions for using the case materials in Chapters 2 through 5. Following Part II is a set of appendices that contain sample responses for selected activities presented in the case chapters in Part I. The contents of Parts I and II and the appendices are described in more detail in the sections that follow.

Part I: Using Cases to Enhance Learning

The centerpiece of Part I is a set of narrative cases of classroom mathematics lessons developed under the auspices of the NSF-funded COMET (Cases of Mathematics Instruction to Enhance Teaching) Project. The goal of COMET was to produce professional development materials for teachers based on data (including more than 500 videotaped lessons) collected on mathematics instruction in urban middle school classrooms with ethnically, racially, and linguistically diverse student populations in six schools that participated in the QUASAR (Quantitative Understanding: Amplifying Student Achievement and Reasoning) Project (Silver, Smith, & Nelson, 1995; Silver & Stein, 1996). QUASAR was a national project (funded by the Ford Foundation) aimed at improving mathematics instruction for students attending middle schools in economically disadvantaged communities. The teachers in schools that participated in QUASAR were committed to increasing student achievement in mathematics by promoting conceptual understanding and complex problem-solving.

Chapters 2 through 5 each feature a case and related materials for engaging the reader in analyzing the teaching and learning that occur in the classroom episode featured in the case. Each case portrays a teacher and students engaging with a cognitively complex mathematics task in an urban middle school classroom. By examining these instructional episodes, readers can wrestle with key issues of practice, such as what students appear to be learning and how the teaching supports or inhibits students' learning opportunities. The cases are based on real teachers and events, drawing on detailed documentation (videotapes and write-ups) of classroom lessons and interviews with teachers about the documented lessons. At times, the cases enhance certain aspects of a lesson in order to make a particular idea salient. However, every attempt has been made to stay true to the dispositions and general teaching habits of the teacher who inspired the case. Although the names of the teachers, their schools, and their students have been changed so as to protect their anonymity, the teachers portrayed in the cases agreed to share their stories so that others might learn from their efforts to improve mathematics teaching and learning.

As an opening to Part I, Chapter 1 describes how the case chapters can be used as a resource for professional learning. In each case chapter, readers are guided through a set of coordinated experiences that encourage reflection on, analysis of, and inquiry into the teaching and learning of mathematics in the middle grades. Readers of the cases also are encouraged to use the particular episodes portrayed in the cases as a base from which to generalize across cases, from cases to general principles, and, when applicable, from the cases to their own teaching.

Teachers of mathematics, individuals preparing to become teachers of mathematics, or other readers using this book as learners will want to focus on Part I. A reader might learn from our materials as an individual, but, if at all possible, we encourage interaction with others around the cases. Through careful reading of the cases in this volume, accompanied by thoughtful analysis and active consideration of the issues raised by the cases, readers have an opportunity to learn a great deal about mathematics and the teaching of mathematics. Readers also have a chance to learn about student thinking because examples of student thinking about mathematical ideas are embedded in each case.

Part II: Facilitating Learning from Cases

In Part II, teacher educators or other professional development providers who work with teachers will find materials that are intended to support the use of the cases presented in Part I. As an opening to Part II, Chapter 6 provides a rationale for selecting narrative cases as a vehicle for helping mathematics teachers, prospective mathematics teachers, or others interested in exploring issues in mathematics teaching and learning to develop more thoughtful and ambitious notions about the teaching and learning of mathematics. After a short explanation of how participants learn from cases and what we expect participants to learn from our cases in particular, a description of the kinds of support that can be found in each of the facilitation chapters is provided.

Chapters 7 through 10 provide support for facilitating the cases and related materials presented in Part I. The suggestions in these facilitation chapters are based on our own experiences using the cases. They reflect the lessons that we have learned about what works well and what does not with respect to preparing participants to read the case, guiding their discussion of the case, and designing follow-up activities that will help practicing teachers connect the case experience to their own classrooms.

Each facilitation chapter begins with a short synopsis of the case. The heart of the facilitation chapter is the "Case Analysis" section, which specifies the key mathematical and pedagogical ideas embedded in each case and identifies where in the case those ideas are instantiated. Other sections of the facilitation chapters help the facilitator to prepare for activities related to the case discussions such as the Opening Activity and the follow-up activities.

Part II will be of special interest to case facilitators— those who intend to use the materials to assist preservice and/or inservice teachers to learn and improve their practice, or who provide professional development to other individuals interested in improving mathematics teaching and learning. Case facilitators include any professionals who contribute to improving the quality of mathematics teaching and learning through their work in diverse settings: schools (e.g., teacher leaders, coaches, mentors, administrators); school district offices (e.g., curriculum coordinators, staff developers); regional intermediate units and state agencies; or colleges and universities (e.g., instructors of mathematics or methods courses).

Building on Extensive Research and Prior Experience

As noted earlier, the cases in this volume are based on research conducted in middle schools that participated in the QUASAR Project. A major finding of this research was that a teacher's actions and interactions with students were crucial in determining the extent to which students were able to maintain a high level of intellectual engagement with challenging mathematical tasks (see Henningsen & Stein, 1997). More specifically, the quality and quantity of student engagement in intellectually demanding activity sometimes conformed to a teacher's intentions but often did not (see Stein, Grover, & Henningsen, 1996). Our research also showed that there were consequences for student learning when teachers were able or unable to maintain high intellectual demands (Stein & Lane, 1996). In classrooms where high-demand tasks were used frequently, and where the intellectual demands usually were maintained during lessons, students exhibited strong performance on a test assessing conceptual understanding and problem-solving. In contrast, in classrooms where intellectually demanding tasks were used rarely, or where the intellectual demands frequently declined during lessons, student performance was lower.

This research also identified characteristic ways in which cognitively demanding tasks either were maintained at a high level or declined. For example, tasks sometimes declined by becoming proceduralized; in other cases, they declined due to unsystematic and non-productive student exploration. In the casebook *Implementing Standards-Based Mathematics Instruction: A Casebook for Professional Development* (Stein, Smith, Henningsen, & Silver, 2000), we present six cases that serve as prototypes to illustrate these distinct patterns.

The cases in this volume build on that earlier work in at least two important ways. First, they make salient key instructional factors and pedagogical moves that affect the extent and nature of intellectual activity in classroom lessons involving cognitively complex mathematics tasks. For example, the cases illustrate how a teacher might uncover student thinking and use it productively to encourage students to explain and justify their thinking or to make connections among ideas. Second, the cases extend the earlier work by sharpening the focus on the specific mathematical ideas at stake in the lesson and by explicitly calling attention to ways in which the instructional actions of the teacher support or inhibit students' opportunities to learn worthwhile mathematics. In particular, the cases in this volume draw attention to key aspects of geometry and measurement.

The Appendices

The appendices following Part II contain sample responses for the Opening Activity and for the professional learning tasks in the "Analyzing the Case" section in each of the case chapters (Chapters 2–5). These sample responses are often products from our work in using the case materials in professional development settings. In some instances the sample responses are the work of the participants in the professional development session; sometimes the sample responses were generated by the case facilitator in preparation for using the case. References to the appendices are made in the case and facilitation chapters when appropriate.

Each case chapter in Part I is related to a facilitation chapter in Part II and to a set of sample responses in an appendix. The relationship between case chapters, facilitation chapters, and appendices is as follows:

- The Case of Barbara Crafton: Chapter 2, Chapter 7, and Appendix A
- The Case of Isabelle Olson: Chapter 3, Chapter 8, and Appendix B
- The Case of Keith Campbell: Chapter 4, Chapter 9, and Appendix C
- The Case of Nancy Upshaw: Chapter 5, Chapter 10, and Appendix D

Now that we have described the contents of this book, in the following section we provide a rationale for selecting geometry and measurement as the content focus.

WHY GEOMETRY AND MEASUREMENT?

As noted previously, geometry and measurement have received far less attention than algebra in public and professional conversations and in policy mandates aimed at enhancing the teaching and learning of mathematics in the middle grades. Yet these topic areas are equally important. Geometry and measurement constitute an important part of the middle-grades mathematics curriculum, one in which the poor performance of American students is well documented (Kenney & Lindquist, 2000). A disproportionate focus on algebra in the middle grades could diminish attention to these other important topic areas. Thus, we have devoted this volume to cases that engage readers with a slice of the geometry/measurement content treated in the middle grades—namely, perimeter, area, surface area, and volume.

The teaching and learning of perimeter, area, surface area, and volume often have focused exclusively on formulas to be memorized and applied in routine problems, with far less attention to the development of meaning for the formulas and the associated concepts or to the application of the concepts and skills in nonroutine settings (Bright & Hoeffner, 1993). Thus, it is probably not surprising that students may be confused about the difference between the concepts of perimeter and area (Bright & Hoeffner, 1993; Chappell & Thompson, 1999) or of surface area and volume (Martin & Strutchens, 2000). Students also have difficulty applying their knowledge of these concepts to solve nonroutine problems, as is clear from the fact that only 1 out of every 100 8th-grade students was able to produce a satisfactory solution to an NAEP (National Assessment of Educational Progress) problem that asked students to determine the dimensions of a dog pen with maximum area, given a fixed amount of fencing (Kenney & Lindquist, 2000).

Principles and Standards for School Mathematics (NCTM, 2000) recommends that far more attention be paid to geometry and measurement than typically has been the case in the middle grades. Despite the need for increased emphasis on geometry and measurement, many middle school teachers have limited experience in teaching these topics to their students in any fashion other than one that focuses on memorizing formulas and applying them to solve routine tasks. Moreover, most teachers of mathematics in the middle grades lack personal experience in learning these topics in a nonformulaic manner, and many have had no learning experiences with this content since they were in high school. Thus, teachers of mathematics in the middle grades need some help in order to gain greater proficiency in teaching this important cluster of mathematical ideas.

The materials in this volume are intended to provide some assistance in teaching and learning a particular slice of the geometry/measurement domain. In particular, they help teachers and other readers to focus on how students might develop an understanding of area and volume that is not limited to memorizing and applying standard formulas. Through the exploration of the tasks and analyses of the cases in this volume, readers encounter problem situations that involve measuring perimeter, area, surface area, and volume, and see how students can learn to analyze these situations and generalize relationships between and among attributes, dimensions, and units. The cases also highlight a set of pedagogical moves that support students as they work to make sense of the mathematics without removing the challenging aspects of the tasks.

THIS VOLUME AND ITS COMPANIONS

This is one of three volumes of materials intended to help readers identify and address some key challenges encountered in contemporary mathematics teaching in the middle grades. This volume provides opportunities for readers to delve into and inquire about the teaching and learning of geometry and measurement, particularly in relation to the topics of perimeter, area, surface area, and volume. Two companion volumes focus on other familiar and important mathematics topic domains in the middle grades. These volumes are entitled *Improving Instruction in Rational Numbers and Proportionality: Using Cases to Transform Mathematics Teaching and Learning, Volume 1,* and *Improving Instruction in Algebra: Using Cases to Transform Mathematics Teaching and Learning, Volume 2.* We encourage readers of this volume to use the cases provided in the companion volumes to investigate the teaching and learning of mathematics across a broader spectrum of topics in the middle grades.

The materials in this volume and its companions are designed to be used flexibly. As a complete set, the three volumes provide a base on which to build a coherent and cohesive professional development program to enhance readers' knowledge of mathematics, mathematics pedagogy, and students as learners of mathematics. These materials, either as individual cases, separate volumes, or the entire set of volumes, also can be used as components of other teacher professional development programs. For example, many users of preliminary versions of these materials have included our cases in their mathematics methods and content courses for preservice teachers, in their professional development efforts for practicing teachers, in their efforts to support implementation of reform-oriented curricula, and in their efforts to communicate reform-oriented ideas of teaching and learning of mathematics to school administrators. Our most sincere hope is that they will be used in a wide variety of ways to enhance the quality of mathematics teaching and learning in the middle grades.

Improving Instruction in Geometry and Measurement

Using Cases to Transform Mathematics Teaching and Learning, Volume 3

Part I

USING CASES TO ENHANCE LEARNING

In the Introduction, we provided a rationale for this volume and an overview of the materials it contains. In Part I of this book (Chapters 1–5), we turn our attention to using cases to enhance learning. Chapter 1 introduces this part of the book and describes how to use the case materials presented in Chapters 2 through 5. These chapters are intended to engage teachers, prospective teachers, or other readers in analyzing and reflecting on important ideas and issues in the teaching and learning of mathematics.

1

Using Cases to Learn

In this chapter, we describe the cases presented in this volume and discuss the opportunities for learning they afford. We then provide suggestions for using the cases and related materials for reflection and analysis and, when applicable, as springboards for investigation into a teacher's own instructional practices.

THE CASES

Each of the four cases in this book portrays the events that unfold in an urban middle school classroom as a teacher engages his or her students in solving a cognitively challenging mathematical task (Stein et al., 2000). For example, in Chapter 3, Isabelle Olson (the teacher featured in the case found in this chapter) and her students determine the maximum area of a rectangular rabbit pen (with three sides enclosed by a fixed, but unknown, amount of fence and the fourth side provided by the school building). Since the problem contains no numeric data and there are no suggestions regarding what to attend to in constructing the rabbit pen, students need to identify which aspects of the problem are and are not important, devise and test different configurations of fencing, and prove when they have found the configuration which will yield the maximum area, all of which are features of high-level thinking and reasoning (Resnick, 1987).

Each case begins with a description of the teacher, students, and school so as to provide a context for understanding and interpreting the portrayed episode. The case then presents the teacher's goals for the lesson and describes the unfolding of the actual lesson in a fairly detailed way. To facilitate analysis and discussion of key issues in relation to specific events in

a case, the paragraphs in each case are numbered consecutively for easy reference.

Each case depicts a classroom in which a culture has been established over time by the implicit and explicit actions and interactions of a teacher and his or her students. Within this culture, a set of norms have been established regarding the ways in which students are expected to work. The cases illustrate authentic practice—what really happens in a mathematics classroom when teachers endeavor to teach mathematics in ways that challenge students to think, reason, and problem-solve. As such, the cases are not intended to be exemplars of best practice to be emulated but rather examples to be analyzed so as to better understand the relationship between teaching and learning and the ways in which student learning can be supported.

The cases in this volume have been created and organized so as to make salient important mathematical ideas related to geometry and measurement and a set of pedagogical ideas that influence how students engage in mathematical activity and what they learn through the process. Each of these is described in the sections that follow.

Important Mathematical Ideas

Perimeter, area, surface area, and volume represent important middle school topics that cut across the strands of geometry and measurement. According to *Principles and Standards for School Mathematics* (NCTM, 2000), students need to be able to choose and use appropriate units for the attributes being measured, estimate measurements, and solve problems involving the attributes of two- and three-dimensional shapes. In addition, students need to be able to generalize relationships between and among attributes (e.g., the dimensions of a rectangular prism that maximize surface area for a fixed volume), dimensions (e.g., the possible values of length and width for a rectangle with a fixed perimeter), and units (e.g., the conversion factor between centimeters and square centimeters).

Developing the capacity to solve problems and generalize relationships, however, requires more than memorizing and applying formulas for perimeter, area, surface area, and volume. According to Battista (2003), instructional tasks must provide students with opportunities to construct and represent two- and three-dimensional arrays of objects and to invent, test, and discuss strategies for determining area, surface area, and volume "in a spirit of inquiry and problem solving" (p. 135). Such experiences help establish the structural relationships in a set of objects and build an understanding of the processes and units for measuring length, area, and volume (Schifter, Bastable, Russell, & Woleck, 2002).

The cases feature students working on such tasks. For example, students are challenged to determine the dimensions of a rectangular pen that yield the maximum area; make conjectures regarding the dimensions, surface area, and volume of rectangular prisms built with the same number of cubes; estimate and calculate the number of 1,000-cube blocks and soccer balls that would be needed to fill a room; and to use different representations (e.g., context, diagrams, concrete models, tables, symbolic expressions) to organize, record, and communicate their mathematical ideas. As a collection, the tasks help develop an understanding of attributes that goes beyond the application of standard formulas, make salient the effect of unit size on measurement, and focus on the ways in which making connections between different representations can help students make sense of mathematical ideas.

The teacher featured in a case usually solicits several different approaches for solving a problem so as to help students develop a flexible set of strategies for recognizing and generalizing relationships. For example, in "The Case of Nancy Upshaw" (Chapter 5) we see one group of students determining the number of blocks that would fill their classroom by finding the volume of the classroom (i.e., $V = W \times L \times H$) and then dividing that number by the volume of one big block. Another group began by determining the number of blocks that would fit along each dimension of the classroom and then multiplied to calculate how many blocks would fill the entire room.

Pedagogical Moves

Each case begins with a challenging mathematical task that has the potential to engage students in high-level thinking about important mathematical ideas related to perimeter, area, surface area, and volume (e.g., the surface area of a rectangular prism is minimized when it is shaped as a cube). Throughout each case, the teacher endeavors to support students as they work to make sense of the mathematics, without removing the challenging aspects of the task. This support includes pressing students to explain and justify their thinking, encouraging students to use and connect different representations for problematic situations, and providing students with sufficient time and resources to wrestle with and make sense of emerging mathematical ideas.

As such, each case highlights a set of pedagogical moves that support (or in some cases inhibit) student engagement with important mathematical ideas. For example, in "The Case of Keith Campbell" (Chapter 4) students are asked to determine the volume of rectangular prisms and compare the characteristics of rectangular prisms with the same volume but different surface areas. Mr. Campbell supports his students' learning by using a table to organize data and to aid in discovering patterns and relationships; by having students make connections between the context of the problem (i.e., moon gems), drawings, descriptions based on physical models, and the formula for calculating volume; and by pressing students to provide more thorough explanations of their solution strategies and to clarify ideas presented by others. By orchestrating the lesson as he does, Mr. Campbell advances his students' understanding about the relationship between the shape of a prism and its surface area and helps them build meaning for the volume formula—the ultimate goal of the lesson.

THE CASES AS LEARNING OPPORTUNITIES

Reading a case is a unique experience. Although it bears some similarities to reading other narratives (e.g., the reader has a story line to follow, may identify with the joys and dilemmas experienced by the protagonist, and may end up glad or sad when the story concludes), it differs from other narrative accounts in an important way. Cases are written to highlight specific aspects of an instructional episode in order to stimulate reflection, analysis, and investigation into important issues in teaching and learning. By analyzing the particular ideas and issues that arise in a case, readers can begin to form general principles about effective teaching and learning. Cases can foster reflection on and investigation into one's own teaching and, in so doing, help teachers or prospective teachers continue to develop their knowledge base for teaching. Cases also can help those in administrative roles to gain greater insight into important issues in teaching and learning mathematics.

By reading and discussing a case and solving the related mathematical task, readers can examine their own understanding of the mathematics in the lesson and how the mathematical ideas are encountered by students in the classroom. Through this process, readers can develop new understandings about a particular mathematical idea, make connections that they previously had not considered, and gain confidence in their ability to do mathematics. In addition, readers may begin to develop an appreciation of mathematical tasks that can be solved in multiple ways and allow entry at various levels. Take, for example, "The Case of Isabelle Olson" (Chapter 3). As readers encounter the strategies Ms. Olson's students use to determine that all rabbit pens made with the same amount of fence do not have the same area, they may begin to see for the first time that approaches such as drawing diagrams of different pens, physically modeling the dimensions of the pens, and organizing the data about different pens in the same table can help students to make sense of the problem situation. These approaches serve as first steps in students' development of a generalization that yields the maximum area for a rabbit pen built with any amount of fencing.

Cases also provide the reader with an opportunity to analyze the pedagogical moves made by the teacher in the case. Through this analysis readers are encouraged to investigate what students are learning about mathematics and how the teaching supports that learning. For example, in Chapter 5 Nancy Upshaw's students appear be developing an understanding of volume that goes beyond the ability to find the product of width, length, and height. A deeper analysis requires the reader to account for what Nancy Upshaw does to help her students develop an understanding of the concept of volume.

Finally, cases can provide readers with an opportunity to focus on the thinking of students as it unfolds during instruction and to offer explanations regarding what students appear to know and understand about the mathematics they are learning. Through this process, readers expand their views of what students can do when given the opportunity, develop their capacity to make sense of representations and explanations that

may differ from their own, and become familiar with misconceptions that are common in a particular domain. For example, in reading "The Case of Isabelle Olson" (Chapter 3) readers may see that some students do not realize that area can vary for rectangles with a fixed perimeter (or in this case, pens that are made from a fixed amount of fence). As readers analyze the responses given on the first day by Tommy's group (which was convinced that "if the amount of fencing is the same, then the area will be the same") and consider Ms. Olson's concern about their understanding, they come to realize that the group's confusion is more than a simple incorrect answer. Rather, it represents a well-documented source of confusion for students in the middle grades (Chappell & Thompson, 1999; Kenney & Lindquist, 2000).

Reading and analyzing a case thus can help a teacher or prospective teacher to develop critical components of the knowledge base for teaching—knowledge of subject matter, pedagogy, and students as learners—through the close examination of classroom practice. Although this is a critical step in developing knowledge for improved practice, the payoff of learning from cases is what teachers take from their experiences with cases and apply to their own practice.

USING THE CASE MATERIALS

It is important to note that learning from cases is not self-enacting. Reading a case does not ensure that the reader automatically will engage with all the embedded ideas or spontaneously make connections to his or her own practice. Through our work with cases we have found that the readers of a case need to engage in specific activities related to the case in order to maximize their opportunities for learning. Specifically, readers appear to benefit from having a lens through which to view the events that unfold during a lesson that signals where they might profitably direct their attention. For that reason we have created a set of professional learning tasks that provide a focus for reading and analyzing each case.

In the remainder of this chapter we provide suggestions for using the cases and related materials found in Chapters 2 through 5. These suggestions are based on our experiences in a range of teacher education settings over several years. For each case, we describe three types of professional learning tasks: solving the mathematical task on which the case is based; analyzing the case; and generalizing beyond the case (i.e., making connections to teachers' classroom practices and to the ideas of others).

Although it is possible to read through the cases and complete the accompanying professional learning tasks independently, we recommend working with a partner or, better yet, a group of peers who are likewise inclined to think about and improve their practice. In this way, readers will not only feel supported, but also develop a shared language for discussing teaching and learning with their colleagues.

Solving the Mathematical Task

Each case begins with an Opening Activity that consists of the same mathematical task that is featured in the case (or a similar task). It is important to spend sufficient time solving the task, ideally working through it in more than one way. This is a place in which working with colleagues is particularly advantageous. Different people will approach and solve the tasks in different ways; seeing a variety of approaches will help to enrich the readers' understanding of the mathematical ideas in the task and expand their repertoire of applicable strategies for solving the task.

We have found that it is important to engage with the mathematical task before reading the case. By engaging with the mathematical ideas themselves, whether individually or with the help of colleagues, readers will be primed for and able to recognize many of the solution strategies put forth by students in the case, making it easier to understand and follow students' thinking, identify students' misconceptions, and recognize the mathematical possibilities of the task.

For each of the cases in Chapters 2 through 5, there is a corresponding appendix (A through D, respectively) that provides a set of solutions to the Opening Activity. We encourage the reader to review these solutions after she or he has completed the task, and we encourage readers to try to make sense of and find relationships between the different approaches.

Analyzing the Case

We have found it helpful to focus the reading and analysis of the case by providing a professional learning task (PLT). The professional learning task begins in the "Reading the Case" section of Chapters 2 through 5, with the intention of focusing the reader's attention on some aspect of the teaching and learning that occurs in the case. The analysis continues in the "Analyzing the Case" section as the reader, after reading the case, is asked to ex-

plore the pedagogy in a deeper way, focusing on specific events that occurred in the classroom and the impact of these events on students' learning. For example, in the PLT in Chapter 3, readers initially are asked to identify, by paragraph numbers, pedagogical moves Isabelle Olson made during the lesson. The PLT stimulates a deeper analysis of the case by asking readers, after reading the case, to indicate whether each move on the list served to support or inhibit students' opportunities to engage with the mathematical ideas in the task. For each case, we have identified a specific focus of analysis for the PLT. This focus is intended to highlight what each case can best contribute to the reader's investigation of teaching and learning. For example, in "The Case of Barbara Crafton" (Chapter 2) readers are asked to identify the moves Barbara Crafton made to promote discussion during the lesson, and to indicate how these moves (and the subsequent discussion) may have contributed to students' learning of mathematics. Since the lesson features a debate that is skillfully orchestrated by the teacher, this case provides a unique opportunity to analyze what the teacher did to stimulate and sustain the debate and what impact this appeared to have on students' learning.

Additional questions are provided in the "Extending Your Analysis of the Case" section. These questions focus the reader's attention on specific events depicted in the case and invite the reader to critique or explain what occurred. Readers may want to review the questions and identify one that resonates with their experiences or interests. These questions vary greatly from case to case and represent our best effort to bring to the fore a wider set of issues that might be explored within the context of each case.

The true value of the case analysis is realized when readers share their ideas about the professional learning task with others during a group discussion. It is through these discussions that teachers, future teachers, or other readers of the case will begin to develop a critical stance toward teaching and learning. If there is not an opportunity for a face-to-face group discussion about the case, the reader may want to consult the sample responses to the PLT provided in the appendix that corresponds to the case. Alternatively, new technologies may make it reasonable to conduct a discussion about a case via email or a web-based discussion group.

Generalizing Beyond the Case

Following the analysis of each case, readers are invited to engage in one or more activities in which the mathematical and pedagogical ideas discussed in the case are connected to their own teaching practice (when applicable) or to other related ideas and issues regarding mathematics teaching and learning. In the section entitled "Connecting to Your Own Practice" readers who currently are teaching are provided with opportunities to move beyond the specifics of a case and task and begin to examine their own practice in light of new understandings about mathematics, instruction, and student learning. This process is critical to the transformation of a teacher's practice.

While the specific activities vary from case to case, there are three general types of connections to practice that we recommend: enacting high-level tasks in a mathematics lesson, analyzing one's own teaching, and working on specific issues that were raised during the case reading and analysis. The activities in this section are intended to build upon the reader's analysis of the case and extend this analysis to his or her own classroom. For example, following the analysis of the ways in which Isabelle Olson's pedagogy supported or inhibited students' opportunities to engage with the mathematical ideas in Chapter 3, readers are asked to select one of the moves Ms. Olson made that supported her students' learning and to plan, teach, and reflect on a lesson in which a concerted effort is made to focus on this move. In doing so, teachers can become more aware of the extent to which their actions and interactions influence students' learning opportunities.

In the section "Exploring Curricular Materials" readers are invited to investigate mathematics curricula to determine the ways in which mathematical ideas related to geometry and measurement are developed and the opportunities that are provided for students to think and reason about mathematics. In this section, readers also are encouraged to explore mathematical tasks from other curricula that make salient the mathematical ideas featured in the case.

In the last section of each chapter, "Connecting to Other Ideas and Issues," we identify a set of readings from teacher-oriented publications (e.g., *Mathematics Teaching in the Middle School*) and other sources that elaborate, extend, or complement the mathematical and pedagogical content in the case in some way. The readings report findings from research on student learning (e.g., the Battista article referenced in Chapter 4); present actual activities that could be used in the classroom in a unit on geometry and measurement (e.g., the NCTM *Addenda* or *Navigations* Series referenced in Chapters 2–5); and provide additional lenses through which to analyze a case (e.g., the Rittenhouse article referenced in Chapter 2). In each case chapter, a specific set of suggestions are given regarding how to use the cited material to support the reader's understanding of the case or the ideas and issues that arise from the case.

The remaining chapters in Part I (Chapters 2--5) each feature a case and the related materials intended to engage the reader in analyzing important issues in teaching and learning mathematics. We feel that the suggestions for using the case materials presented in this chapter will allow readers to gain the most from our cases and case materials. We hope that readers find the experience of engaging in the case-based activities rewarding, challenging, and insightful.

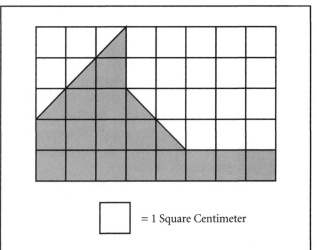

Reasoning About Units for Linear and Area Measure

The Case of Barbara Crafton

This chapter provides the materials to engage readers in reading and analyzing the teaching and learning that occurred in the classroom of Barbara Crafton as she and her 6th-grade students discuss how to determine the area of an irregular figure, first in square centimeters and then in square millimeters. Prior to reading "The Case of Barbara Crafton"—the centerpiece of this chapter—we suggest that you begin by completing the Opening Activity. The primary purpose of the Opening Activity is to engage you with the mathematical ideas that will be encountered when reading the case.

OPENING ACTIVITY

The Opening Activity for "The Case of Barbara Crafton" is shown in Figure 2.1. The first problem in the Opening Activity is the same problem that Barbara Crafton and her students discuss during the lesson. The second problem is the homework problem that Mrs. Crafton assigns at the end of the lesson. By comparing the mathematical ideas in these two problems, you will have the opportunity to explore the relationship between linear and area measurements when converting between units.

Once you have completed the Opening Activity, you may want to refer to Appendix A, which contains some solutions generated by teachers who completed the Opening Activity as part of a professional development experience featuring "The Case of Barbara Crafton." You are encouraged to examine the different solutions provided and to consider the relationship between your solution and those produced by others.

FIGURE 2.1. The Opening Activity for "The Case of Barbara Crafton"

= 1 Square Centimeter

Solve

1. Find the area of the shaded region of the irregular shape shown above in square centimeters and square millimeters.

2. How many square inches are in a square foot? Draw a diagram and write a few sentences to explain how you determined your answer.

Consider

What mathematical ideas do Problems 1 and 2 have in common?

Illustration from *Visual Mathematics Course Guide, Volume II* published by The Math Learning Center. Copyright © 1991 by The Math Learning Center, Salem, Oregon. Reprinted by permission.

READING THE CASE

As you read the case, we encourage you to make a list of the pedagogical moves Barbara Crafton made during the lesson in order to promote discussion in her classroom. (You may want to use a highlighter or Post-it note to keep track of these as you read the case.) For example, you may notice general features of the ways in which Mrs. Crafton manages the discussion (e.g., she provides students with opportunities to talk to one another) as well as more specific aspects of her role in the discussion (e.g., she redefines the poles of the debate by summarizing Charlene's and Larry's thinking).

The list of moves Barbara Crafton made to promote discussion can serve as the basis for a discussion with a colleague who also has read the case, as issues to investigate as you read additional cases, or as starting points for exploration in your own classroom. For example, you might wonder whether students in your class would benefit from engaging in a mathematical debate. We will discuss additional connections to your own practice at the end of the chapter.

THE CASE OF BARBARA CRAFTON

1.   This is Barbara Crafton's third year of teaching mathematics in a manner that stresses conceptual understanding, reasoning, and communication. Along with her colleagues, Barbara has been using a new curriculum that aims to build students' abilities to think, interpret, and analyze, not simply rehearse and repeat. It has not been easy. Not only has she had to change her way of teaching, which previously had emphasized the memorization and application of facts and formulas, but her students have had to undo years of learning regarding how they should act, talk, and think in a mathematics classroom.

2.   Barbara feels that she has made a lot of progress with her 6th-graders since the beginning of the year. Any observer would be struck immediately by the nature of the verbal interactions in her classroom. Students talk nearly as much as the teacher does, and often to one another, as well as to the teacher. In order to set the stage for productive discussion, Barbara has learned the importance of selecting tasks that are at an appropriate level of challenge for her students. She spends a lot of time identifying or designing tasks that are challenging yet build on students' prior knowledge. If tasks are difficult—but not beyond her students' reach—she has found that her students definitely will join in. Barbara also has found that tasks that have visual diagrams to point to and think with are good for stimulating discussion. Barbara enjoys it when students begin talking animatedly to one another, but she has found it to be challenging as well. She really has to know the mathematical content well because she often needs to think on her feet. In addition, she has had to devise a whole new way of interacting with (and subtly steering) the ongoing conversation. She has told her colleagues that she sometimes feels more like an orchestra conductor than a teacher.

3.   An established routine in Barbara's class is for students (sometimes selected by the teacher, sometimes self-selected) to come to the overhead projector to explain their solutions and reasoning for a task that they have worked on with partners or in a small group. The students know that they are expected to explain *how* they arrived at their answers, instead of simply providing the solution. After the presenters have finished, the other students ask them questions, propose different solutions, and/or present alternative ways of coming up with the same solution. If Barbara has chosen good tasks and prepared her students well, these exchanges can be rich in mathematical conjecturing, questioning, and justification. Barbara sees these discussions as opportunities to develop good discussion and argumentation skills and sound mathematical reasoning.

Barbara Crafton Talks About Her Class

4.   This week we started a series of lessons on area measurement using nonstandard and metric units. We began yesterday with the students using an outside wrapper from a stick of gum (unopened) and then a playing card to measure the area of an 8½- by 11-inch sheet of paper. Because the area of one playing card was equal to that of four gum

wrappers, they also were able to measure the area with either wrappers or playing cards and then divide (or multiply) to obtain the number of units that it would take to cover the area with the other. My goal for this introductory lesson was for students to understand the inverse relationship between the size of the unit and the number of units it will take to cover a given area. This idea is important when selecting appropriate units of measurement, and by the end of this unit I hope they will have that concept nailed down—in metric, as well as nonstandard, units.

5.   In today's lesson, we will be going over yesterday's homework assignment in which students were asked to find the area of irregular shapes, first in square centimeters and then in square millimeters. As with the gum wrapper/playing card task, the inverse relationship between the size of the unit and the number of units it takes to express a given area will become evident as students observe that it takes many more square millimeters than square centimeters to express the area of these shapes.

6.   In order to reason through last night's homework, students must recognize that each of the sides of any given square (i.e., a square centimeter) can be measured as 1 centimeter or 10 millimeters. (I don't expect them to have difficulty with this, since we've spent lots of time on metric linear measurement.) The tricky part will be applying this knowledge to figuring out the area of the irregular shape in square millimeters. First, they must reason that the area of each 1-centimeter square would be 10 millimeters × 10 millimeters, or 100 square millimeters. To successfully complete the problem, then, they will need to multiply the total area of the irregular shape as measured in square centimeters by 100.

7.   I think that the tasks I assigned will provide the basis for lots of good discussion. I have found that the routine of explaining your thinking and asking questions sometimes can lead to pretty superficial interactions. When students don't get excited about and take ownership of their ideas, the discussion tends to fall flat. My hunch is that this won't happen today because I expect that the students will have different answers—answers that they will want to defend—for the area of the irregular shapes in square millimeters. I expect that some students will think that changing from square centimeters to square millimeters involves multiplying by 10 (as was done in earlier lessons on linear measurement). Others, however, will have figured out that changing from square centimeters to square millimeters involves multiplying by a factor of 100. Having two possible solutions on the table is useful; in aligning themselves with one or the other, students become more invested in defending their claims.

The Class

8.   Last night, I gave the class four homework problems, each of which involved finding the area of an irregular shape. One of these is shown in Figure 2.2. Students were asked to determine the area of each shape in square centimeters and square millimeters. Since the figures were given on grid paper marked in square centimeters, I knew that it would be easy for them to determine the areas of these irregular shapes in square

FIGURE 2.2. The Irregular Shape Whose Area Students Were Asked to Determine in Square Centimeters and Square Millimeters

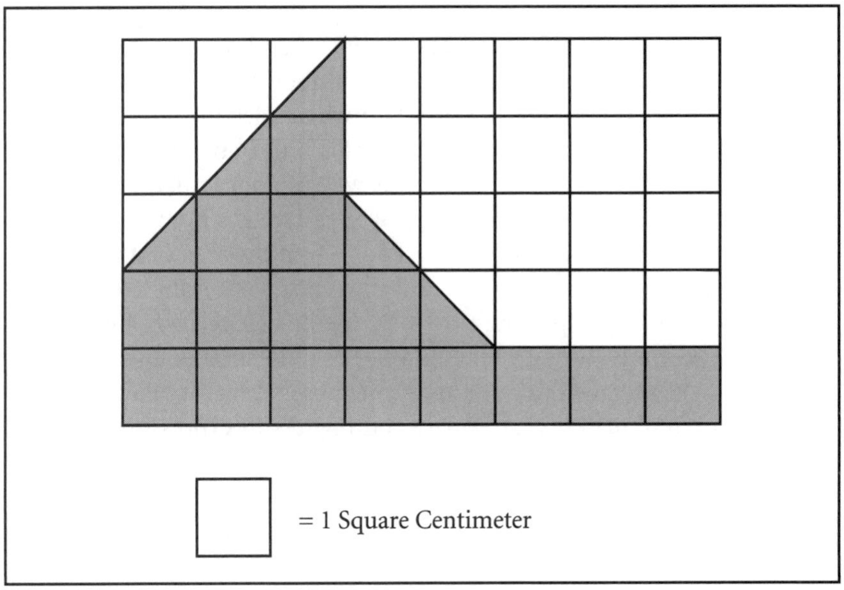

☐ = 1 Square Centimeter

centimeters. Although they may use formulas, the grid makes it possible to find the area by counting. I don't expect that they will get thrown by the irregular shapes or the half-shaded squares; they've had lots of experience in 4th and 5th grade with manipulating irregularly shaped figures in order to more easily find their areas, and they know that the area will be conserved. What I really want to focus on here is the difference in converting between units for linear measurement and for area measurement.

9. As the students were settling into their seats before the period began, I quickly walked around the room scanning the homework papers that were already out on most of the students' desks. I noticed that many students had found that the area of the irregular shape was 17.5 square centimeters, but—as I suspected—their answers varied with respect to the area of the same shape in terms of square millimeters. Many of the students had 175 square millimeters; an almost equal number, however, had 1,750 square millimeters. I decided that I would try to orchestrate a discussion in which students felt obligated to determine which was the correct answer and to convince others of their position. Basically, I wanted to set up an argument and let them play it out. This would give them practice in citing mathematical evidence to back up their own claims or to dispute the claims of others. The fact that different students would be taking up specific positions seemed to be a good way to get such an exchange going.

10. I decided to begin by establishing what we all agreed upon. I asked Ellen to come to the overhead projector and explain her solution and her strategy for finding the area in square centimeters. She explained that she "just counted" to obtain 17½ square centimeters, and she pointed to each square or half square as she counted up to a total of 17½

squares. Joelyne asked her to go over again how she knew to count the half squares. Ellen indicated that she knew that "two halves make a whole," and that the diagonal line divided a square into two halves. Although the class unanimously agreed with Ellen's answer, I asked if anyone had arrived at the same answer using a different strategy. Michael said that he had used the "length times width formula." I asked him to come to the overhead projector to show us what he had done.

11.   After drawing the heavy black line marking off a rectangle within the irregular shape (as shown in Figure 2.3), he said that he knew that the area of "that part" was 8 because it was 2 × 4. Then, he explained, he added 7 for the remaining whole squares and 2½ for the 5 half squares to get 17½. I reminded him that it was 17½ *square centimeters*. I asked if anyone else had done it Michael's way and no one raised a hand. I pointed out to the students that Michael's way of doing it saved a little time because he didn't have to actually count those 8 blocks.

12.   At this point, I decided that the students should have some time to think about and, if necessary, practice defending their solutions to the second part of this problem. I asked the students to form pairs with the student directly across from them and to discuss the area in square millimeters. The students had a variety of materials available to them, including centimeter square pieces, metric rulers, and calculators. As they talked, I tried to encourage conversation by continually asking, "What have you decided?" and "How did you decide?" I was able to observe most of the pairs. Although a few seemed lost as to how to proceed, many pairs had come to an agreement regarding which answer was correct and why, while equally as many appeared to be having their own mini-debates, with one student claiming the answer was 1,750 and the other claiming that it was 175.

13.   After about 10 minutes, I decided that the pair conversations were no longer productive and that it was time to open it up to a whole-class

FIGURE 2.3. Michael's Diagram for Determining the Number of Square Centimeters That Are Shaded

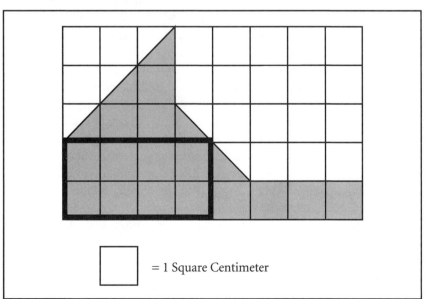

= 1 Square Centimeter

discussion. I decided to begin with Larry. Although his answer was incorrect, it was shared by at least half of the class.

14. I asked Larry to come to the overhead and explain his solution. He said that since there were 17½ centimeters, and since there were 10 millimeters for every 1 centimeter, he multiplied 17 by 10 to get 170. As he was talking, I gently interrupted at a couple of points to correct his language to *square centimeters* instead of centimeters. I did this with some hesitation because I was worried that by doing so I might be pointing directly to the flaw in his reasoning. Since reminding students to state the units was something I normally did, however, the words were out of my mouth before I could stop them. It didn't seem to matter. Larry confidently repeated his answer: "170 square millimeters."

15. After he had finished, he asked the students at their desks if they had any questions. All was quiet for a long 10 seconds and then Jerome asked why he multiplied by 10, to which he replied that there were 10 millimeters for 1 centimeter. "Anybody have a question about that?" I asked. "Did everybody get 170 square millimeters for their answer?" Only one or two students were shaking their heads affirmatively. I continued, "How many of you got 170 square millimeters?" This time, about eight students raised their hands. "How many of you got something else?" A few hands timidly climbed into the air. "If you got something else, I don't understand why your hand isn't in the air asking him how he got what he did." I had to admit this "debate" was getting off to a slow start. Despite all of our work on risk-taking and trust-building, students were still hesitant to challenge or disagree with one another. My job was to figure out how to get them to understand that arguing was part of what it means to do mathematics in this classroom.

16. Bonita was the first student who was brave enough to challenge Larry's reasoning and his answer. However, what she challenged was not what I had hoped for. She asked him why he used 17 rather than 17½ or 17.5. He answered, "'Cause there are 17½ and the ½ or .5 would make it complicated so I just dropped that, and for every centimeter there's 10 millimeters." Although appropriate levels of precision was a topic that I had hoped to touch upon later in the week, I didn't see it as useful for the debate I was trying to set up at the moment. I decided that I'd let Bonita's comment and Larry's response to it slide and hope that the next comment was more on track.

17. Next, Charlene raised her hand. Referring to Larry's original explanation, she asked, "If every centimeter is 10 millimeters, then the dimensions of a 1-centimeter square would be 10 by 10, right? So that makes every centimeter worth 100 millimeters, right?" I chimed in, "Do you mean that every *square centimeter* is worth 100 *square millimeters?*" "Yeah," Charlene continued, "One hundred square millimeters. So, if you add them all up, each centimeter being a hundred, you would get 1,700. You know, like, when you come to the end of something, you move the decimal over."

18. I was basically happy with Charlene's explanation. It started with something that Larry knew (that there were 10 millimeters in every centimeter) and then applied it appropriately to find the corresponding linear measures of the length and width of the square in millimeters. Then she went on to explain that, in order to find the area, you'd need to

take the length times the width, so the corresponding answer would be 10 millimeters × 10 millimeters, or 100 square millimeters. I looked around the room, trying to read students' faces. Were others starting to get it?

19.   Larry, for one, didn't seem to be. Unfortunately, he hadn't picked up on the same part of Charlene's explanation that I had. Instead, he gravitated to the "moving the decimal" part. "Which way?" he asked. Actually, I had found this part of Charlene's explanation to be unclear, but not for the same reasons Larry was asking about. Before I could think of what to say, another student chimed in that Larry should not have dropped the .5 because multiplying wasn't so complicated since you just have to "move the decimal." Suddenly, I felt that this discussion could go down an unproductive path, so I intervened again and tried to redefine the poles of the debate. "We still have some discussion here," I said. "Charlene is saying that each individual square centimeter is not 10 square millimeters but is 100. Larry and a few others are still saying that each square centimeter is 10."

20.   I called on Natalie, whose hand had been patiently in the air for quite a while now. From her desk, she said, "The things are 1 by 1 and 10 by 10. It's 100 each. So, you multiply by 100 instead of 10." I decided that things were getting a little too abstract and that we could use some concrete diagrams. I asked Natalie if she could come up to the overhead projector to show us what she meant. At the overhead projector Natalie illustrated her assertion with a 10 by 10 square (shown in Figure 2.4), which she asked her classmates to think of as 1 square centimeter that was "blown up" to make it clear that it was also a 10-millimeter by 10-millimeter square.

21.   Like Charlene, Natalie argued that each square centimeter had the linear dimensions of 10-millimeter by 10-millimeter and so its area, by

FIGURE 2.4. Natalie's Diagram to Show That One Square Centimeter Is Also a 10-Millimeter by 10-Millimeter Square

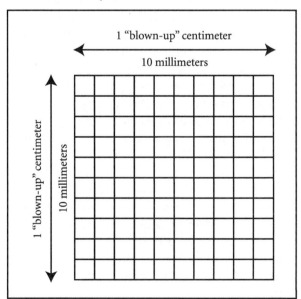

counting or by using the formula "length times width," would be 100 square millimeters. My belief in visual diagrams as an aid to discussion and explanation was further strengthened!

22.   I still had the feeling that not everyone was on the same page. I asked, "How many of you agree with Natalie? Because if you don't, we need to go further. How many of you *do not* agree with that? How many of you still think it's 175? It's okay to think differently. I think we need more discussion here." I was right. Steve said to Natalie, who was still standing at the overhead projector, "I thought it took 10 millimeters to make up a centimeter." I was happy that Steve had the courage to admit his confusion and I was quite certain that he was giving voice to several other students' continuing misunderstandings. Before Natalie could respond, Steve's partner, Dave, said, "When we were working in the Powers-of-Ten unit, we learned that you should move the decimal point one place to the right when you go from centimeters to millimeters."

23.   Steve and Dave appeared to be having difficulty breaking out of their memorized rule for converting centimeters to millimeters. They needed to somehow start to connect their thinking to the problem, actually seeing that they were dealing with area—not linear—measurement. As I was trying to think of the best way to help them do this, Natalie regained the floor and did it better than I ever could. "You can still do it by moving the decimal point, but this time you need to move it two places. Look. Like I was saying, each one of these squares is 1 centimeter by 1 centimeter so this is 10-millimeters by 10-millimeters (as she talked she pointed to two sides of one square). For each length, which is 1 centimeter, it's just the same as we learned before—move the decimal one place. But there are *two* lengths so you need to move the decimal point *two* places, one place for each length."

24.   Natalie was drawing connections between a conceptual and an algorithmic way of tackling the problem. In essence, her explanation showed *why* you would need to move the decimal point not one but two places. Given some students' tendencies to rely on "moving the decimal point," this explanation, I thought, should give them something to think about. I wanted to reinforce what she had said so I added, "So, Natalie is saying that you need to move the decimal point *two* powers of 10 when you're working with area measurement." "Yeah," she replied, "because you have two sides and you multiply each times 10."

25.   I suddenly realized that this insight regarding moving the decimal point one place for converting between linear units versus two places for converting between square units was entirely dependent on the fact that we were using two different units of *metric* measurement. In the metric system, different units are always related by powers of 10 and conversions can be accomplished by using the shortcut method of moving the decimal point. If the problems we did in class continued to involve only metric units, students might think that moving the decimal point one versus two places was the important connection in converting linear and area measurement between different units (rather than the fact that if the linear units are related by a factor of x, then their corresponding square units are related by a factor of x^2). I decided that I had better give problems that went beyond converting between two different units of the metric system, such as converting between square feet and square yards.

26.   I looked back at Steve and his partner who were busily conferring with their heads bent over their homework papers. I decided to take a quick assessment of the rest of the class. "How many of you think the answer is 1,750 square millimeters?" I asked. Every hand went up, except Steve's and Dave's—they were still busy conferring. This seemed too good to be true. I decided to move on to the next homework problem and called on Beth, a student who began the period not differentiating between linear and area measurement. She came to the overhead projector at the front of the room and not only provided the correct answers, but also gave a convincing explanation regarding how to change from square centimeters to square millimeters. I was also satisfied with the solutions and explanations provided by the next two students for the remaining homework problems, although I knew that I would need to check back for understanding in the days to follow (especially with Steve and Dave).

27.   I hadn't planned on giving homework since the entire period was going to be devoted to reviewing last night's assignment. But I decided that students could benefit from looking at a problem that involved converting linear and area measurements between two nonmetric units of measurement. With this in mind, I told students to take out their journals and write down two problems for homework.

1. How many square inches are in a square foot? Draw a diagram and write a few sentences to explain how you determined your answer.
2. How is this problem similar to the problems we discussed today in class?

28.   I hoped that an observation regarding the $1:x$ relationship between linear units and the $1:x^2$ relationship between the corresponding square units would arise in tomorrow's discussion of how the first problem was related to the homework problems we discussed today in class. Over the course of the next few lessons, I would want students to see that the area ratio was the square of the linear ratio, not only when converting between different units of measure but also when comparing linear and area measurements in similar figures.

ANALYZING THE CASE

Now that you have had an opportunity to "visit" Barbara Crafton's classroom and note what she does to promote discussion in her classroom, we invite you to consider how the actions on your list served to foster students' learning. Here are a few suggestions on how to proceed.

- Review the list you created during your initial reading of the case in which you identified the moves Barbara Crafton made to promote discussion during the lesson. For each item on your list indicate *how* this may have contributed to students' learning of mathematics. Be sure to cite specific evidence (i.e., paragraph numbers) from the case to support your claims.
- Consider what Barbara Crafton did (or may have done) prior to the discussion. How might these actions have contributed to students' learning? Cite specific evidence from the case to support your argument.
- If you have colleagues who also are reading this case, compare and contrast the ideas in your individual lists and possibly generate a master list. Note points of disagreement since these are likely to be fruitful topics for further discussion and debate. If you are working on this activity alone, we encourage you to refer to Appendix A, which includes a list that was produced by teachers who previously participated in a discussion of Barbara Crafton's teaching practices. You may want to note points of agreement and disagreement and flag issues that you wish to investigate.

You may wish to extend your analysis of the case by considering the questions in the next section. Alternatively, you can skip the next section and proceed directly to the "Connecting to Your Own Practice" section in which you are encouraged to relate the analysis of the ideas and issues raised in the case to your own teaching practice.

EXTENDING YOUR ANALYSIS OF THE CASE

The questions listed in this section are intended to help you focus on particular aspects of the case related to teacher decision-making and student thinking. You may want to focus on one that addresses an issue with which you have been grappling. If you are working in collaboration with one or more colleagues, the questions can serve as a stimulus for further discussion and debate.

1. When Mrs. Crafton summarizes or restates what a student has said, she often makes a point of using the mathematically correct terminology, even if this language was not used initially by the student. For example, as Larry explains his solution (para. 14), Mrs. Crafton points out that he is referring to *square* centimeters instead of centimeters. When is focusing on terminology appropriate and when might students' imprecise or inaccurate language be overlooked?
2. In response to Steve's and Dave's confusion about moving the decimal point, Natalie says that there are two lengths, so you need to move the decimal point two places, one for each length (para. 23). How does Natalie's explanation make a connection between a conceptual and an algorithmic way of tackling the problem? What are the limitations to Natalie's explanation?
3. Mrs. Crafton anticipates that students will have two different answers to the homework problem that she plans to discuss during the lesson (para. 7). If no students had recognized the correct relationship, what questions could Mrs. Crafton have asked to help students identify their misconception?
4. Some may argue that the problem featured in the case is rather procedural. Why would Mrs. Crafton, who claims to focus on conceptual understanding (para. 1), select this task?
5. Mrs. Crafton has established norms in her classroom that promote mathematical argumentation. What are the advantages and challenges for students and teachers in classrooms in which mathematical argumentation is the norm?
6. Mrs. Crafton chose to devote an entire class period to examine one problem. What are the advantages and disadvantages of this decision?
7. Mrs. Crafton states that the lesson featured in the case is one in a series of lessons on area measurement (para. 4). How are the problems in this series of lessons (measuring a sheet of paper using nonstandard units, finding the area of irregular shapes in square centimeters and square millimeters, the two homework problems assigned at the end of the lesson) mathematically related? How does each problem build on the previous problem(s)?

CONNECTING TO YOUR OWN PRACTICE

This section is intended specifically for readers who currently are teaching mathematics. In this section, we offer ways to connect the specific ideas investigated in "The Case of Barbara Crafton" to a set of larger issues that can be explored in your own classroom. The activities described in this section are designed to help you consider the ways in which issues identified in Mrs. Crafton's classroom have implications for your own teaching of mathematics.

The ability to communicate mathematically is regarded as an essential component of mathematical understanding. Students who have opportunities to practice their communication skills (i.e., speaking, writing, listening) during mathematics class reap dual benefits: They learn mathematics and they learn to communicate mathematically (NCTM, 2000). In particular, "students who are involved in discussions in which they justify solutions—especially in the face of disagreement—will gain better mathematical understanding as they work to convince their peers about differing points of view" (NCTM, 2000, p. 59). Here are a few activities that will help you move from consideration of Barbara Crafton's teaching to a focus on your own classroom practices.

- Review the list you created during the case analysis in which you indicated what Barbara Crafton does to promote discussion. Select one of the teacher actions from this list that you feel has implications for your own teaching. Plan and teach a lesson in which you purposefully address the identified action. For example, you may be curious about what your students could learn from having them share their solutions with partners and justify their points of view.
- Plan and teach a lesson in which you make a concerted effort to encourage mathematical argumentation by having students consider two different solutions to a problem (using either the problem featured in "The Case of Barbara Crafton" or another problem that addresses one of your mathematical goals and has the potential for debate—that is, one that you would expect some students to solve correctly and others to exhibit a common misconception about). If possible, audio- or videotape the lesson or have a colleague observe and take notes. As you go back over the lesson, reflect on the ways in which you set up and managed the debate and the impact it appeared to have on students' learning. Also indicate what you still need to work on with respect to encouraging mathematical argumentation.

Prior to teaching this lesson, you might want to consider how you will create a classroom environment in which your students feel comfortable disagreeing with one another. Students in the middle grades are often reluctant to share their thinking and publicly disagree with one another (NCTM, 2000). Consider the following: How will you encourage your students to participate in the mathematical debate? How will you assure them that they are in a "safe" environment and that "they will not be criticized personally, even if their mathematical thinking is critiqued" (NCTM, 2000, p. 270)?

EXPLORING CURRICULAR MATERIALS

You may want to explore your curriculum for ideas related to linear and area measurement by considering the following questions: Are there tasks in your curriculum that promote students' understanding of the relationships between different units of measure? If not, could the curriculum be modified (i.e., by adapting existing tasks or inserting new tasks) so as to provide students with such experiences? What might be the potential benefits of including such tasks?

You also may want to explore additional tasks that make salient the mathematical ideas that were the focus of the case. The following list identifies resources that contain problems considered to be mathematically similar to the task used in "The Case of Barbara Crafton."

Billstein, R., & Williamson, J. (1999a). *Middle grades maththematics: Book 1*. Evanstown, IL: McDougal Littell.

Of particular interest is an exploration activity (pp. 455–456) in which students explore the relationships between square inches, square feet, and square yards in the context of a real-world situation.

Education Development Center, Inc. (1998b). *MathScape: Gulliver's worlds: Measuring and scaling* (Student guide). Mountain View, CA: Creative Publications.

Of particular interest is Lesson 11 (Gulliver's Worlds Cubed, pp. 30–31), in which students explore how length, area, and volume change when the scale changes.

Foreman, L. C., & Bennett, A. B., Jr. (1996). *Visual mathematics: Course II, Lessons 1–10*. Salem, OR: The Math Learning Center.

Of particular interest in Lesson 2 (Shape and Surface Area) are Actions 8–10 in the Focus Teacher Activity (pp. 24–25). Students explore the effects of changing the unit with respect to linear measurement, surface area, and volume.

Lappan, G., Fey, J. T., Fitzgerald, W. M., Friel, S. N., & Phillips, E. D. (1998d). *Looking for Pythagoreas: The Pythagorean theorem*. Menlo Park, CA: Dale Seymour.

> Of particular interest is Problem 2.1 (p. 17), in which students determine the areas of regular and irregular figures drawn on grids.

The Mathematics in Context Development Team. (1998c). Mathematics in context: Reallotment (Student guide). In National Center for Research in Mathematical Sciences Education & Freudenthal Institute (Eds.), *Mathematics in context*. Chicago: Encyclopaedia Britannica.

> Of particular interest are Problems 4, 5, 8, 9, and 10 (pp. 30–32), in which students use diagrams to convert between metric units of measurement.

CONNECTING TO OTHER IDEAS AND ISSUES

If you have additional time, you may want to explore some aspect of the case in more depth. The resources identified in the following list provide some possibilities for exploring the pedagogical issues raised in "The Case of Barbara Crafton." For example, you might: (1) use Rittenhouse's (1998) analysis of Lampert's teaching to consider what Barbara Crafton might have done at the beginning of the school year to help her students learn how to engage in mathematical talk; (2) read the excerpt of Lampert's lesson (pp. 732–736) described in Lampert, Rittenhouse, and Crumbaugh (1996) and note the ways in which Lampert's structured debate are similar to and different from how Barbara Crafton structured her debate; (3) continue to explore the relationships between the length, surface area, and volume of cubes using the activity provided in Pugalee, et al. (2002); (4) use Sherin's (2000) framework to analyze the class discussion in the case; or (5) use Stein (2001) to consider the role of the teacher in a classroom in which students effectively engage in mathematical argumentation.

Lampert, M., Rittenhouse, P., & Crumbaugh, C. (1996). Agreeing to disagree: Developing sociable mathematical discourse. In D. R. Olson & N. Torrance (Eds.), *The handbook of education and human development: New models of learning, teaching, and schooling* (pp. 731–764). Cambridge, MA: Blackwell.

> In this book chapter, the authors argue that teachers need to be aware that students' concerns about social acceptance may interfere with the teachers' goal of engaging students in mathematical argumentation. They illustrate this phenomenon by comparing and contrasting two examples from Lampert's 5th-grade classroom: a whole-group discussion in which children engage in a mathematical debate and a small-group discussion in which children resist engaging in an argument and decide to "agree to disagree," in order to preserve social relationships.

Pugalee, D. K., Frykholm, J., Johnson, A., Slovin, H., & Preston, R. (2002). *Principles and standards for school mathematics navigations series: Navigating through geometry in grades 6–8*. Reston, VA: National Council of Teachers of Mathematics.

> This book contains resources to assist teachers in providing geometry instruction consistent with the expectations outlined in the "Geometry Standard" of the *Principles and Standards for School Mathematics* (NCTM, 2000). The extension to the activity entitled "Minimizing Perimeter" (pp. 73–75) provides a task in which the ratio of the side lengths of two cubes is compared to the ratio of their surface areas and to the ratio of their volumes.

Rittenhouse, P. S. (1998). The teacher's role in mathematical conversation: Stepping in and stepping out. In M. Lampert & M. L. Blunk (Eds.), *Talking mathematics in school: Studies of teaching and learning* (pp. 163–189). New York: Cambridge University Press.

> In this book chapter, the author uses a series of lessons from Lampert's 5th-grade classroom that occurred at the beginning of the school year to investigate how the teacher helped her students learn to engage in mathematical talk and debate. The author provides detailed examples of how Lampert introduced this way of doing mathematics to her students.

Sherin, M. G. (2000). Facilitating meaningful discussion of mathematics. *Mathematics Teaching in the Middle School, 6,* 122–125.

> In this article, the author introduces a framework for organizing classroom discussions that are based on students' ideas and are mathematically productive. The author describes three phases of effective whole-class discussions: generating ideas, comparing and evaluating ideas, and focusing the range of ideas. A lesson from an 8th-grade classroom is used to illustrate these three phases.

Stein, M. K. (2001). Mathematical argumentation: Putting umph into classroom discussions. *Mathematics Teaching in the Middle School, 7,* 110–112.

> In this article, the author uses the task featured in "The Case of Barbara Crafton" to frame a discussion of how teachers can engage their students in mathematical argumentation. The author also highlights the role of the teacher in such lessons.

3

Exploring Area and Perimeter

The Case of Isabelle Olson

This chapter provides the materials to engage you in reading and analyzing the teaching and learning that occurred in the classroom of Isabelle Olson as she and her 7th-grade students determine the maximum area of a rectangular rabbit pen. Prior to reading "The Case of Isabelle Olson"—the centerpiece of this chapter—we suggest that you begin by completing the Opening Activity. The primary purpose of the Opening Activity is to engage you with the mathematical ideas that you will encounter when you read the case.

OPENING ACTIVITY

The Opening Activity for "The Case of Isabelle Olson" is presented in Figure 3.1. The task in the Opening Activity is similar to the problem Ms. Olson's students solve in the case and involves finding the length and width of the pen that yields the greatest area. By exploring the "Consider" questions, you will have an opportunity to think about the relationship between area and perimeter.

Once you have completed the activity, you may want to refer to Appendix B, which contains some solutions generated by teachers who completed the Opening Activity as part of a professional development experience that focused on "The Case of Isabelle Olson." You are encouraged to examine the different solutions provided and to consider the relationship between your solution and those produced by others.

READING THE CASE

As you read the case, we encourage you to make note of the pedagogical moves made by Isabelle Olson during

FIGURE 3.1. The Opening Activity for "The Case of Isabelle Olson"

Solve

You are going to build a rectangular pen for your rabbit, Euclid. You have decided to build the pen using some portion of the back of your house as one side of the pen and enclosing the other three sides with a length of fencing that was left over from another project. If you want Euclid to have as much room as possible (after all he spends most of the day in his pen), what would the length and width of the pen be?

Consider

1. Can you have 2 rectangles that have the same perimeter but different areas?

2. Can you have 2 rectangles with the same area but different perimeters?

3. Can you determine the perimeter of a rectangle if the area is known?

4. Can you determine the area of a rectangle if the perimeter is known?

the lesson. (You may want to use a highlighter or Post-it notes to keep track of these as you read the case.) For example, you may notice general features of her instruction (e.g., she used an open-ended task, she provided students with a variety of tools to use) as well as more specific aspects of her teaching (e.g., she revised her questioning strategy on the first day when students were not making progress, she asked Tommy's group to share their thinking on the second day).

We encourage you to write down the moves that you identify. These can serve as topics for discussion with a colleague who also has read the case, as issues to investigate as you read additional cases, or as starting points for exploration in your own classroom. For example, you might wonder about how much time you should allow students to struggle with a problem and how to help them make progress if they are struggling. We will discuss additional connections to your own practice at the end of the chapter.

THE CASE OF ISABELLE OLSON

1. Isabelle Olson teaches at Roosevelt, a middle school located in a large urban school district. She left a position at Lakeview, a more affluent suburban district, 3 years earlier to teach at Roosevelt. She had been using a new curriculum in her classes at Lakeview but found no support within her school for her efforts. Most of her colleagues were still using traditional textbooks and wanted no part of Isabelle's approach, which focused more on actively engaging students in mathematical activities and less on teacher talk. They saw it as too time-consuming and not necessary. Lakeview students were doing just fine with the program they had.

2. Isabelle knew that the teachers at Roosevelt shared her enthusiasm for the new curriculum and that she would have colleagues with whom to collaborate. This was very important to her. Enacting a new curriculum was hard work and she no longer wanted to do it alone. At Roosevelt she would be a member of a team that met frequently to discuss the mathematics they were teaching, what students were learning, and how to best facilitate student learning of mathematics.

3. Isabelle had not planned to stay at Roosevelt. She had taken a one-year leave of absence from Lakeview and had planned to return there, recharged, she hoped, by her experiences with Roosevelt teachers. But at the end of her first year at Roosevelt she decided to stay. She had come to believe that all students were more likely to succeed if they had access to a good curriculum and quality instruction from committed teachers. At Roosevelt, Isabelle felt that she could really make a difference in the students' lives—something that she had never felt at Lakeview.

4. Isabelle knew that the tasks in the curriculum often presented challenges to her students. Most tasks could not be solved by a simple algorithm or procedure, and many were pretty open-ended. She had worked hard to help her students understand that it is all right to struggle with mathematics, and that through struggling you often learn something important. She believed that students gain confidence in themselves as learners and doers of mathematics by having success with problems that they first have to struggle to figure out. This, she thought, was how you really empowered students.

Isabelle Olson Talks About Her Class

5. It is the end of April and in 6 weeks school will be over for the year. I've been really pleased with the progress that my third-period, 7th-grade class has made over the past 8 months. Of course, I can't take all the credit; the groundwork had been laid last year when, as 6th-graders, they were introduced to a more active, inquiry-oriented way of thinking about and doing mathematics. They have now had almost 2 years of mathematics classes in which they have been expected to think hard about the problems they were given, to represent their ideas and solutions in a variety of ways, and to communicate their understandings in clear and mathematically convincing ways. My students have made steady progress in unit after unit of challenging material, learning to solve complex mathematical tasks. I am hopeful that the mathematical

experiences they have had over the past 2 years will prepare them to tackle algebra next year as 8th-graders.

6.   The biggest challenge that I have been faced with this year has been helping students to gain the confidence and skills to deal with more open-ended problems. I want my students to be able to impose structure on under-specified or ill-structured situations. This is an important goal of mine. After all, most of the world's problems are like that! Furthermore, I firmly believe that we all learn through a process that begins when we confront a problem and don't know what to do. I really want my students to learn how to deal with the uncertainty and frustration that they often feel when they first encounter a problem they do not immediately know how to tackle head on, rather than running and hiding from it. I've seen too many kids simply throw up their arms and say, "I can't do this!"

7.   We currently are working in a unit on measurement. One of my goals for the unit is to help my students create meaning for concepts such as area, perimeter, surface area, and volume. Too often, students' experiences in learning measurement have been limited to memorizing and applying formulas. In order to remedy this situation, I have decided to give my students the opportunity to explore the relationship between area and perimeter.

8.   The task I have selected is the most open-ended task that I have ever given to this group of students. Like many of the tasks that I use in my class, I adapted it from a more well-defined problem. The first part of the original problem is as follows:

THE ORIGINAL FENCING PROBLEM

Each of the 7th-grade classes in Franklin Middle School will raise rabbits for their spring science fair. Each class will use the school building as one of the sides of its rectangular rabbit pen, and each class wants its rabbits to have as much room as possible.

Ms. Brown's class has 24 feet of fencing to enclose the other three sides of the pen. If Ms. Brown's class wants the rabbits to have as much room as possible, what would the area of the pen be? How long would each of the three sides of the pen be? Try to organize your work so that someone else who reads it will understand it.

9.   The problem also had additional parts that asked students to consider pens that were constructed from various lengths of fencing (i.e., 18 ft., 20 ft., 15 ft., 19 ft.). It finally asked students to look for patterns in the pens they constructed for each part of the problem. While I liked the problem, I felt that it led students to the generalization rather than letting them explore the situation presented and impose their own structure on the problem. I decided to restate the problem so as to leave the amount of fencing unspecified and omit the question regarding the need to determine the length of the three sides.

MY VERSION OF THE FENCING PROBLEM

Ms. Olson's 7th-grade class at Roosevelt Middle School will raise rabbits for their spring science fair. The class will use some portion of the school building as one of the sides of its rectangular rabbit pen and will use the fencing that was left over from the school play to enclose the other three sides of the pen.

    If Ms. Olson's class wants its rabbits to have as much room as possible, what would the dimensions of the pen be? Try to organize your work so that someone else who reads it will understand it.

10.   I have no doubt that this problem will cause a great deal of discomfort for my students. I expect that, initially, the students won't have a clue as to how to solve the problem since no numbers have been given. But I want them to begin to appreciate the fact that real-world problems often involve defining what the problem is and identifying the critical pieces of information needed to solve it. Sometimes students just pull numbers from problems and perform operations without much thought about what is really going on in the problem. This time I want them to first think about the problem qualitatively—deciding what variables are important to consider, what needs to be held constant, and what to allow to vary—and then to quantify the relationships by using specific lengths of fence.

11.   Of course, I hope that the students arrive at the generalization that for any amount of fencing, the maximum area will be obtained by constructing a pen where the width is one-half the length. In order to arrive at this conclusion, students will need to consider how to maximize the area of the rabbit pen and how to generalize their findings to apply to any amount of fencing. In addition to my mathematical goals, I am also very interested in the process by which they arrive at these conclusions. Specifically, I want the students to have firsthand experience with making conjectures and gathering evidence to support or refute their conjectures. I hope that the students will see the need to pick a length of fence, build pens with different dimensions while holding the amount of fencing constant, come up with a conjecture regarding the dimensions of the pen that has the maximum area, and then test that conjecture by trying additional cases. However, I expect that this will take several class periods.

The First Day

12.   I told students that they were going to begin work on a project that would take several days. As I passed out a sheet of paper containing the problem, I indicated that they would be working in their groups to solve the problem. I told them that they needed to consider only pieces of fence that were whole numbers. The ultimate product that I expected was a 36×24 poster (one for each group) that stated the claim they were making about the dimensions of the pen that would give the most room and showed, in some systematic fashion, the evidence that supported their claim. This notion of having evidence to support a claim was not new to my students. Since the first day of 6th grade when my students encountered the handshake problem they had been working on problems that led to a generalization of some type.[1] This process always involved looking at a specific example, making conjectures, and then trying additional cases. The new twist in this problem was the need for the students to add structure to a vaguely stated, open-ended task.

13.   I told students that I expected that initially the problem would cause
some frustration and that they probably would experience some disequilibrium. This was a word that I had introduced to them at the beginning
of the year. I wanted them to have a way of describing what they were
feeling and to come to view this as an important part of the learning
process. I went on to explain that the group would have to make some
decisions regarding how to proceed. I told them to discuss any questions
they might have within their group rather than approach me for the
answer. I reminded them that they could help themselves to any tools
they needed (e.g., graph paper, tiles, calculators) to solve the problem. I
promised to periodically stop by and check on their progress. With those
simple directions, I set the groups loose on the problem.

14.   *Getting started.* Students initially exhibited a great deal of confusion,
not knowing where to begin. As I visited each group, I asked, "What are
you trying to decide?" With this question, I was trying to steer them
toward a critical appraisal of the problem goal and important information
needed to address the goal. After several attempts, however, I noticed that
my question didn't seem to be working. Instead of answering it, most
students responded with requests for more specific information: "How
many rabbits will we raise?" "How much space does each rabbit need?"
"How big is the school building?" "How much fencing was left over from
the school play?" To each question, I responded in the same way: They
had all of the information that they needed to solve the problem and they
needed to think about what was most critical for solving the problem.

15.   *Deciding on an approach.* Frustrated by my refusal to provide more
specific information, most groups arbitrarily selected a length for the
school building. For example, the group that included Tommy, Michael,
Tanya, and Beatriz had decided that the side of the school building was
100 yards long and that the pen should be square. When I stopped by,
they were in the process of constructing a poster that featured a scale
drawing of the proposed pen, with ½ inch equal to 10 yards (as shown in
Figure 3.2). They were taking great care to produce an accurate picture.

16.   I was concerned, however, that they showed no signs of moving in a
direction that would lead them toward a solution. Reluctantly, I decided
to change my questioning strategy. I asked the group how much fencing
they had used for the pen. Tommy responded that they had used 300
yards of fence and that the rabbits would have 10,000 square yards of
space. I asked, "How do you know that this is the largest amount of
room possible with 300 yards of fence?" With that I left the group to
continue to think about the problem.

17.   I then stopped by the group that included Jessica, Jamal, Toby, and
Michele. They had drawn the pen shown in Figure 3.3. I asked them if
they could explain how they were thinking about the problem. Jessica
began by saying that they had decided that the side of the school building was 50 yards long (the bold line) and therefore one side of the pen—
the one opposite the building—would have to be 50 yards too. I then
asked what the dotted lines on the other two sides represented. Toby
went on to explain that it would depend on how much fencing was
available. I asked what he meant by this. He continued, "Well, you take

FIGURE 3.2. Tommy, Michael, Tanya, and Beatriz's Scale Drawing of a Square Rabbit Pen

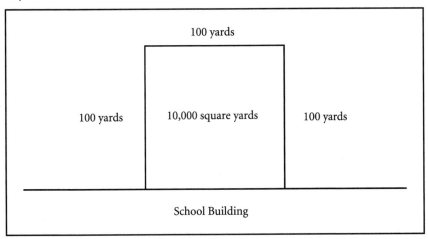

however much fence you have and you subtract 50 for one side. Then you take what is left and divide it by two. That will tell you how long each of the other two sides are." Michele added, "Since we don't know how much fence there is, this is all we can do."

18.   While I was pleased to see that this group realized that there were many possible pen configurations, by constraining the length of the side of the building they too were missing an important point of the problem. I asked, "Does the building have to be 50 yards? What if you didn't know how long it was? What if you just had a certain amount of fence?" Again, I left the group to consider my questions.

19.   I stopped for a minute to consider my interactions with Tommy's and Jessica's groups. Was I giving away too much with these questions by identifying what was and wasn't important in the problem? I had hoped to be able to ask more open-ended questions, but the students seemed to need this push. At this point, I began to toy with the idea of going back to the original problem and telling them that they had 24 feet of fencing, but then forced myself to remember my goal for the lesson:

FIGURE 3.3. Jessica, Jamal, Toby, and Michele's Drawing of a Rabbit Pen

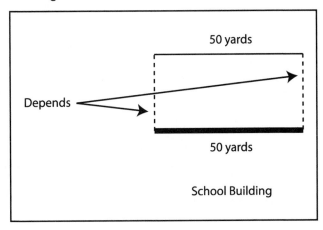

to give students the opportunity to struggle in order to learn that perseverance would lead to satisfying conclusions.

20.   As I continued my rounds of the small groups, I asked the question, "How do you know that your enclosure has the most area?" I began to realize that even this question appeared to be too remote to steer the students in the right direction. Most of the students insisted that their particular construction covered the most area. When I pushed them to tell me how they knew, they said, "We just know!"

21.   I returned to Tommy's group after stopping to check on each of the other groups. They appeared not to have made much progress since my first visit. I again asked the group how they knew that the pen they had built provided the largest amount of room possible with 300 yards of fence. Beatriz said that if the amount of fencing is the same, then the area will be the same. I replied, "Are you sure that there is no other way to give the rabbits more room?" In unison they replied that they were sure. In fact, I noticed that they had added a statement to their poster that read, "We think that no matter how you shaped the pen it will still be the same area if you keep the same perimeter every time." I said, "Well, I am not convinced. You need to prove it to me. I want to see the evidence that supports your claim." I went on to say that since they had chosen 300 yards, I wanted them to build rectangles with different dimensions that used the same amount of fence. I left the group with Tommy pleading, "I swear this is the only way!"

22.   As I did a brief tour of the room to assess where students were, I noticed that no other group had made progress. Most continued to have only one pen and it seemed as though they were at a loss as to what to try next. With a heavy sigh, I glanced at the clock and noted that the bell would be ringing within 10 minutes. I knew that the problem would be a struggle for the kids, but I had expected that they would have made a little more progress than this by the end of the period.

23.   *Reconsidering the question.* On my way back to the front of the room, I passed by Tommy's group and stopped quickly in my tracks. The group was very engaged again. I overheard Tanya ask, "Is there anything else we can do with 300 yards of fence that would be bigger?" She suggested that maybe they could make a circle. Beatriz reminded the group that it had to be a rectangular pen. Michael said maybe the pen could be 125×50. Tanya asked where those numbers came from. Michael explained that he was just trying out different numbers that would add up to 300. Beatriz said that if the side of the building was 100 yards you would be using only half of the side. Michael added, "No one said we had to use it all. Maybe it doesn't matter."

24.   Tommy, who had remained quiet during the discussion up to this point, started arguing that the area would still be 10,000 yards. Michael punched the numbers (125×50) into the calculator and reported that he got 6,250. Tommy said, "No, no, no! That can't be right. Give me that calculator." He then punched in the numbers and came up with the same number Michael had reported. Tommy and the other members of the group looked puzzled by this finding.

25.   At this point I noticed that the bell would ring any minute. I told students that for homework they should continue to think about the

problem, consider what steps their group should take the next day, and come to class prepared to share some ideas with their group.

26.   *Reflecting on the first day.* Although I thought that the open-endedness of the problem might throw students, I was really surprised that they didn't know that two figures could have the same perimeter but have different areas. Helping them to see this was not my main goal. In fact, I assumed they would have no trouble with this idea, but it seemed to be a roadblock. Their confusion with this basic notion kept them from reaching my goals—adding structure to an ill-defined situation and coming up with a generalization for the dimensions of the pen that would give maximum area for any amount of fence.

27.   There were a few indicators of movement in the right direction toward the end of class. For example, Tommy's group finally realized that there was at least one rectangle that could be built with 300 yards of fence that had an area different from the square they had built originally. Also, Debra's group decided to not worry about the size of the building since that wasn't getting them anywhere and instead pretended they knew how much fence was left from the school play. Other groups were getting close to this point as a result of my encouraging them not to worry about the length of the building. But I am not sure if this is basis enough to expect more progress tomorrow without some additional intervention on my part. Should I just let the students continue to struggle with the problem and see if they can come up with a solution on their own? Should I continue to demand that students prove that their pens enclose the most area, as I had with Tommy's group? But, I wondered, would that be taking the challenge and the opportunity to discover away from the other students? Indeed, after today's class, I was not sure if I had done Tommy's group a favor or a disservice. I know that sometimes I just have to be patient and let students struggle. But it is really hard trying to decide when the struggle is likely to lead to productive activity and when the struggle is likely to lead to frustration and unwillingness to persevere. How can I help my students make progress?

The Second Day

28.   I started class the next day by telling my students that they would have a few minutes to share with their group members any new ideas they had about the problem and how they thought the group should proceed. I planned to listen in on these discussions and decide whether it might be helpful to have one of the groups share their thinking with the class. I thought that by having one group talk about what they were doing, other groups might get some ideas to pursue. If nothing new emerged from the discussions, I thought that I would ask Debra to talk about why her group decided to pick a length of fence and ask Michael to discuss what he had found out about the two rectangles his group had built the previous day.

29.   *Getting started, again.* As I walked around the room, I noticed that most groups were now building pens with a fixed length of fence and a few had started to notice that not all the areas were the same. When I got to Tommy's group, they were in the middle of a debate about what to do

next. Michael was saying that he thought they should try other rectangles. Beatriz and Tanya were nodding in agreement. Tommy, however, had a different idea. He said that he thought they should prove that the two they created yesterday really had different areas. He said he had been thinking about this last night and wanted to try something out. He asked me if they could go out into the hall because they would need more room. The other members of the group seemed willing to go along with this, so I agreed. As they went into the hall I moved to the door so I could keep one eye on Tommy's group and one eye on the rest of the class.

30.   In the hall Tommy told the group that he wanted them to build the square they had talked about yesterday. He paced off a square that was 10 × 10 and asked Tanya, Beatriz, and Michael to each stand in one of the corners. He said that each square of the linoleum counted as 10 yards, so each side was 100 yards and the area was 10,000 square yards. The group agreed. He then suggested that they build the rectangle that Michael had suggested at the end of the class.

31.   Michael paced off a rectangle that was 125 yards (12.5 linoleum squares) by 50 yards (5 linoleum squares). Michael then proceeded to count linoleum squares in the area. He got confused while counting, but Tanya was ready to step in. She said it would be five rows of 12 squares, which was 60, plus 2.5 more when you put the half tiles together. This would be 62.5. Beatriz added that you then had to multiply 62.5 by 100 since each tile had an area of 100. Tommy announced, "We still have 300 yards of fence, but the area is definitely smaller." He continued, "So we were wrong about everything." The other members nodded in agreement. They returned to the classroom and the group started to work on the task again.

32.   I was thrilled to see that they were finally making progress. They had been so sure that they were right, but now they seemed poised to really explore the problem. I thought the other students might benefit from the group's experience and asked them privately if they would be willing to share with the rest of the class what they were thinking about and what they did. They agreed. I called the class together.

33.   *Considering one group's approach.* Tanya, serving as spokesperson for the group, explained, "When we started the problem we decided that the building would be 100 yards and that each side would be 100 yards. This would give the rabbits 10,000 square yards of space, which was a lot. We thought we were done but we weren't. Ms. Olson said we needed evidence. So we finally tried another rectangle that used 300 yards and got a different area. We didn't think that could happen."

34.   I asked the class if they had any questions for Tanya and her group. Kendra said that she didn't understand how you could have two rectangles with 300 yards of fence but different areas. Michael asked if he could draw it on the overhead. Michael drew the diagrams shown in Figure 3.4 and explained that both pens had 300 yards of fence but that they didn't have the same area. He said they didn't believe it at first either. "So now," he explained, "we are going to try to find other rectangles we can make with 300 yards of fence and see if any areas are bigger than 10,000."

FIGURE 3.4. Michael's Diagrams That Show Two Rectangles Made from 300 Yards of Fence but Which Have Different Areas

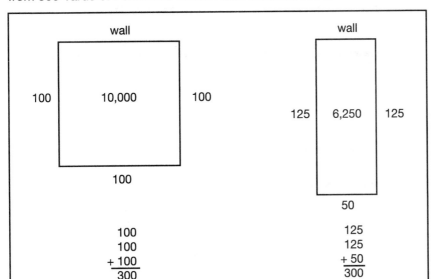

35.   Several students looked puzzled by this revelation and more hands shot up around the room. Rather than discuss the questions in whole group, I suggested that at this point students should go back to their groups and continue to think about the problem and talk about what Tanya's group had done. I wanted to give students something new to consider, but I didn't want to solve the task completely. I thanked Tanya and her group for sharing their thinking.

36.   *Rethinking the task at hand.* I gave the groups a few minutes to get back on task and then started my journey around the classroom. My first stop was the group that included Robert, Kenneth, Ty, and Cassandra. They were in the process of constructing pens that used 24 feet of fence on graphing paper (as shown in Figure 3.5). I asked them to explain what they were doing. As I recalled, the last time I visited this group they had built a square pen that was 8 × 8. Like most groups, they had decided on one configuration and wouldn't budge. Cassandra explained that they were trying to see if what Michael said was true. She went on to say that they decided to draw the pens on graph paper because then they could count the distance around the outside and count the squares on the inside.

37.   They had created three pens—the original 8 × 8, a 6 × 12, and a 4 × 10. I asked them what they had found out about these pens. Kenneth said that they found out that the area was not always the same. He explained, "You can use the same amount around the outside but get different amounts on the inside." Ty added that they found a pen that had a bigger area than the one they had built the previous day. I asked what they planned to do next. Kenneth said that they were going to find all the pens you can make with 24 feet of fence so they could see which was the biggest. "As you do that," I suggested, "think about how you can organize the data so you can see when you have the largest one."

FIGURE 3.5. Robert, Kenneth, Ty, and Cassandra's Rabbit Pens Made with 24 Feet of Fence

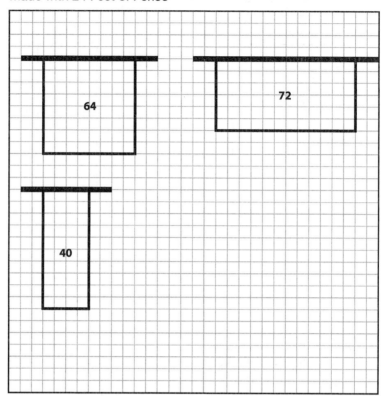

38.   Next, I stopped by the group that included Marcus, Luther, Denise, and Liz. They were working with 20 feet of fence, and had drawn all possible pens (shown in Figure 3.6). I asked them what they had learned from this. Marcus said that they had proven that Michael's conjecture about the area not being the same was true. Luther explained, "The skinniest ones have the smallest area." I asked what he meant by "the skinniest." He went on to say that the rectangles that had a 1 or 2 had the smallest area. Liz explained that the biggest area was the rectangle that had a width that was half the length. I indicated that this was an interesting observation and wondered if it would always be true. I encouraged them to continue to explore the problem and consider other lengths of fence.

39.   I visited a few more groups, noting that most were making progress. Unlike yesterday, students were definitely exploring—some were building pens with tiles, some were drawing configurations on graph paper, and others were just sketching pens freehand. But the important thing was that they were collecting data that were going to help them answer the question.

40.   The group that consisted of Jessica, Jamal, Toby, and Michele had chosen a different approach to the problem. Rather than drawing or building the pens, they had made a table (shown in Table 3.1). I asked them how they had selected this strategy. Toby explained that they started drawing the pens, but couldn't keep track of them—they couldn't tell if they had missed any. By making a table, he explained, they could make sure they had all of them. Recalling that yesterday they

FIGURE 3.6. Marcus, Luther, Denise, and Liz's Diagrams of All Possible Rabbit Pens with 20 Feet of Fence

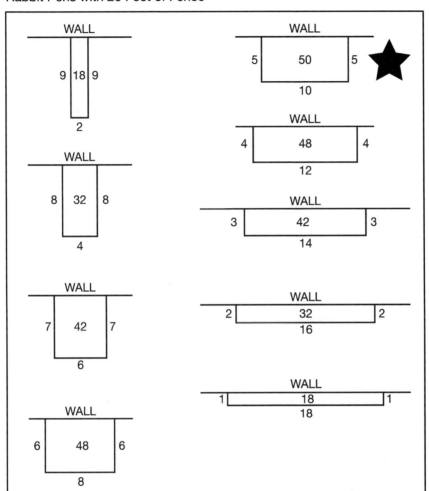

had fixed the size of the building at 50, I wondered how they had gotten to this point. Jamal said that they decided to pick an amount of fence to try, since they weren't getting anywhere with the other way. I asked why they picked 40. Michele said she thought that Michael's group picked a number that was too high—it would be hard to do all the pens. They wanted one that was smaller.

41.   I asked what they had found out from the table. Michele said that they found out that the 20 × 10 pen had the biggest area. Jamal added that the wall lengths decreased by two each time and the side length increased by one. Jessica said that if you look at the area it keeps getting bigger and bigger until you get to the biggest, then it starts going down. Toby said that they were going to try some other ones to see if they noticed any patterns. "But," Jamal added, "if we do it the same way, we can stop once the numbers start going down because we know there won't be any bigger ones." I told them they had done some interesting thinking on the problem, and encouraged them to continue their explorations.

42.   The groups were making good progress today. In another day they should be ready to look for patterns across different cases. As I walked back to the front of the room, I noticed that Tommy's group was hard at

TABLE 3.1. Jessica, Jamal, Toby, and Michele's Table That Shows All Possible Rabbit Pens with 40 Yards of Fence

Wall Length	Side Lengths	Amount of Fencing	Area
38	1	40	38
36	2	40	72
34	3	40	102
32	4	40	128
30	5	40	150
28	6	40	168
26	7	40	182
24	8	40	192
22	9	40	198
20	10	40	200
18	11	40	198
16	12	40	192
14	13	40	182
12	14	40	168
10	15	40	150
8	16	40	128
6	17	40	102
4	18	40	72
2	19	40	38

work exploring different pens with 300 yards of fence. Michael and Tanya were drawing rectangles, Beatriz was using the calculator to find the areas, and Tommy was putting the data into a table. I wished they had picked a smaller number, but I did not want to interfere at this point. Maybe tomorrow I would suggest they try a shorter length of fence.

43.   With about 5 minutes left in the class, I called the groups together again. I told them that I was really pleased with their thinking and how hard they were working on the problem. I asked them to individually write down what they had discovered today and what they thought the group should do next. I told students that we would continue work on the problem the next day.

NOTE

[1] The handshake problem my students worked on asked them to determine how many handshakes there would be if each of 10 guests at a party shook hands with every other guest only once. Once students had solved this problem, the number of guests was increased to 25, then to 100, and finally students were asked if they could determine the number of handshakes with any number of guests.

ANALYZING THE CASE

Now that you have had an opportunity to "visit" Isabelle Olson's classroom and note the pedagogical moves she made during the lesson, we invite you to consider how these moves influenced students' opportunities to engage with the mathematical ideas in the task. Here are a few suggestions on how to proceed.

- Review the list you created during your initial reading of the case in which you identified the pedagogical moves Isabelle Olson made during the lesson. For each item on your list, indicate whether this move supported or inhibited students' opportunities to engage with the mathematical ideas at the heart of the lesson. We also encourage you to consider *why* the pedagogical moves you identified are important in terms of students' opportunities to learn. Be sure to cite specific evidence (i.e., paragraph numbers) from the case to support your claims.
- If you have colleagues who also are reading this case, compare and contrast the ideas in your individual lists and possibly generate a master list. Note points of disagreement since these are likely to be fruitful topics for further discussion and debate. If you are working on this activity alone, we encourage you to refer to Appendix B, which includes a chart that was produced by teachers who participated in a professional development experience that focused on "The Case of Isabelle Olson." You may want to note points of agreement and disagreement and flag issues that you wish to investigate.

You may wish to extend your analysis of the case by considering the questions in the next section. Alternatively, you can skip the next section and proceed directly to the "Connecting to Your Own Practice" section in which you are encouraged to relate the analysis of the ideas and issues raised in the case to your own teaching practice.

EXTENDING YOUR ANALYSIS OF THE CASE

The questions listed in this section are intended to help you focus on particular aspects of the case related to teacher decision-making and student thinking. If you are working in collaboration with one or more colleagues, the questions can serve as a stimulus for further discussion and debate.

1. Ms. Olson states that she is most interested in giving her students "firsthand experience with making conjectures and gathering evidence to support or refute their conjectures" (para. 11). Given her goal, do you think that the rabbit pen problem was appropriate for this purpose? Why or why not?
2. Although Ms. Olson recognizes that students do not understand that all rectangles with the same perimeter do not necessarily have the same area, she chooses not to deal with this directly. How important is students' confusion regarding this relationship in solving this task?
3. Ms. Olson notices that her questions aren't working in that students "showed no signs of moving in a direction that would lead them toward a solution" (para. 16), and later that her questions "appeared to be too remote to steer the students in the right direction" (para. 20). What questions might Ms. Olson have asked in order to help students make better progress on the task throughout the first day of the lesson? How could Ms. Olson balance generic questions (e.g., para. 37, "think about how you can organize the data so you can see when you have the largest one") and task-specific questions (e.g., para. 38, "I asked what he meant by 'the skinniest'") to maximize student learning?
4. Ms. Olson consciously makes the decision to use a task that does not have clear expectations. However, if she had used the task in its original form (para. 8), much of the confusion that students experienced might have been avoided. What are the advantages and disadvantages of using the more open version of the problem?
5. At the end of the first day, Ms. Olson realizes that her students do not know that two rectangles that have the same perimeter can have different areas (para. 26). How could Ms. Olson have determined students' prior knowledge about area and perimeter *before* presenting this problem?
6. During the first day, students struggle to make sense of the problem and at times become frustrated with their inability to satisfy Ms. Olson. In your view, does Ms. Olson make the right decision in continuing to press students to explain why the solution they pose satisfies the conditions of the problem—that the rabbits will have "as much room as possible"? Should she have provided additional information to students? How do you know when a task is too open-ended to support

students' learning and when, with more persistence, students will make progress toward the mathematical goal you have set for them?

7. At the end of the first day, Ms. Olson asks students to "continue to think about the problem, consider what steps their group should take the next day, and come to class prepared to share some ideas with their group" (para. 25). Was this a reasonable homework assignment given the difficulties that students had experienced during class? How could the homework assignment be modified in order to help focus students' attention more squarely on the key mathematical ideas in the problem?

8. During the first day, Tanya suggests that her group should try building a circular pen (para. 23). If the pen did not have to be rectangular, what shape would maximize the area? Would the same generalization still hold?

9. As it turned out, Ms. Olson's students selected only lengths of fence that resulted in pens that had whole-number dimensions. If, however, students had selected 30 feet as the amount of fencing available for building the pen and had used only whole numbers for the length and width of the pen, they may have falsely concluded that two different pens—7 feet by 16 feet and 8 feet by 14 feet—both yielded a maximum area of 112 square feet. How might Ms. Olson have handled such a claim? Are there other fence lengths for which this issue will occur?

CONNECTING TO YOUR OWN PRACTICE

This section is intended specifically for readers who currently are teaching mathematics. The activities described in this section are designed to help you consider the ways in which issues identified in Ms. Olson's classroom have implications for your own teaching of mathematics. One of the complexities of teaching with which teachers (including Ms. Olson) grapple is the need to "balance purposeful, planned classroom lessons with the ongoing decision making that inevitably occurs as teachers and students encounter unanticipated discoveries or difficulties that lead them into uncharted territory" (NCTM, 2000, p. 17). Here are a few activities that will help you move from consideration of Isabelle Olson's teaching to a focus on your own classroom practices.

• In the "Analyzing the Case" section, you considered how Ms. Olson's pedagogical moves sup-

ported and/or inhibited students' opportunities to engage with the mathematics. Select one of the pedagogical moves from this chart that you feel has implications for your own teaching. For example, you may be concerned about how to maintain a balance between challenging your students and providing them with enough direction so that they can make progress on a task. You then might plan and teach a lesson in which you make a concerted effort to maintain the challenge of a task and offer help to students in a way that does not diminish their opportunities to think and reason about mathematics. If possible, audio- or videotape the lesson or have a colleague observe and take notes. As you reflect on the lesson, consider whether or not you maintained the challenge of the task and how this influenced what students learned. Also indicate what you still need to work on with respect to this pedagogy.

• Teach a lesson using the problem featured in the case (you might use Smith and Boston [2003] as a resource in designing the lesson). Compare and contrast the work produced by your students with that produced by Ms. Olson's students. For example, did your students also struggle to impose structure on the problem? How were the strategies produced by your students similar to or different from those produced by Ms. Olson's students?

EXPLORING CURRICULAR MATERIALS

You may want to explore your curriculum for ideas related to area and perimeter by considering the following questions: Does your curriculum focus on learning and applying formulas for solving problems involving area and perimeter? Does your curriculum develop students' understanding of area and perimeter (e.g., that rectangles with a fixed perimeter do not necessarily have the same area or that different rectangles with a fixed area do not necessarily have the same perimeter) through the use of problems set in a real-world context? What might be the potential benefits of including such tasks?

You also may want to explore additional tasks that make salient the mathematical ideas that were the focus of the case. The following list identifies instructional resources that contain problems that are considered to be mathematically similar to the task used in "The Case of Isabelle Olson."

Education Development Center, Inc. (1998a). *MathScape: Family portraits: Comparing function families* (Student guide). Mountain View, CA: Creative Publications.

> Of particular interest is Lesson 9, "Fenced In" (pp. 26–27), in which students explore a problem similar to the one that Ms. Olson's students solved. However, in this problem, students identify rectangles that can be constructed with a particular length of fencing (32 feet). Students also use a graph to determine the rectangle that has the greatest area.

Lappan, G., Fey, J. T., Fitzgerald, W. M., Friel, S. N., & Phillips, E. D. (1998a). *Covering and surrounding: Two-dimensional measurement.* Menlo Park, CA: Dale Seymour.

> Of particular interest is Problem 4.1 (pp. 35–36), in which students identify rectangular pens with a perimeter of 24 meters and determine the pen that has the greatest area.

The Mathematics in Context Development Team. (1998a). Mathematics in context: Get the most out of it (Student guide). In National Center for Research in Mathematical Sciences Education & Freudenthal Institute (Eds.), *Mathematics in context.* Chicago: Encyclopaedia Britannica.

> Of particular interest are Problems 1–5 (pp. 39–40), in which students identify rectangles with a perimeter of 100 meters and determine the rectangle that has the greatest area.

CONNECTING TO OTHER IDEAS AND ISSUES

If you have additional time, you may want to explore some aspect of the case in more depth. The resources identified in the following list provide some possibilities for exploring the mathematical and pedagogical issues raised in the case. For example, you might: (1) draw on Boston and Smith (2003) to discuss the opportunities for student learning afforded by tasks such as the Fencing Problem; (2) explore the set of mathematics problems presented in Chappell and Thompson (1999); (3) discuss the ways in which Ms. Olson might have used Activity 9A in Geddes and colleagues (1994) with her students prior to the lesson; (4) discuss how Ms. Olson might have used technology in her lesson as described in Hersberger and Frederick (1995) and/or Jones, Thornton, McGehe, and Colba (1995); (5) use Hirstein, Lamb, and Osborne's (1978) discussion of student misconceptions to analyze Ms. Olson's students' thinking; (6) compare and contrast the Build a Doghouse task described in Kenney and Lindquist (2000) with the task featured in the case; or (7) use Smith and Boston (2003) as a resource in designing a lesson around the Fencing Problem.

Boston, M., & Smith, M. S. (2003). Providing opportunities for students and teachers to "measure up." In D. H. Clements & G. Bright (Eds.), *Learning and teaching measurement* 2003 yearbook of the National Council of Teachers of Mathematics (pp. 209–220). Reston, VA: National Council of Teachers of Mathematics.

> The authors present two classroom vignettes that illustrate benefits of problem-centered instruction in developing student understanding of measurement concepts. Each lesson provides students with the opportunity to explore a mathematical task in which one attribute of a geometric figure remains constant while another attribute varies. The first vignette, "Designing Rabbit Pens," is based on the same problem used by Isabelle Olson.

Chappell, M. F., & Thompson, D. R. (1999). Perimeter or area? Which measure is it? *Mathematics Teaching in the Middle School, 5,* 20–23.

> The authors describe a study that examines middle school students' work on a set of open-ended perimeter and area tasks similar to the problem used by Isabelle Olson. Additional tasks described in the article include drawing figures with a given area or perimeter, recognizing real-world applications of area and perimeter, and exploring the relationship between area and perimeter. The authors also discuss students' visual representations, students' ability to create authentic word problems, and student reasoning.

Geddes, D., Berkman, R., Fearon, I., Fishenfeld, M., Forlano, C., Fuys, D. J., Goldstein, J., & Welchman, R. (1994). *Curriculum and evaluation standards for school mathematics addenda series, grades 5–8: Measurement in the middle grades.* Reston, VA: National Council of Teachers of Mathematics.

> The authors present a variety of activities related to measurement, including Activity 9, which focuses on the perimeters and areas of figures. The challenge problem in Activity 9A is nearly identical to the Fence in the Yard task which appeared on the 1996 NAEP (see the Kenney and Lindquist, 2000, reference provided in this list for a discussion of student performance on this task). In this activity, students are asked to consider whether shapes having the same perimeter must have the same area and whether shapes that have the same area must have the same perimeter—the same questions asked in the "Consider" portion of the Opening Activity for "The Case of Isabelle Olson."

Hersberger, J., & Frederick, B. (1995). Flower beds and landscape consultants: Making connections in middle school mathematics. *Mathematics Teaching in the Middle School, 1,* 364–367.

> The authors provide suggestions on how teachers could use a problem in which the area of a flowerbed built from a fixed amount timber must be maximized. Of particular interest is their suggestion that spreadsheets be used to explore students' conjectures.

Hirstein, J. J., Lamb, C. E., & Osborne, A. (1978). Student misconceptions about area measure. *Arithmetic Teacher, 6,* 10–16.

> The authors identify several common misconceptions that students have about area. For example, when comparing areas of two rectangular figures, students often state that the areas are equal if one dimension from one rectangle is equal to one dimension from the other. The authors conclude by suggesting several ways in which teachers can help students overcome these misconceptions.

Jones, G. A., Thornton, C. A., McGehe, C. A., & Colba, D. (1995). Rich problems—big payoffs. *Mathematics Teaching in the Middle School, 1,* 520–525.

> The authors discuss students' solutions to a set of problems that involve maximizing the area of a rectangular hotel atrium built from a fixed amount of railing under three different conditions: (1) the railing encloses all four sides; (2) the railing encloses only three sides; and (3) the railing encloses all four sides minus a 40-foot section on one of the sides. Of particular interest is the use of the graphing calculator to determine the maximum value, the connections among numeric and geometric patterns, and the connections made across the three variations of the problem.

Kenney, P. A., & Lindquist, M. M. (2000). Students' performance on thematically related NAEP tasks. In E. A. Silver & P. A. Kenney (Eds.), *Results from the seventh mathematics assessment of the National Assessment of Educational Progress* (pp. 343–376). Reston, VA: The National Council of Teachers of Mathematics.

> The authors describe sets of items that were developed around a common context and students' performance on these items. One of these contexts, "Building a Doghouse," involves a task similar to the problem used by Isabelle Olson. In the task, students are asked to construct a dog pen built from 36 feet of fence that encloses the largest area.

Smith, M. S., & Boston, M. (2003). Making rabbit pens. In G. W. Bright & D. H. Clements (Eds.), *Classroom activities for learning and teaching measurement* (*2003 Yearbook of the National Council of Teachers of Mathematics*) (pp. 47–49). Reston, VA: National Council of Teachers of Mathematics.

> The authors present teaching notes to accompany a task similar to the problem used by Isabelle Olson (described in Boston & Smith [2003]). In particular, the authors discuss how to implement the lesson, suggest questions to ask students as they work on the task, and describe typical student responses.

Exploring Volume and Surface Area

The Case of Keith Campbell

Chapter 4 has been designed to engage readers in considering important issues in the teaching and learning of mathematics related to surface area and volume. Prior to reading "The Case of Keith Campbell"—the centerpiece of this chapter—we suggest that you begin by completing the Opening Activity. The primary purpose of the Opening Activity is to engage you with the mathematical ideas that will be encountered when reading the case.

OPENING ACTIVITY

The Opening Activity, shown in Figure 4.1, poses questions similar to those explored by students in the lesson featured in "The Case of Keith Campbell." After you have determined all of the ways that each fixed number of cubes can be arranged into rectangular prisms; sketched the prisms; and determined their dimensions, volume, and surface area you are encouraged to complete the "Consider" portion of the activity. The "Consider" questions provide an opportunity for you to reflect on your work in creating the prisms in order to form generalizations about maximum and minimum values of surface area and about the common formulas for surface area and volume of rectangular prisms.

Once you have completed the activity, you may want to refer to Appendix C, which contains a set of solutions generated by teachers who completed the Opening Activity as part of a professional development experience that focused on "The Case of Keith Campbell." You are encouraged to compare your solutions with those that are provided in order to consider different approaches and reasoning that you may not have used in your own work on the task.

FIGURE 4.1. The Opening Activity for "The Case of Keith Campbell"

Solve

Find all of the ways that the following fixed numbers of cubes can be arranged into rectangular prisms: 8, 9, 10, 11, and 12. For each fixed number of cubes, sketch the rectangular prisms you create, and record their dimensions, volume, and surface area. You may want to organize your information into a table.

Consider

1. For each fixed number of cubes, how do you know that you have found all the rectangular prisms that can be constructed?

2. Explain why the formulas $SA = 2LW + 2LH + 2WH$ and $V = L \times W \times H$ can be used to determine the surface area and volume (respectively) of a rectangular prism.

3. For each of the fixed number of cubes, compare the prism with the greatest surface area to the one with the least surface area. Make observations about the characteristics of these prisms that appear to affect their surface area. Would the observations you made continue to be true for any set of rectangular prisms that share a constant volume?

READING THE CASE

As you read the case, we encourage you to make note of the mathematical ideas Keith Campbell's students appear to be learning. (You may want to use a high-lighter or Post-it notes to keep track of these as you read the case.) For example, you may identify a specific for-mula that students were learning (e.g., the formula for finding the volume of rectangular prisms) or concep-tual understandings students were developing (e.g., connections between physical models, tables of data, and symbolic formulas).

Your list of the mathematical ideas Keith Campbell's students are learning can serve as topics for discussion with a colleague who also has read the case or as topics to investigate as you read additional cases. If you currently are teaching mathematics, issues that surface in reading "The Case of Keith Campbell" might serve as starting points for exploration in your own classroom. For exam-ple, you might consider how using different representa-tions for a concept (e.g., diagrams, concrete models, tables, equations) might influence students' learning of mathe-matics in your own classroom. We will discuss additional connections to your own practice at the end of the chapter.

THE CASE OF KEITH CAMPBELL

1.   Keith Campbell is in his 17th year of teaching mathematics and reading to middle school students. For the past 4 years, he has been a member of the faculty at Franklin Middle School. Although certified as an elementary/physical education teacher, Keith took a variety of mathematics courses in both high school and college. He describes mathematics as "extremely interesting and challenging."

2.   Students at Franklin learn mathematics through problem-solving and discussion. In Keith's eyes, this approach provides the ideal setting to pass his excitement for mathematics along to his 7th-grade students. Keith enjoys how this approach has changed his role in the classroom. After years of simply telling mathematical ideas to students—who then were expected to memorize, practice, and reproduce exactly what they were given—Keith now has the opportunity to guide his students as they create and explain their own mathematical ideas to him. For the first time in his teaching career, Keith feels that he is helping to "develop students' minds." Keith credits strong support from his colleagues with helping him to make this transition.

3.   Another change Keith experienced in his move to Franklin was in the demographics of the students. For 13 years, Keith taught in a private school populated mainly by White students from suburban communities. In contrast, Franklin's population is predominantly minority students from economically impoverished, urban neighborhoods. Although the students at Franklin are disadvantaged in many ways, Keith does not see this as a barrier to their success in mathematics. In fact, he is insulted when others so quickly associate low achievement with students from poor communities. Keith believes that *all* students can learn challenging mathematics when given the opportunity.

Keith Campbell Talks About His Class

4.   My 24 7th-grade students and I are currently working in a unit that integrates measurement and geometry concepts. Over the past few days, students have been exploring surface area and volume of rectangular prisms in the context of covering "moon gems" (1-inch cubes) to keep them from disintegrating on the journey back to Earth. "Astronauts" have discovered moon gems occurring both individually and grouped together in the form of rectangular prisms. The number of gems being packaged or covered corresponds to volume, and the cost of covering the package, at $1 per square unit of special paper, corresponds to surface area. This context builds upon the intuitive notions of volume and surface area that my students have developed from working with 3-D shapes in earlier grades. Today's lesson definitely extends this foundation as students discover the formula for volume of a rectangular prism and compare the characteristics of rectangular prisms with the same volume but different surface areas.

5.   Before I came to Franklin, my approach to teaching surface area and volume can be summarized as, "Here are the formulas, here is a shape, now find its surface area and volume." I was always sure to tell my

students exactly what these terms meant in everyday language, although I clearly emphasized memorizing and applying the formulas rather than understanding the concepts. What's exciting about this unit is that the students are developing an understanding of the concepts first and then are developing the formulas based on their understanding. I used to enjoy presenting surface area and volume to my students. Now, I enjoy listening to my students present surface area and volume to me and to their classmates.

6.   We have covered some exciting territory over the past few days and have made some great discoveries. First, students used graph paper to attempt to find all of the possible covers for a single gem. My initial directions stated that the covers should be constructed from non-overlapping squares sharing one or more adjacent sides. One student suggested that if we split one of the outer squares into fractional pieces or fancy designs, we could never find *all* of the possible covers. With the added requirement that covers must consist of whole squares, students identified 10 covers for a single gem, as shown in Figure 4.2. We discovered that all of these covers, even the fancy ones, have a cost of $6 since they all must contain exactly 6 squares. We then moved on to designing covers and finding the costs of packages with 2 and 3 gems, and concluded the lesson by comparing the covers for the 1-, 2-, and 3-gem packages.

7.   Our focus then shifted from creating covers to exploring the notion that different rectangular prisms with the same volume can have different surface areas. More specifically, with arrangements of 4 gems, students discovered that the package (the rectangular prism) could have two different shapes ($4 \times 1 \times 1$ and $2 \times 2 \times 1$), each of which resulted in a different cost (surface area). Students confirmed this finding by looking at different arrangements of 6 gems that also had different costs. We concluded yesterday's lesson by organizing our information, as shown in Table 4.1, which students copied into their notes.

8.   I also have this information copied onto an overhead transparency, since we will be adding to it both today and tomorrow. In labeling the columns, I chose to introduce the terms *volume* (and cubic units), *surface area* (and square units), and *dimensions*, but to maintain the student-generated terms *front edge* and *side edge*. These words seemed

FIGURE 4.2. Covers or "Nets" for a Single Moon Gem Created by Mr. Campbell's Students

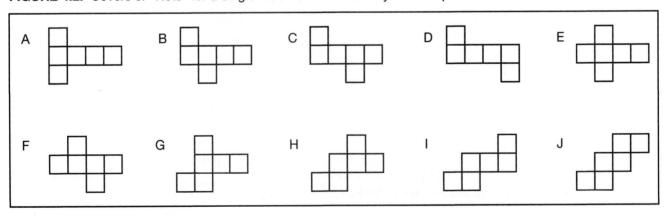

TABLE 4.1. The Volume, Dimensions, and Surface Area of Rectangular Prisms Consisting of 1 to 6 Moon Gems

Volume in cubic units (# of gems)	Dimensions			Surface Area in square units (Cost)
	Front Edge	Side Edge	Height	
1	1	1	1	6
2	2	1	1	10
3	3	1	1	14
4	2	2	1	16
	4	1	1	18
6	3	2	1	22
	6	1	1	26

more descriptive than the traditional use of length and width. Considering students' perspective of rectangular prisms constructed on their desks (see Figure 4.3), front edge and side edge appear to be very natural choices.

9.   Last night's assignment was to explore the various ways of packaging 8 gems (stated in our new terminology as "different rectangular prisms with a volume of 8 cubic units"), to add this information to the chart, and to begin to make some observations and conjectures about the data we have recorded so far. After our work with 4 and 6 gems in class yesterday, students should not have had difficulty tackling this assignment.

10.   Students also have a running list of observations and questions in their notebooks that have surfaced during class discussions, which are listed on the side chalkboard.

• Packages with 1, 2, and 3 gems have only one shape, but you can make different shapes out of 4 gems. (Cameron) —as long as they are rectangular prisms. (Maria)
• Both packages held 4 gems, but one cost more than the other. (Rochelle)
• The different packages of 4 gems have different costs because in one package the gems have more sides touching than in the other. (Antonio)

FIGURE 4.3. Mr. Campbell's Students' Perspective of Rectangular Prisms Constructed on Their Desks

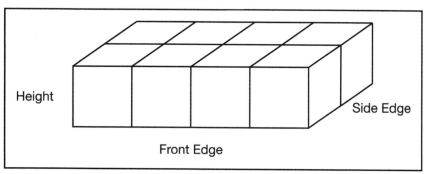

Height

Side Edge

Front Edge

- If you put the gems in a row, each new gem will add $4: 1 gem costs $6, 2 gems cost $10, 3 gems cost $14, 4 gems cost $18. (Charlise)
- This pattern works because if you think of putting the new gem in the middle, where two of its sides would be touching the other gems, only four new sides would be on the outside to be counted in the cost. (Rochelle) —or, if you think of adding the new gem on the end, you cover up one side that you had with one side of the new gem, so you are adding five new sides, but taking away one. (Curtis)
- Will all the packages with more than 4 gems also have more than one shape? (Tyrone)
- Do our observations for packages of 4 gems also seem to be true for packages of 6 gems? (Mr. Campbell)
- How do you know when you have found all of the different packages? (Mr. Campbell)
- Why did we skip 5 and 7? (Cameron)

11.   Today, after discussing the homework, we will look at packages that hold 12 gems. There are two primary goals for today's lesson: (1) students will develop the formula for volume of a rectangular prism, and (2) students will generalize that for different rectangular prisms with the same volume, the elongated prisms have a greater surface area than the more compact prisms (or, conversely, that surface area decreases as the prisms become more cube-like). Additionally, I hope that students will begin using the mathematical terminology rather than the context of the moon gems. Making this transition will confirm that students have associated the familiar ideas in the moon-gem model with the concepts of surface area and volume. Most of what I've heard students say so far in this unit indicates that they are building on their intuitive understanding of volume and surface area to form conceptions about how these attributes are measured.

12.   I am still concerned, however, that students seem to be overlooking square and cubic units, and that they instead are treating surface area and volume as strictly numeric quantities. I was alerted to this oversight when the class did not challenge a student's observation that "surface area will always be bigger than volume." I emphasized to students (and noted on the chart) that volume is measured in cubic units and surface area is measured in square units. We then discussed how these units relate back to the moon gems. I also explained that because the edges of the gems that we are working with measure 1 inch, our units would be cubic inches for volume and square inches for surface area.

The Class

13.   As students entered the room, last night's homework was displayed on the overhead:

1. Determine the possible surface areas for different rectangular prisms with a volume of 8 cubic units. Add this information to your chart.
2. Look over the information in your chart. Write down any interesting observations or patterns to share with the class.

I was impressed to see students gathering their materials and moving their desks into pairs without being reminded to do so. Once everyone was settled in, I began class by telling students that today we were going to explore packages of 12 gems, although I first wanted to talk about their findings from last night's homework. Several hands shot up, and I selected Sheila to present her solution.

14.   Sheila came up to the overhead with 8 blocks and built a 4 × 1 × 2 prism. She explained, "Since we didn't have the blocks to work with, I tried making sketches like we did in class. The easiest way was to draw a rectangle with 8 squares, then make it look like blocks." She proceeded to draw a 4 × 2 rectangle (Figure 4.4.a) and then added the extra lines to give it a 3-D appearance (Figure 4.4.b). Many students had experienced difficulty in sketching rectangular prisms earlier in the week, so I asked Sheila to identify the dimensions. She pointed to the drawing to indicate "4 along the front edge, 1 along the side edge, and 2 for the height."

15.   "And what did you find for the surface area, for the cost of covering this package?" I asked, still hesitant to completely abandon the moon-gem context. Sheila pointed to the faces of the prism as she counted out the surface area. "Eight on the front and the back gives $16, 2 on each side is $4, plus 4 on the top and the bottom is $8. So, 16 + 4 + 8 is $28 total." Before asking for questions from the class, I wanted to somehow hint that Sheila's method of totaling the surface area was directly related to the formula. I asked Sheila to repeat her procedure, and suggested that the class listen closely to her *system* for finding the cost, or surface area. I indicated that this would be important later, and left it at that. I thanked Sheila for sharing her work and asked if anyone had questions.

16.   Immediately Jamal raised his hand. "Sheila said that she drew a picture because we didn't have blocks to work with at home. Well, I just used the blocks we made out of graph paper the other day." I affirmed that this was a good approach and asked whether he had come up with a prism different from Sheila's. "I have two that are different than the one Sheila has. I'll show you the one I like the best," Jamal responded. He built a 2 × 2 × 2 prism and said, "Four squares on each side times 6 sides is $24." As Jamal sketched the package on the overhead, he acknowledged Maria's hand in the air. "Why do you like this one the best?" she asked. Jamal replied, "It makes a cube."

FIGURE 4.4. (a) The 4 × 2 Rectangle Drawn By Sheila; (b) Sheila "Adds Extra Lines" to Make the 4 × 2 Rectangle into a 4 × 1 × 2 Prism

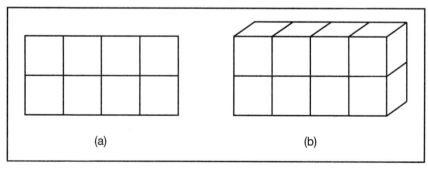

(a)   (b)

17.   There were no more questions, so I selected Antonio to present the next prism. "I used the observation from our list that each new gem adds $4 to the cost if the blocks are in a row. I just continued the table to 7 gems, which cost $30, and 8 gems, which cost $34. If you draw the pictures like this (Figure 4.5), then it's easy to find the cost, I mean the surface area."

18.   Antonio drew the picture, then explained the calculations he had written next to it: "For 8 gems in a row, you have four sides with 8 squares each, plus one square on the top and one on the bottom. So, 4 times 8 is 32, plus 2 is 34." "Wow," I responded, "that's a great observation and a new way of modeling the prism. How can we use Antonio's picture to confirm that covering 7 gems in a row costs $30?" Antonio began to cross out the bottom row of cubes, but I indicated to him that I would like to hear from someone else. Devon's hand shot up. "Like how Antonio was scratching out the last row of squares. Each side would have 7 instead of 8. You would have four sides of 7, plus 2," he said. I wanted to continue in this direction because I think that it is valuable for students to make generalizations, even though the generalization I was after did not contribute to the goals of today's lesson. I asked, "What would the picture look like for 6 gems in a row?" "Four sides of 6 plus 2," Maria offered, and I again countered with, "How about for a million in a row?"

19.   Still at the overhead, Antonio wrote "4 × GEMS + 2," and concluded, "This will always work, even for a million gems." Rather than asking Antonio how he had reached this conclusion, I directed the question toward the rest of the class. Cameron contended, "Once you know you've found a pattern, it will always work or else it wouldn't be a pattern." I asked if anyone could offer an explanation based on Antonio's sketch on the overhead. Sharee suggested, "It's like we said for 6 in a row, 7 in a row, 8 in a row—when you get to a million in a row, you will have four sides of a million, plus 2. The picture would look the same, only with a million squares for each side." After some giggling about how Sharee's sketch wouldn't fit on the overhead, I asked the class whether Rochelle's observation about this pattern yesterday somehow related to Antonio's new explanation today. No one volunteered any ideas, so we added both

FIGURE 4.5. Antonio's Illustration of the Surface Area of an 8-Gem Prism

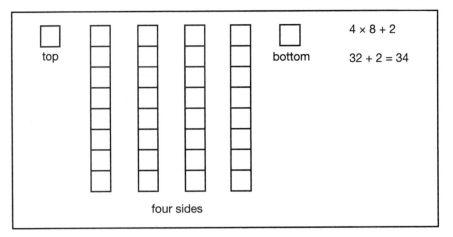

Antonio's formula and my question to our list of observations, with a promise to revisit them tomorrow.

20.   I thanked Antonio for his contribution and asked for a volunteer to present another prism. The class seemed content that we had found all of the possible prisms, so I reiterated a question from our list that had remained unanswered: "How do you know when you have found all of the different packages?" Other than responses of "that's just all there is," and "we just know," no one could offer any real justification at this point.

21.   I decided to see if we had successfully dispelled an earlier misconception that a prism perceived from a different orientation was a completely different prism. I quickly sketched a $2 \times 1 \times 4$ prism, the "tall" version of Sheila's prism, and asked, "What about this one? I don't see it up here anywhere." Students were quiet for a minute; then I could hear mumblings of, "it costs $28," and "that's already up there," and "it's the same as Sheila's, it's just turned a different way."

22.   Angelique seemed particularly eager to speak. "You don't have to find the cost to show that two prisms are the same or different, just look at the dimensions." She was referring to our decision to use cost as the criterion for determining whether two packages were the same or different (based on the conjecture that if two packages of the same number of gems had the same cost, then they must be the same package). Angelique continued, "If the dimensions are the same three numbers, then it's the same prism. It's just turned differently." She proceeded to show how Sheila's shape could be thought of as "2 along the front edge, and 1 along the side edge. So when you write it in the chart, the dimensions will be exactly the same, but the 2 and the 4 will be switched." I indicated that looking at the dimensions would be a very quick and useful way of determining whether two shapes were the same or different and noted how our chart made this feature easier to see. I also asked Angelique to add her observation to our list.

23.   Angelique's comment reminded me that we still needed to enter today's information into the overhead chart, so I asked the volunteers to come back up and do so. Our chart now included prisms up to a volume of 8 cubic units, as shown in Table 4.2.

24.   Almost half of the period was gone, and I wanted students to begin exploring packages of 12 gems. Immediately, Cameron raised his hand to ask why we were skipping packages of 9, 10, and 11 gems. I praised his curiosity and conceded to have one pair work with 9 gems and one pair work with 10 and 11 gems (and to add this information directly to our chart when they had completed their work). The rest of the class was instructed to create different rectangular prisms with a volume of 12 cubic units.

25.   As students began their investigations, I observed many pairs that were busy building and sketching prisms. One pair didn't appear to be building any prisms and had proceeded directly to listing dimensions on their chart. Another pair, Rochelle and Brian, had built a $3 \times 2 \times 2$ prism and found the cost of $32. They were debating how this could be true if one of the 8-gem packages had cost $34. "Look at the chart," said Rochelle. "One of the packages with 6 gems cost $26 and one with 8 cost $24. It doesn't make sense, but packages with more gems can actually

TABLE 4.2. The Volume, Dimensions, and Surface Area of Rectangular Prisms Consisting of 1 to 8 Gems

Volume in cubic units (# of gems)	Dimensions			Surface Area in square units (Cost)
	Front Edge	Side Edge	Height	
1	1	1	1	6
2	2	1	1	10
3	3	1	1	14
4	2	2	1	16
	4	1	1	18
6	3	2	1	22
	6	1	1	26
8	2	2	2	24
	4	1	2	28
	8	1	1	34

cost less." I told them to see if they could find anything in common about the ones that cost the most or the ones that cost the least. "Perhaps you can make some sense out of it," I offered, hoping that their interest in making sense out of their observation would uncover a relationship between the shape of a prism and its surface area.

26.   After about 10 minutes, I began selecting pairs to sketch one of their prisms on the board and to write the cost underneath. Once all four prisms were represented, we would add the information to our chart with the lowest cost first. By now, most pairs had found four different prisms and were discussing whether or not they had found them all. I listened in on a few conversations and heard many students reaching an informal consensus as we had in class. Only a few students were basing their arguments on using different combinations of the factors of 12. Sheila was one of these, and I made a note to call on her later in the discussion.

27.   Soon all four prisms with a volume of 12 cubic units and those with volumes of 9, 10, and 11 cubic units were drawn on the board and added to the chart, as shown in Table 4.3. I asked whether everyone agreed that our list was correct and complete, and Latisha hesitantly raised her hand. "We have $38 in the chart twice," she said in a questioning tone, "and I thought that if the cost was the same then it was the same package." I pointed out that the two prisms she was referring to had different volumes and therefore would have to be different prisms. Wrinkling her forehead, Latisha looked at the list of observations and asked, "But didn't Angelique say that if the cost was the same, then the dimensions will be the same, too?" I restated Angelique's observation to stress that the surface area *and* the volume had to be the same, and Latisha seemed contented by this explanation. I thanked Latisha for voicing her concern and giving us the opportunity to clarify Angelique's observation.

28.   I asked if we were ready to begin making observations about the chart and Antonio, as usual, seemed eager to assume center stage. "If you take three numbers that multiply to 12, like 6 times 2 times 1, then your dimensions would be 6 along the front edge, 2 along the side edge,

TABLE 4.3. The Volume, Dimensions, and Surface Area of Rectangular Prisms Consisting of 9 to 12 Gems

Volume in cubic units (# of gems)	Dimensions			Surface Area in square units (Cost)
	Front Edge	Side Edge	Height	
9	3	3	1	30
	9	1	1	38
10	5	2	1	34
	10	1	1	42
11	11	1	1	46
12	3	2	2	32
	3	4	1	38
	6	2	1	40
	12	1	1	50

and 1 for the height. We proved it by building it, and it takes 12 blocks. The same is true for 4 times 3 times 1, 12 times 1 times 1, and 3 times 2 times 2."

29.　　　I didn't know how to rephrase Antonio's explanation without giving away the formula, so I turned it over to the class. "Did anyone else make this same observation? Can anyone explain it to us again?" Erica chimed in, "If you multiply the dimensions together, you get the volume. Look," she said, coming up to the overhead, "it works for every one we have listed in our chart." Erica began moving her finger across the rows of our chart and multiplying the dimensions aloud.

30.　　　I questioned further, "Can anyone describe more precisely what it is that we are multiplying together to get the volume?" "Front edge, times side edge, times height," Tyrone responded. I handed Tyrone the marker and asked him to write what he had just said on the overhead, and he wrote "FE × SE × H = Volume."

31.　　　"Congratulations!" I said, addressing the entire class. "We have just put together a formula for finding the volume of a rectangular prism. This means that if I gave you the dimensions of any rectangular prism, you could tell me the volume. And, in your homework tonight, you'll be able to list the possible dimensions without having to build a prism or draw a picture!" I didn't have time to go through any examples at this point. Perhaps tomorrow, though, I would be curious to see whether they really could find the volume of any rectangular prism if just given the dimensions. I continued, "If we change 'front edge' to length and 'side edge' to width, then our formula becomes Length × Width × Height = Volume. Does this sound familiar to anyone?"

32.　　　Cameron was quick to respond: "That's exactly what my dad said when I told him we were working on volume. He said, 'Volume is length times width times height,' and I told him that Mr. Campbell said that volume was the number of gems that a package can hold." "Well, you were both right," I laughed, thinking to myself how pleased I would have been in the past if a student had provided this formula as the definition of volume. "Your dad was saying how to find volume and you were explaining to him what volume is. Well, that's what volume is when you are working with the moon gems. How would you explain what volume is without using moon gems?" Cameron responded with "the number of cubes in a package," which Maria restated as "the number of cubic units in a rectangular prism." I added, ". . . or any 3-D shape, for that matter," and I asked Maria to add this definition of volume to our list.

33.   Sheila now had her hand in the air, and I remembered that I had wanted to include one of her ideas into the discussion. "We noticed that the three numbers multiplied together is always 12. So, like, all of the different ways of getting an answer of 12 become all of the different packages." "Different prisms," I interrupted. Before prompting Sheila to continue, I restated her first observation: "You noticed that the dimensions are always factors of 12, and . . ." Sheila responded, "That's why there was only one package for 2 and 3—because they don't have any factors." "They don't have *any* factors?" I asked. "Well, I mean, besides 2 times 1, and 3 times 1," Sheila concluded, "they don't have any *other* factors."

34.   I addressed the class with, "What do we call numbers that don't have any factors besides themselves and 1?" Many students chimed, "Prime." "So, if the volume is a prime number—I mean, if the number of cubic units of volume is a prime number—how many different prisms can you make?" Sheila led the response of "one" with a few others joining in. I asked Sheila to add this observation to our list. We could return to it tomorrow by looking at Cameron's question of why we skipped 5 and 7. Right now, I wanted to discuss the maximum and minimum surface areas, and we didn't have much time left.

35.   I knew Brian and Rochelle were close to being able to make a conjecture about this, so I decided to begin the discussion with them. "Brian, did you and Rochelle discover anything special about the prisms that always seem to have the most surface area?" "Yeah," Brian said, "the ones with the blocks in a row, the ones in our 'add four each time' chart. They always have the highest cost." Again, I interjected, "the most surface area," and asked Brian to show that this was the case for volumes of 4, 6, 8, and 12 in our chart.

36.   I next inquired, "Which prisms seem to have the least surface area?" Motioning toward the sketches on the board, Rochelle suggested, "Well, the ones with blocks in a row are longer and skinnier than the other prisms, and they have the most surface area. So it looks like the short, fat prisms have the lowest cost—surface area." Although she was right on the mark, I wanted more descriptive words than "short, fat" prisms. "What do you mean by short, fat prisms?" I asked. Rochelle continued, "They're more scrunched together, they have more sides touching, like we said the other day."

37.   I was hoping for Rochelle to mention cubes, so I probed further. "Okay, so can anyone use other words that give this same idea?" "More compact?" Sheila offered, then added, "The numbers for the dimensions are closer together." Although this wasn't exactly what I was looking for, Sheila had at least provided a description that I could build on. "What type of prism would be the most compact, or would have its dimensions closest together?" Now quite a few hands shot up. "A cube," Tyrone called out, "because the dimensions would be the same!" We only had one cube in our list, a $2 \times 2 \times 2$. I was again at a loss for how to rephrase

this idea without giving everything away, and it seemed like the perfect time for a quick journal entry. I instructed students to think about the relationship between the shape of a prism and its surface area, and then to write these ideas down in their journals.

38.　　　As students were writing, I posted the following homework questions on the overhead:

1. a) Predict how many rectangular prisms will have a volume of 24 cubic units. How do you know?
   b) Predict which one will have the greatest surface area and which one will have the least surface area. How do you know?
   c) Now add rectangular prisms with a volume of 24 cubic units to your chart. Check your answers above to see if they agree with the information in your chart.
2. How can you use the dimensions of a rectangular prism to find its surface area?

39.　　　With a minute or so left, I hinted that students should think about Sheila's method of systematically counting out surface area at the beginning of the lesson. I also suggested that drawing prisms, as Antonio had, might be helpful as well. I praised the class for today's efforts, indicating that they now could answer all of the questions on our list. We would attempt to do this tomorrow during our final discussion and summary of this unit.

ANALYZING THE CASE

Now that you have had the opportunity to read the case and identify the mathematics that Keith Campbell's students were learning, we invite you to consider how Keith Campbell supported or inhibited students' learning. Here are a few suggestions on how to proceed.

- For each mathematical idea that you identified as you read the case, indicate the pedagogical moves Mr. Campbell made that appeared to support (or inhibit) his students' learning of the mathematical idea and provide evidence (i.e., paragraph numbers) from the case to support your claims. (You may want to organize your work into a two-column chart—one column for mathematical ideas, the other for Mr. Campbell's pedagogical moves.)
- If you have colleagues who also are reading the case, compare and contrast the ideas in your individual charts and possibly generate a master chart. Note points of disagreement since these are likely to be fruitful topics for further discussion. If you are working on this activity alone, we encourage you to refer to Appendix C, which includes a chart that was produced by a group of teachers who engaged in this activity. You may want to note points of agreement and disagreement and identify issues that you wish to investigate.

You may wish to continue your analysis of the case by considering the questions in the next section. If you currently are teaching mathematics, you might want to proceed to the "Connecting to Your Own Practice" section in which you are encouraged to relate the analysis of the ideas and issues raised in "The Case of Keith Campbell" to your own teaching practice.

EXTENDING YOUR ANALYSIS OF THE CASE

The questions listed in this section are intended to help you focus on particular aspects of the case related to teacher decision-making and student thinking. If you are working in collaboration with one or more colleagues, the questions can serve as a stimulus for further discussion.

1. In what ways do the stacking cubes help to support students' thinking during this and prior lessons in the Moon Gems Task? In what ways is the "moon gem" context conceptually helpful?

2. Compare the different diagrams for representing rectangular prisms presented in the case: net diagrams (Figure 4.2), Sheila's diagram (Figure 4.4), and Antonio's diagram (Figure 4.5). How does each type of diagram support students' thinking about surface area and volume? For what purposes might one type of diagram be more useful to students than the others?

3. Identify points in the lesson where Mr. Campbell leads students toward specific responses. What might Mr. Campbell have done differently to foster more inquiry on the part of the students?

4. Mr. Campbell builds on Antonio's drawing to help students develop the formula $4 \times n + 2$ for determining the surface area of a rectangular prism with dimensions $n \times 1 \times 1$ (paras. 18–19). Was this a worthwhile sidetrack from the lesson's primary goals? How does Antonio's formula relate to Rochelle's or to Charlise's observation (para. 10)?

5. Students use Antonio's sketch to justify that the "$4 \times \text{GEMS} + 2$" formula will always work (para. 19). However, the formula for volume is justified only through numeric examples. What issues does this raise about mathematical proof? How else might students have proven that their formula for volume would always work?

6. Identify opportunities in the lesson where Mr. Campbell could have encouraged student-to-student interaction. What might Mr. Campbell do, or do differently, to establish student-to-student interaction as a norm in class discussions?

7. Approximately 10 students in Mr. Campbell's class offer explanations that provide a window into their thinking and understanding of surface area and volume. What evidence in the case suggests that students who did not offer explanations were or were not understanding these concepts? In what ways did Mr. Campbell appear to be assessing the understanding of the whole class? What could he do to get a better idea of what all of his students were understanding?

8. Why is Mr. Campbell concerned that his class "did not challenge a student's observation that 'surface area will always be bigger than volume'" (para. 12)? Identify opportunities where Mr. Campbell could have reinforced proper units for surface area and for volume. What role should the use of proper units and terminology have played in this lesson? What might Mr. Campbell

have done differently to foster the use of proper units and terminology throughout the lesson?

9. Why did Mr. Campbell think that it was important to include factors and prime numbers into the discussion (paras. 33–34)? How do factors and prime numbers relate to the question of whether students have found all of the possible rectangular prisms of a constant volume? How do factors and prime numbers relate to the question of why Mr. Campbell skipped volumes of 5, 7, and 11 cubic units?

10. Students conjecture that two packages with the same number of gems and the same cost must be the same package (para. 22). Is it true that if two rectangular prisms have the same volume and surface area, they must be congruent? What about other shapes?

CONNECTING TO YOUR OWN PRACTICE

This section is intended specifically for readers who currently are teaching mathematics. The activities described in this section are designed to help you consider the ways in which issues identified in Mr. Campbell's classroom have implications for your own teaching of mathematics. One of the challenges that teachers like Mr. Campbell have to grapple with is how to help students develop an understanding of mathematical ideas that goes beyond being able to memorize and apply procedures and formulas. Here are a few activities that will help you move from a consideration of Keith Campbell's teaching to a focus on your own classroom practices.

• One aspect of Mr. Campbell's pedagogy that supported his students' learning of mathematics was the way in which he used and connected different representations for surface area and volume. By exploring prisms with cubes, drawing diagrams of prisms, and displaying and analyzing data in tables, students were able to understand what volume and surface area are and to derive the formula for volume themselves. Plan a lesson in which you can incorporate different representations (e.g., diagrams, concrete models, tables, graphs, real-world contexts, equations) of the mathematical concept you are teaching. Consider how you will introduce the representations and how you will make specific connections between representations so that students develop an under-

standing of the key ideas in the lesson. Prepare specific questions in advance that you can ask to determine what students currently understand and to advance their understanding.

• Teach the lesson you planned in the previous activity. If possible, videotape your teaching or have a colleague observe and take notes. Then reflect alone or with a colleague on the lesson and identify the mathematical ideas your students appeared to be learning and the pedagogical moves you made that supported (or inhibited) students' learning. For each inhibiting move identified, consider how the move could be avoided in future lessons. For each supporting move identified, consider how the move could be used in other lessons.

EXPLORING CURRICULAR MATERIALS

You may want to explore your curriculum for ideas related to surface area and volume by considering the following questions: Does your curriculum include tasks that go beyond the rote application of formulas? Does your curriculum provide opportunities for students to make sense of surface area and volume? What might be the potential benefits of including tasks that provide opportunities for students to build prisms, collect data, and make conjectures about the patterns they observe?

You also may want to explore additional tasks that make salient the mathematical ideas that were the focus of the case. The following list identifies instructional resources that contain problems that are considered to be mathematically similar to the task used in "The Case of Keith Campbell."

Billstein, R., & Williamson, J. (1999b). *Middle grades math thematics: Book 2*. Evanston, IL: McDougal Littell.

Of particular interest are Problems 8 and 9 (p. 438), in which students are asked to construct different rectangular prisms from 36 cubes, to determine the surface area and volume for these prisms, and to consider maximum and minimum values of surface area.

Education Development Center, Inc. (1998c). *MathScape: Shapes and space: Thinking three-dimensionally* (Student guide). Mountain View, CA: Creative Publications.

Of particular interest is Lesson 4, entitled "Move the Cube" (pp. 12–13), in which students are challenged to find the greatest possible surface area for different numbers of cubes.

Foreman, L. C., & Bennett, A. B., Jr. (1996). *Visual mathematics: Course II, Lessons 1–10*. Salem, OR: The Math Learning Center.

Of particular interest in Lesson 2 (Shape and Surface Area) are Actions 1–7 in the Focus Teacher Activity (pp. 21–24), in which students construct different rectangular prisms made from 24 cubes and explore how the surface area changes as the shape of the prisms changes.

Lappan, G., Fey, J. T., Fitzgerald, W. M., Friel, S. N., & Phillips, E. D. (1998c). *Filling and wrapping: Three-dimensional measurement.* Menlo Park, CA: Dale Seymour.

Of particular interest are Problems 2.1 and 2.2 (pp. 16–17). In Problem 2.1, students explore different ways that 24 cubes can be arranged into rectangular prisms and determine the amount of material needed to cover each prism. Problem 2.2 asks students to make conjectures about the rectangular arrangement of cubes that requires the least amount of packaging material.

The Mathematics in Context Development Team. (1998c). Mathematics in context: Reallotment (Student guide). In National Center for Research in Mathematical Sciences Education & Freudenthal Institute (Eds.), *Mathematics in Context.* Chicago: Encyclopaedia Brittanica.

Of particular interest is Problem 21 in Section E, where students are asked to find different-sized boxes that will hold 24 cubes and to determine how much cardboard would be needed to make each box.

CONNECTING TO OTHER IDEAS AND ISSUES

If you have additional time, you may want to explore some aspect of the case in more depth. The resources identified in the following list provide some possibilities for exploring the mathematical and pedagogical issues raised in the case. For example, you might: (1) complete additional activities found in Del Grande and Morrow (1993), Geddes and colleagues (1994), or Stern (2000) that extend and reinforce the mathematical ideas in the case; (2) analyze student thinking in the case with respect to the common misconceptions identified in Ben-Chaim, Lappan, and Houang (1985) and Battista and Clements (1996); (3) compare Mr. Campbell's teaching and the lesson presented in Battista (1999) and discuss the impact of inquiry-based instruction on students' learning of surface area and volume; or (4) connect the case to ideas featured in Principles and Standards for School Mathematics (NCTM, 2000) using Chappell (2001), or to "The Case of Isabelle Olson" using Boston and Smith (2003).

Battista, M. (1999). Fifth-graders' enumeration of cubes in 3-D arrays: Conceptual progress in an inquiry-based classroom. *Journal for Research in Mathematics Education, 30,* 417–448.

This research article examines students' thinking and common errors in working with and understanding the volume of cubic arrays. The study provides research support for the effectiveness of inquiry-based instruction in developing students' understanding of surface area and volume.

Battista, M., & Clements, D. (1996). Students' understanding of 3-D rectangular arrays of cubes. *Journal for Research in Mathematics Education, 27,* 258–292.

This research article discusses students' solution strategies and errors in perceiving, enumerating, and constructing 3-D arrays of cubes during instruction and pairwork in an inquiry-based classroom. The authors analyze the development of students' thinking in determining the surface area and volume of "boxes" represented first as 2-D nets (pattern pictures), then as 2-D diagrams (box pictures).

Ben-Chaim, D., Lappan, G., & Houang, T. (1985). Visualizing rectangular solids made of small cubes: Analyzing and effecting student performance. *Educational Studies in Mathematics, 16,* 389–409.

This research article discusses students' difficulties in (a) relating diagrams to the 3-D shapes they represent, (b) determining the volume of rectangular prisms represented by diagrams of small cubes (based on the 1977–78 NAEP data and released tasks), and (c) spatial ability in general. The authors also discuss the effects of instruction in spatial visualization on the performance of middle school students, with the intent of making practical suggestions for instruction.

Boston, M., & Smith, M. S. (2003). Providing opportunities for students and teachers to "measure up." In D. H. Clements, & G. W. Bright (Eds.), *Learning and teaching measurement* (2003 Yearbook of the National Council of Teachers of Mathematics) (pp. 209–220). Reston, VA: National Council of Teachers of Mathematics.

The authors present two classroom vignettes that illustrate the benefits of problem-centered instruction in developing student understanding of measurement concepts. One of the vignettes featured in the article depicts a classroom and lesson similar to the one upon which "The Case of Keith Campbell" is based. The article might be used to stimulate a discussion of problem-centered instruction in geometry and measurement, or as a connection between this case and "The Case of Isabelle Olson."

Chappell, M. (2001). Geometry in the middle grades: From its past to its present. *Mathematics Teaching in the Middle School, 6,* 516–519.

In this article, the task that was featured in "The Case of Keith Campbell" is used to portray how spatial reasoning can be used to foster conjecturing and can connect to other important mathematical ideas. Figure 2 in the article presents nets for rectangular prisms of 1 through 4 cubes that correspond to the "$4n + 2$" formula discussed in the case (para. 19). The article might be used to connect ideas in the case to the NCTM principles and standards or to focus the discussion on nets of rectangular prisms or other solids.

Del Grande, J., & Morrow, L. J. (1993). *Curriculum and evaluation standards for school mathematics addenda series, grades 5–8: Geometry and spatial sense in the middle grades*. Reston, VA: National Council of Teachers of Mathematics.

Activity 1 from this book provides some foundational explorations involving cubes, networks for cubes, and visual arrays of cubic structures. These activities relate to and extend the mathematical ideas in "The Case of Keith Campbell" and hence might serve as additional explorations for participants or for participants to use with their students.

Geddes, D., Berkman, R., Fearon, I., Fishenfeld, M., Forlano, C., Fuys, D. J., Goldstein, J., & Welchman, R. (1994). *Curriculum and evaluation standards for school mathematics addenda series, grades 5–8: Measurement in the middle grades*. Reston, VA: National Council of Teachers of Mathematics.

This book contains a variety of activities related to measurement. Activity 14 provides an opportunity to look at the surface area of a variety of 3-D shapes;

Activity 22a provides further exploration of how the shape of a solid is related to its surface area; and Activity 22b uses the context of creating buildings with different numbers of rooms (cubes) and windows (faces of cubes) to explore the connection between surface area and volume of rectangular prisms and other cubic structures.

Stern, F. (2000). Choosing problems with entry points for all students. *Mathematics Teaching in the Middle School*, 6, 8–11.

The author of this article frames the discussion around a task with many of the same features as the Moon Gems Task. Students explore several questions arising from the context of icing a cube-shaped cake and then cutting this cake into cube-shaped pieces. Similar to the case, students in the article encounter the ideas of surface area and volume and create a data table that is utilized later in the lesson to look for patterns and make generalizations. The article might be used as an extension to the case to revisit surface area and volume, to focus on the discovery of patterns and generalizations, or to discuss how a task can be accessible to all students.

5

Estimating and Calculating Volume

The Case of Nancy Upshaw

Chapter 5 has been designed to engage the reader in considering important issues in mathematics teaching and learning. Prior to reading "The Case of Nancy Upshaw"—the centerpiece of this chapter—we suggest that you begin by completing the Opening Activity. The primary purpose of the Opening Activity is to engage you with the mathematical ideas that will be encountered when reading the case.

OPENING ACTIVITY

The Opening Activity, presented in Figure 5.1, is similar to the task explored by Nancy Upshaw's students in the lesson featured in the case. After you have determined how many blocks and how many balls would be needed to fill a room, we encourage you to compare the methods you used when working with the blocks and the balls, to consider other ways of approaching the problem, and to reflect on whether the different approaches are mathematically related.

Once you have completed the activity, you may want to refer to Appendix D, which contains a set of solutions generated by teachers who completed the Opening Activity as part of a professional development experience that focused on "The Case of Nancy Upshaw." You are encouraged to compare your solutions with those that are provided in order to consider how other approaches or reasoning relates to your own solution strategies.

READING THE CASE

As you read the case, we encourage you to make note of what Nancy Upshaw's students are doing in order to make sense of and ultimately complete the activities in the Large Numbers Lab. (You may want to use a highlighter or Post-it notes to keep track of these as you read the case.) For example, you may identify ways in which her students are using diagrams and manipulatives to support their thinking or ways in which groups of students are working together to solve the problems.

Your list of observations regarding students' sense-making activities during the lesson can serve as topics for discussion with a colleague who also has read the case or as topics to investigate as you read additional cases. If you currently are teaching mathematics, these might serve as starting points for exploration in your own classroom. For example, you might consider how the use of diagrams and manipulatives might support students' sense-making activities in your own classroom. We will discuss additional connections to your own practice at the end of the chapter.

FIGURE 5.1. The Opening Activity for "The Case of Nancy Upshaw"

LARGE NUMBERS LAB

1,000 Cubes

Picture a big block that has been formed by making a 10 × 10 × 10 cube from 1,000 small 2-cm cubes. Circle the number that you think would be closest to the number of big blocks it would take to fill up this room:

100   1,000   10,000   100,000   1,000,000

Determine as accurately as you can how many big blocks are needed to fill up this room. Explain your method.

1,000 Balls

Circle the number that you think would be closest to the number of tennis balls it would take to fill up this room:

100   1,000   10,000   100,000   1,000,000

Determine as accurately as you can the number of tennis balls it would take to fill up this room. Explain your method.

Consider

- Think about the methods you used to determine the number of blocks and balls needed to fill the room. Are your two methods mathematically related? If so, how are they related? If not, how are they different?

- Think about another way to determine the number of blocks or balls needed to fill the room. What are the mathematical similarities and differences between this method and the method(s) you originally used?

- Suppose we wanted to fill the room with balls that were twice the diameter of the ball that was used originally. How would this change the number of balls that would fit in the room? What if we used a ball that was half the diameter of the original ball?

THE CASE OF NANCY UPSHAW

1. Nancy Upshaw is in her 18th year of teaching mathematics and science. For the past 5 years, she has been teaching mathematics at El Toro Middle School. Nancy loves children and mathematics and science, so she cannot imagine a more perfect way to be spending her time. The majority of the students at El Toro live in the surrounding low-income community and about 90% of the students speak Spanish as a native language.

2. This is El Toro's third year of participating in a mathematics reform project, and Nancy has tried to participate earnestly despite some concerns she has about the curriculum. She and her colleagues have drawn material from a variety of sources because at the time they began their reform effort there were few, if any, commercial curriculum programs available that addressed their desire to engage students in activities that were more oriented toward inquiry and problem-solving.

3. Prior to their involvement in the new project, the teachers at El Toro had been using a textbook series that was 7 years old. Although Nancy feels the exploratory nature of many of the new tasks has rejuvenated her classroom and she enjoys teaching math more than ever before, she worries that there is not enough basic skills review folded into the new curricular units they are using. She tries to supplement the new units in order to address her concern, and she looks for opportunities to include basic skills practice in the context of the new units as much as possible.

Nancy Upshaw Talks About Her Class

4. This is my smallest class of 7th-graders, with only 30 students. Nearly all of them speak English as a second language, so I often give directions in both English and Spanish. As 7th-graders, my students are taking the first half of a mathematics course originally designed for 9th-grade pre-algebra. My students will have the second half of the course in the fall as 8th-graders. I am new at teaching this part of the course.

5. This class is part of a 90-minute math/science block. One nice thing about block scheduling is that it gives me the flexibility to sometimes spend a little extra time on mathematics or on science, as needed. Yesterday and today we are devoting all our time to math. This is the second day we've been working on the Large Numbers Lab activity in the Large Numbers unit (see Figure 5.2). Students have the following materials available: up to 400 2-cm cubes, up to 10 soccer balls, rulers, meter sticks, tape measures, a formula sheet, and paper.

6. I like this activity because it has a "science lab" feel to it. I enjoy that aspect of the task because it gets students engaged. The students have been working in groups of four or five. Because there are not enough materials for each group to work on the same lab at the same time, I asked about half the class to begin with the 1,000 Cubes Lab and half to begin with the 1,000 Balls Lab.

7. The Large Numbers unit is designed to help students build their understanding of the relative size of large numbers through concrete

FIGURE 5.2. The Large Numbers Lab Activity Used in "The Case of Nancy Upshaw"

LARGE NUMBERS LAB

1,000 Cubes

Picture a big block that has been formed by making a 10 × 10 × 10 cube from 1,000 small cubes. Circle the number that you think would be closest to the number of big blocks it would take to fill up this room:

| 100 | 1,000 | 10,000 | 100,000 | 1,000,000 |

Determine as accurately as you can how many big blocks are needed to fill up this room. Sketch any cubes your group builds and label their dimensions. Write an explanation of your method.

Find the volume in cubic centimeters or cubic meters of a box that would hold exactly 1,000 of these big blocks. Explain how you determined the volume needed.

1,000 Balls

Circle the number that you think would be closest to the number of soccer balls it would take to fill up this room:

| 100 | 1,000 | 10,000 | 100,000 | 1,000,000 |

Determine as accurately as you can how many soccer balls are needed to fill up this room. Write an explanation of your method.

Find the volume of a box in cubic centimeters or cubic meters that could be filled up with 1,000 soccer balls. How did you determine this?

How much volume would *not* be filled by the soccer balls in the box? Explain the process you used to determine this.

Adapted from *Investigating Mathematics: An Interactive Approach* by Larry Hatfield. Copyright © 1994 by the Glencoe Division of Macmillan/McGraw-Hill. Used with permission.

investigations of situations involving numbers such as 1,000 and 1,000,000. These are important benchmarks to add to their repertoire. The Large Numbers Lab activities my students are working on are in the context of estimating and measuring the volume of rectangular solids. I like this approach because I think students should be using measurement skills throughout the curriculum, rather than as an isolated unit of study.

8.   I also saw this activity as a good opportunity to help to improve their volume sense and their estimation and measurement skills. My students are proficient with area measure and have some familiarity with the concept of volume for a variety of different solids, so completing the activities provides an opportunity for them to reinforce some important ideas about 3-D units and dimensions. In these activities students have the chance to spend some time estimating volume measures, rather than relying solely on physically counting cubic units in order to find the volume. I want to see them using a multiplicative process for finding the volume (using Length × Width × Height, a "layering" approach, or area of the base × the height) in order to solve the lab problems, and I want them to gain some insight into the relationships underlying the formula for volume of a rectangular prism. Students also can get some practice with linear and area measure, something they should have had plenty of experience with in 5th and 6th grades.

9.   As students calculate the volumes, they also will be getting some practice with computation, something that I try to work on whenever possible. I think computation skills get reinforced best when students use them in the process of solving problems, rather than as an isolated activity. Yesterday I started by encouraging students to organize their work on the labs so that they can easily show all the details of how they are arriving at their answers. I think that in a complex task like this, it is vital for students to record what they have done and to be able to retrace their steps. If there is no record, it is hard to reflect on what they have done. This is something I encourage in science, and it is just as important for math. I did not let the students have calculators for these activities because I wanted to encourage estimation and I wanted students to practice computation in the context of the tasks. I find that when they have calculators, their tendency is not to estimate because they think there isn't really a need to do so. The students also have available to them an information sheet for the entire unit that contains diagrams and area and volume formulas for a range of two- and three-dimensional shapes.

10.   Yesterday most of the students got through at least one of the labs. Several groups got off to a slow start organizing their materials and figuring out how to begin. Most of them were making wild guesses about how many balls or blocks would fit in the classroom, with only a few groups really attempting to make a reasonable prediction. One of those was Rolando's group. They used 5 soccer balls, stacked them in a corner, and estimated that the ceiling was going to be about 10 balls high. In a previous unit, we had measured the room to be 6.5 meters in length, 4.5 meters in width, and 2.33 meters in height, and these dimensions remained posted on a side bulletin board. Using these measurements, Rolando's group estimated that the length of the room was almost three

times the height and the width was about twice the height, so the room would be about 30 balls long and 20 balls wide. To make their prediction, they reasoned that they would need 10 layers of balls, each with dimensions 30 by 20, or a total of 6,000 balls, to fill the room. They decided that even though they had rounded up the dimensions of the room and 6,000 balls was probably a bit too high, they still would choose "closer to 10,000" for their prediction. Their reasoning process was just what I was hoping to see. They were able to use a similar reasoning process to find the volume of the box that would be filled by 1,000 balls.

11.   By the end of the day, I want to bring the class together to look at the findings for both labs to see if the students can see any commonalities across the labs. I also want to push their thinking a little and ask them to consider what would happen if we changed the size of the unit of measure.

The Class

12.   I asked the representatives from each group to come up to the front of the room and get what they needed to continue their work on the labs. (Rather than having all seven groups move around the room, I had group representatives bring the lab materials to their tables as needed. This cut down on the number of students roaming around the room at any given time. Three groups started yesterday with the 1,000 Balls Lab and four groups started with the 1,000 Cubes Lab.) I reminded students to make sure that they recorded their initial predictions on the class chart as they started a new lab (see Figure 5.3). I told the students they'd have about 45 minutes to work on the labs and then we would talk about their findings. After all seven groups had their materials, I walked around the room checking in with each group.

FIGURE 5.3. Ms. Upshaw's Students' Predictions for How Many Blocks and Balls Would Fill Their Classroom

How Many Are Needed to Fill Our Classroom?

Please put a tally mark under the number that you think is the closest to the number of blocks or balls it would take to fill our classroom:

	100	1,000	10,000	100,000	1,000,000
1,000-cube blocks		IIII IIII II		IIII	III
Soccer balls	II	IIII IIII IIII	III		I

13.   *1,000 Cubes Lab.* Mariola, Jorge, Roberto, and Jimmy were beginning work on the 1,000 Cubes Lab. I noticed they had built a 15 × 15
base for a big block and were working on adding another layer to it. No
wonder it seemed like there weren't enough 2-cm cubes to go around!
This was really off track, so I asked them to explain what they were
doing. Jorge said, "We are trying to make the 1,000-cube block so we can
see how big one is so we can predict." It was interesting to me that they
were spending so much time on making a prediction. Most groups had a
sense of how big the 1,000-cube block would be and quickly circled their
prediction or just made a wild guess. Regardless, now that they were
stuck on this problem of building a big block, I had to get them past it. I
replied, "OK, so how many little cubes are in that bottom layer?" Jorge
said, "You have to have all the dimensions the same 'cause it's a cube, so
we made this 15 by 15 on the bottom and now we're building it up to
1,000." I asked what they meant by "building it up to 1,000." Roberto
jumped in and said, "The big cube is supposed to be made up of 1,000
little cubes." I asked if they had calculated how many little cubes they
would need in order to build their 15 × 15 layer into a big block. They
looked at one another and back at me and shrugged their shoulders.

14.   Mariola said, "See, I told you guys. Ms. Upshaw, I told them this will
be too many." I asked Mariola to explain. "If it's a cube, it will have to
have 15 layers going up, too, and that will be way more than 1,000 little
cubes. Each layer is 15 by 15, which is 225, so it will be over 1,000 with
only 5 layers." I asked the boys what they thought about what Mariola
was saying. They reluctantly admitted she was right. Mariola continued,
"1,000 is 10 times itself three times. The bottom layer should be 10 by 10
because that would be 100, and 10 layers high would be 1,000 total
cubes." I asked, "Will you have enough cubes to build an entire 1,000-
cube block?" They all said, "No," in unison. I asked them if they could
make a sketch now of what the big block might look like if they actually
could build it, and I reminded them to label the dimensions on their
sketch. Roberto picked up a ruler and measured the length of one edge
of one of the small cubes and said it was 2 cm. Then he said, "So each
dimension is 20 centimeters long." Jorge asked, "Why isn't it 10 cubes?
Why does it have to be centimeters?" I redirected the question back to
the group and walked away. I would get around to some other groups
and come back to them later.

15.   I walked over to another group that was a little farther along on the
1,000 Cubes Lab. Yesterday, they had predicted that they would need
about 7,000 big blocks to fill the room because the blocks were a little
smaller than a soccer ball so it would take more of them to fill the room.
I had been pleased to see them intuitively using the notion that it would
take more of a smaller unit to fill up the volume. At the time I reached
them, they were well into the activity. They had several calculations
written on their paper, as well as a diagram of a big block, and they were
now arguing about what size box would hold 1,000 of the big blocks.
José was pointing to the diagram of the big block and saying, "Look, one
of these big blocks is 8,000 cubic centimeters. . . ." "Wait," I interrupted,
"tell me where the 8,000 came from." José continued, pointing to the
dimensions of the big block in the diagram, "20 times 20 times 20 is
8,000. So 8,000 cubic centimeters. Now a 1-meter box holds a million

cubic centimeters, so that's 125 of these big blocks." He paused to point out a long division problem of 1,000,000 ÷ 8,000 and then continued, "One 1-meter box holds 125 big blocks, so it will take eight 1-meter boxes to hold 1,000 big blocks (again indicating calculations on paper)—or one big box that is 8 cubic meters in volume. The only way to get that is 2 times 2 times 2." Lucia insisted, "NO, you can get it other ways. It doesn't say the big box has to have all three dimensions the same. It can be 8 meters by 1 meter by 1 meter if you want, or 4 by 2 by 1." José said, "But it's CUBIC meters, CUBE-IC. So I don't see why it doesn't have to be a cube." Lucia replied, "But you can get it other ways." I could see they were talking past each other and I was concerned that José had a misconception about the meaning of cubic units of measure. But I wasn't sure what to do about it at that moment. I needed to get around to some other groups, so I just told them that Lucia was right and that the box does not have to be a cube. I made a mental note to come back to this with José at some point.

16.   At that moment, Mariola called me back over to her group and wanted to know if they were on the right track figuring how many big blocks would fit in the room. I asked Jimmy to explain to me what they were doing. I often did this to spot check that some of the less vocal group members were following what was going on. The students knew that every once in a while they would be put on the spot. So Jimmy explained, "The room is 4.5 meters wide, 6.5 meters long, and 2.33 meters high [referring to the dimensions posted in the room]. We rounded them." I asked why they did that. Jimmy was quiet for about 10 seconds. Mariola was squirming to answer, but I told her to let Jimmy think. Then he said, "Because it makes the numbers easier." He continued, "So you have 5 meters wide, about 7 meters long, and 2 meters high. Then we did Length times Width times Height to get the volume." Mariola mumbled, "'Cause it's a rectangular prism." I shot her a glance that again told her to let Jimmy finish. He went on, "We got a room volume of 70 meters." I said, "Meters cubed?" He said, "Yeah, cubed." I told Jimmy it sounded reasonable so far and I asked Roberto to continue. "Since we had the blocks in cubic centimeters, we changed the dimensions of the room to the same units. So it was 70 million cubic centimeters in the room." He pointed to the equation "$500 \times 700 \times 200 = 70,000,000$" written on the group's paper. Then he continued, "Oh, I guess we could have also done 70 times 100 times 100 times 100—times 100 for each dimension. Anyways, since one of the big blocks has 8,000 cubic centimeters, we had to divide 70 million by 8,000 to get the number of big blocks."

17.   I interrupted him and asked Mariola, "So about how many big blocks will fit in the room?" She said, "70 million divided by 8,000. This is like 70 thousand divided by 8." She reached for the group's paper and pointed to where they had written 70,000,~~000~~ ÷ 8,~~000~~. Mariola continued, "So we knew it was between 8,000 and 9,000, but closer to 9,000. We did the division (pointing to the long division problem of 70,000 ÷ 8 on their paper) and found that 8,750 big blocks will fit in the room." Jimmy said, "That's a lot more than I guessed. I thought it would be closest to 1,000. It was just a wild guess." I asked them how accurate they thought their answer was. They all agreed it was probably a little high because they had

rounded two of the dimensions up when they made their estimate. I told them they were doing fine and should keep working.

18.   As I left, I heard Roberto say he thought of another way to calculate the answer. He thought of dividing each of the room dimensions by 20 cm to see how many big blocks fit along each dimension. Then he would multiply the dimensions to find the total number of big blocks it would take to fill the room. This was similar thinking to what I saw happening in another group—Andres, Maria, Juan, and Begonia—except these students did not use metric units. Instead, they had drawn a sketch iterating the big blocks to show that 5 big blocks fit along 1 meter. Then they expressed the dimensions of the room in terms of big blocks by multiplying each dimension by 5 (resulting in length = 4.5 × 5 = 22.5 blocks; width = 6.5 × 5 = 32.5 blocks; height = 2.33 × 5 = 11.65 blocks) and found the volume of the room to be about 8,520 big blocks. I was pleased to see students using this approach to tackling the problem, which was similar to how Rolando's group estimated the number of soccer balls that would fill the room. Perhaps later on in the discussion, it would be interesting to have the class compare approaches that used meters or centimeters as the units versus ones that used the objects (blocks or balls) as the units, and to get students to think about why these different approaches yielded similar, yet different, results. Since almost half an hour had already gone by, I decided that I better check out some of the other groups working on the 1,000 Balls Lab.

19.   *1,000 Balls Lab.* I moved on to a group of boys working on the 1,000 Balls Lab. I asked them to tell me what they had done so far. They said they were sketching how many balls would cover the floor of the class-room. They had a rectangle drawn on the paper and it was filled with circles (as shown in Figure 5.4). Tomás said, "This is representing the bottom layer of balls in the room." I asked how they determined how

FIGURE 5.4. Tomás's Group's Sketch of How Many Balls Would Cover the Classroom Floor

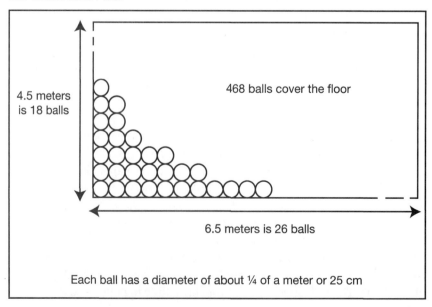

4.5 meters is 18 balls

468 balls cover the floor

6.5 meters is 26 balls

Each ball has a diameter of about ¼ of a meter or 25 cm

many balls would fit along each dimension of the room. They said they had a hard time measuring the diameter of the balls. Rigo picked up a ruler and showed me what they had done. He set the ball next to the ruler and then picked up two pieces of paper. He held the two pieces of paper on either side of the ball, tangent to the ball so that the bottom edges of the paper landed on the ruler. Then Tomás stood up and read the distance on the ruler from one piece of paper to the other. He said, "See, it's a little tiny bit more than 25 centimeters, so we just called it 25. Twenty-five is easy to work with, and it's within half a centimeter anyway." I was happy to see them worrying about accuracy and what kind of error is acceptable in this situation, because yesterday I noticed that several groups were doing things like holding the ruler in the air next to the ball and trying to eyeball the length of the diameter. I talked to the class about this and so it was nice to see that at least one group was listening!

20.   Tomás continued, "The diameter is about 25 centimeters. So you could have four in one meter. So, the width of the room will be 4 balls times 4.5 meters, and the length will be 4 balls times 6.5 meters." He paused a minute to multiply $4 \times 4.5 = 18$, $4 \times 6.5 = 26$, and $18 \times 26 = 468$, and then continued, "So it's 18 by 26—468 balls to cover the floor." I asked how they were going to use that to find the number of balls in the entire room and they said that was easy. Tomás said they just had to multiply by how many layers would fit up to the ceiling. He quickly calculated 2.3×4 on paper, and said, "It's 2.3 meters high, so 2.3 times 4 is 9.2 balls high. So that would be 9.2 layers of 468 balls." I asked, "What does that mean to have 9.2 balls? Can you have .2 of a ball?" I told them to keep going and I moved on to Rolando's group.

21.   Rolando's group was trying to find how much volume would not be filled by 1,000 balls. They said they were completely stuck. Whenever students tell me they have no idea where to begin, I always try to get them to analyze the problem situation and identify what they do know. I want them to realize that they always know something, and that they should not give up so easily. So, I asked them to tell me what they already knew. After about 20 seconds of silence, Angel piped up, "Well, we know there are 1,000 balls and when you pack them in a box, there have to be spaces in between. They don't fit together nicely like the blocks." I said, "OK, anything else? What do we know about the box? Anything?" As I said this, I glanced at the group's paper. They had drawn a box with 10 balls along each dimension and had marked each dimension as 2.5 meters (perhaps they had measured one ball to be .25 meters in diameter?). Written under their drawing was "Volume = $2.5 \times 2.5 \times 2.5$" and the calculations for $2.5 \times 2.5 = 6.25$ and $6.25 \times 2.5 = 15.625$.

22.   Rolando sheepishly offered, "We figured out the volume of it would be 15.625 cubic meters." I said, "So, that's the volume of the box that holds 1,000 balls. What do we need to know to find out how much of that space is taken up by the soccer balls?" Angel seemed to have an epiphany and she blurted out, "Oh, if we get the volume of the balls themselves then we'll know how much of the space they take up." I encouraged them to pursue Angel's idea and see what they could come up with.

23.   Isabel, Guillermo, Maya, and Tran were at this same point in the lab, but Tran had an interesting insight that related to previous classwork.

Tran was showing his group that this was similar to a problem we had done as a warm-up exercise last week in which the students had to decide how much of the area of a rectangle tiled with circles was not being covered by the circles. Tran drew a diagram similar to the one I had seen in Tomás and Rigo's group. He calculated the area of one circle, multiplied it by the total number of circles, and subtracted that result from the area of the rectangle. He said, "See, this is just the same idea except it's 3-D, so instead of areas, we're doing volumes. We have the volume of the box, so now we need the volume of one ball." Isabel said she remembered that problem. I encouraged them, telling them that Tran was on the right track.

24.   *Class discussion.* Now we had about 40 minutes left in the class and I wanted to get started with a discussion about their work on the two labs. To begin the discussion, I told the students to compare the class prediction chart (see Figure 5.5) with their final answers for the number of each object that would fill up the room. The class agreed that the number of 1,000-blocks needed was actually closer to 10,000 and the number of soccer balls needed was closer to 1,000.

25.   A murmur arose around the room. I heard things like, "My prediction was right!" and "I didn't know 1,000 was so small," and "I was way off," and "I guess a million is a lot more than I thought!" I asked Jimmy what he meant when he said he didn't know that 1,000 was so small. He said, "I just always thought 1,000 is a lot, but now it seems much smaller. Especially compared to a million." I asked if any other students felt the same way, and a few raised their hands. Tran commented that "1,000 dollars is a lot of money but a million dollars is a *huge* amount of money." I then asked students if they could tell me why it took more 1,000-blocks to fill the room than soccer balls. Roberto said, "'Cause soccer balls are

FIGURE 5.5. Final Chart of Ms. Upshaw's Students' Predictions for How Many Blocks and Balls Would Fill Their Classroom

How Many Are Needed to Fill Our Classroom?

Please put a tally mark under the number that you think is the closest to the number of blocks or balls it would take to fill our classroom:

	100	1,000	10,000	100,000	1,000,000
1,000-cube blocks		⊞⊞ ⊞⊞	II √	⊞	III
Soccer balls	III	⊞⊞ ⊞III √	⊞	I	III

bigger. They take up more space." I asked, "Why is that important?" He said, "'Cause if they take up more space you need less of them to fill it up." Isabel then blurted out, "But the soccer balls don't fill up all the space the same way the blocks do." I told her that was a good point and to hang on to it until later on in the discussion.

26.   Next, I told students that I would soon be selecting groups to present their strategies for figuring out how many blocks or balls would fill the room, and I asked them to take a minute to think about the processes they used to solve this problem in both labs. The first group that I chose to come to the overhead described how they had found the volume of the room, and then divided by the volume of one big block. I had noticed on my rounds that several groups had used this same basic procedure with only minor differences (i.e., how and when they used estimates instead of exact calculations, how and when they converted from centimeters to meters or from cubic centimeters to cubic meters, and whether they used a layering approach or the volume formula).

27.   I then selected a group that had determined how many blocks would fit along each dimension and then multiplied to see how many blocks would fill the room. As they finished speaking, Rigo chimed in to say that his group had "used the exact same method for the balls, too. The only difference is that there are four balls in each meter instead of five blocks." I asked if any other groups had noticed how the same basic strategy could be used whether we were using blocks or balls. Many nodded their heads, but Isabel raised her hand to say that she thought that the first strategy needed to be changed a little for the balls. "The balls leave spaces, so you can't just divide the volume of the room by the volume of one ball," she said. Tran continued, "Just like when we found the volume of the box that would hold 1,000 balls, you can't just find the volume of one ball and multiply by 1,000 like you can for the blocks. You have to find the diameter of the ball, take that number cubed, then multiply by 1,000. It's like each ball is in its own little box." Rolando picked up from there, saying that his group had thought of the box as being 10 by 10 by 10 blocks or balls, so they just had to multiply the length of a block or the diameter of a ball by 10, "and then cube it to find the volume of the box." Many other groups also seemed to have thought of it in this way.

28.   We then discussed the volume of the box that would not be filled by the balls, and I asked students if they were concerned that different groups came up with different answers. They first suggested that it was because different groups had used different strategies, but Mariola pointed out that Rolando and Tran "gave the same exact answer even though they had used different strategies." Tran then raised his hand and said that he had been thinking that "Rolando pictured the problem different than our group did, but I think we did the same calculations." Tran offered that "if you use the same numbers or estimates in different methods, you should still get the same results." Roberto raised his hand, saying that his group found how many blocks would fill the room by first "changing the length of the blocks to centimeters," but then they also decided to try "changing the dimensions from centimeters to blocks." He concluded by saying, "Both methods gave the same answer, so we knew it had to be right."

29.   I then asked students to take a minute or two to look over all their work so far and to jot down ideas they had about how the labs were similar and how they were different. I then asked the students to share their ideas and I wrote them down in a chart on the overhead.

SIMILAR
- They both show that 1,000 of something can take up a lot of space, but it's still not very much compared to 1,000,000 (Jimmy)
- You didn't really have to count out 1,000 things to get an answer, you could get it faster by multiplying (Rigo)
- They both involved cubing something (Maria)
- Even though the objects were different, we had to use Length × Width × Height in both labs (Lucia)
- They were both three-dimensional problems (Tomás)
- In both you can use metric units or you can use the thing you are measuring with as a unit (Roberto)
- You could find the answers by building layers or by using formulas (Mariola)
- You could use the same strategies with the blocks or the balls (Tran)

DIFFERENT
- We worked with different-shaped objects in each lab (Felipe)
- You could use different volume formulas for each problem: cube, rectangular prism, and sphere (José)
- With blocks you can fill all the volume in the room, but the balls leave space in between (Isabel)
- They each had a different volume for filling up the same room (Belinda)

30.   I asked Mariola to explain more about her observation. I wanted her to explain how building layers related to the volume formulas because this was a key idea I wanted to be sure my students understood. Mariola stated, "When you use the formula, you multiply all three dimensions together at once. When you build layers, you multiply length times width first to find out how many are in the bottom layer, then you multiply by the height because that is the number of layers. So, you still end up multiplying length times width times height either way." Just as she finished, I realized the bell was about to ring, so I told students to put away their materials and that we would continue our discussion the next day. I handed out the following problem for them to think about for homework:

In the 1,000 Balls Lab, suppose we used balls with twice the diameter of a soccer ball. How would this change the number of balls that would fit in the classroom? What if we used a ball that was half the diameter of the soccer ball?

The purpose of the homework questions was to get students to think more deeply about how the size of the unit related to the measurements they obtained in their investigations.

ANALYZING THE CASE

Now that you have had the opportunity to read the case and consider what Nancy Upshaw's students were doing in order to make sense of and ultimately solve the problems in the Large Numbers Lab, we invite you to think about what Ms. Upshaw did to support her students sense-making efforts. Here are a few suggestions on how to proceed.

- Review the list you created as you read the case and consider what Ms. Upshaw did to support her students' efforts to make sense of and solve the problems. In particular, for each student action you identified on your initial list, indicate *what* the teacher did (or appeared to have done) that supported students' efforts to make sense of or to solve the problems and *why* this action served to support their efforts. Be sure to cite paragraph numbers to support your claims.
- If you have colleagues who also are reading the case, compare and contrast the ideas in your individual lists and possibly generate a master list. Note points of disagreement since these are likely to be fruitful topics for further discussion. If you are working on this activity alone, we encourage you to refer to Appendix D, which includes a similar chart that was produced by a group of teachers who engaged in this activity as part of a professional development experience focused on "The Case of Nancy Upshaw." You may want to note points of agreement and disagreement and identify issues that you wish to pursue.

You may wish to continue your analysis of the case by considering the questions in the next section. If you currently are teaching mathematics, you might want to proceed to the "Connecting to Your Own Practice" section in which you are encouraged to relate the analysis of the ideas and issues raised in "The Case of Nancy Upshaw" to your own teaching practice.

EXTENDING YOUR ANALYSIS OF THE CASE

The questions listed in this section are intended to help you focus on particular aspects of the case related to teacher decision-making and student thinking. If you are working in collaboration with one or more colleagues, the questions can serve as a stimulus for further discussion.

1. In this lesson, Ms. Upshaw is using an activity set in the context of volume measurement in order to promote students' large number sense. Ms. Upshaw also comments that the lesson provides an opportunity for students to practice estimation and measurement skills. What are the advantages and disadvantages of incorporating multiple mathematical goals into one lesson? To what extent do you think Ms. Upshaw was successful in meeting each of her mathematical goals?

2. To what extent do you think Ms. Upshaw was successful in balancing high-level thinking and reasoning with practicing computation and measurement skills?

3. Ms. Upshaw reflects on the fact that students' different approaches yielded different results—8,520 versus 8,750 units cubed (para. 18). Why might Ms. Upshaw feel this difference is worth discussing? How would you approach this discussion? Do you think it is important to discuss in this lesson? Why or why not?

4. José insists that only objects shaped like cubes can have measures expressed in cubic units (para. 15). What mathematical idea is at the heart of José's misunderstanding? How might José's misunderstanding be addressed? In what ways does the Large Numbers Lab activity help strengthen students' conceptions of cubic units?

5. Ms. Upshaw asks Jorge and his group to think about whether to label dimensions as the number of cubes or as the number of centimeters (para. 14). How would you have responded to Jorge? Does it matter whether students measure the lengths of the blocks in centimeters or change the dimensions of the room from meters to blocks? Why or why not? What differences between the two methods might be worth addressing with students?

6. Ms. Upshaw discusses why she has decided not to make calculators available in the activity in order to encourage students to practice estimation and computation (para. 9). What are the advantages and disadvantages of this decision?

7. In the 1,000 Balls Lab, students are thinking about stacking the balls as they would cubes, so that the balls appear in neat rows and columns. What if a group thought to arrange the balls in "nested" layers, so that each successive stack fills in the space between the balls in the layers above and below? How, if at all, might this change their estimate or their approach to solving the task?

8. Mariola is eager to answer Ms. Upshaw's question, but Ms. Upshaw asks her to wait for another student to think and formulate an answer (para. 16). What are some ways in which teachers can delay contributions by more talkative students or students who work more quickly in order to give other students a chance to articulate their ideas?

9. Ms. Upshaw comments that Mariola, Jorge, Roberto, and Jimmy were "off track" (para. 13). In what sense do you think Ms. Upshaw meant they were off track? Do you agree with Ms. Upshaw? To what extent did this group make progress on the task during the lesson?

CONNECTING TO YOUR OWN PRACTICE

This section is intended specifically for readers who currently are teaching mathematics. The activities described in this section are designed to help you consider the ways in which issues identified in Ms. Upshaw's classroom have implications for your own teaching of mathematics. One of the challenges that teachers like Ms. Upshaw have to grapple with is how to support students as they work on challenging tasks without taking over the process of thinking for them (NCTM, 2000). Here are a few activities that will help you move from consideration of Nancy Upshaw's teaching to a focus on your own classroom practices.

• In the "Analyzing the Case" section, you considered what Ms. Upshaw did to support her students in making sense of and solving the problems. Ms. Upshaw supported her students' learning in many ways. For example, once she had posed a question, she often walked away and allowed students to continue to explore and make sense of the mathematical ideas on their own. She also provided an opportunity for students to share their ideas and to make important mathematical connections during a whole-group discussion. Choose one aspect of Ms. Upshaw's pedagogy that you would like to work on in your own classroom. Incorporate the new pedagogy into the lessons for one of your classes over a one-week period. After each lesson, write down how the new pedagogy served to support students' learning, what success you had in implementing the new pedagogy, and what you might continue to work on in future lessons.

• In "The Case of Nancy Upshaw," Ms. Upshaw asked her students many questions as they worked in groups and as they presented their ideas at the end of the lesson. Plan a lesson in which you prepare a list of questions that you can ask to support your students as they work on a challenging mathematical task. As you facilitate students' work, consider what was gained (either by you or by the students) from asking each question and consider how each question served to support students' learning. Make note of questions that seemed to work particularly well so that you might use or adapt these questions for future lessons.

EXPLORING CURRICULAR MATERIALS

You may want to explore your curriculum for ideas related to measurement and volume by considering the following questions: Does your curriculum provide opportunities for students to develop an understanding of attributes such as volume? Does your curriculum provide opportunities for students to actively engage in solving problems in which they need to make decisions involving measurement (e.g., what units to use, when to make conversions)? What might be the potential benefits of including lab activities such as those posed by Ms. Upshaw?

You also may want to solve additional tasks to continue to explore the mathematical ideas made salient in the case. The following list identifies resources that contain problems that are considered to be mathematically similar to the task used in "The Case of Nancy Upshaw."

Education Development Center, Inc. (1998c). *MathScape: Shapes and space: Thinking three-dimensionally* (Student guide). Mountain View, CA: Creative Publications.

> Of particular interest are Lesson 3 and Lesson 11. In Lesson 3 (pp. 11–12), students are asked to determine how many centimeter cubes it will take to fill their classroom and to express the volume of the classroom in cubic centimeters and cubic meters. Lesson 11 (pp. 30–31) provides opportunities for students to consider appropriate units of measure for expressing the volume of a variety of real-life objects.

Foreman, L. C., & Bennett, A. B., Jr. (1996). *Visual mathematics: Course II, Lessons 1–10.* Salem, OR: The Math Learning Center.

Of particular interest in Lesson 2 (Shape and Surface Area) are Actions 8–10 in the Focus Teacher Activity (pp. 24–25), in which students explore how the dimensions, surface area, and volume of rectangular prisms change when the unit of volume is changed.

Lappan, G., Fey, J. T., Fitzgerald, W. M., Friel, S. N., & Phillips, E. D. (1998b). *Data around us: Number sense.* Menlo Park, CA: Dale Seymour.

Of particular interest are Problems 4.1 and 4.2 (pp. 38–40), in which students use multiplicative structures to make sense of large numbers, such as a million, a billion, and a trillion.

The Mathematics in Context Development Team. (1998b). Mathematics in context: Power of ten (Student guide). In National Center for Research in Mathematical Sciences Education & Freudenthal Institute (Eds.), *Mathematics in context.* Chicago: Encyclopaedia Britannica.

Of particular interest are Problems 23 and 25 in Section C (pp. 18–19), in which students are presented with different situations that incorporate measures of volume as a way of exploring the relative size of large numbers. Problem 23 asks students to determine the size of a room needed to store a million bricks, and Problem 25 asks students to determine the number of balloons needed to fill the principal's office.

CONNECTING TO OTHER IDEAS AND ISSUES

If you have additional time, you may want to explore some aspect of the case in more depth. The resources identified in the following list provide some possibilities for exploring the mathematical and pedagogical issues raised in the case. For example, you might: (1) consider the understandings and misconceptions that students develop in forming volume sense using students' strategies and errors presented in Battista and Clements (1996) and the thinking of Ms. Upshaw's students in the case; (2) draw on the suggestions in Battista (1998) to design a lesson featuring the Large Numbers Lab activity or a similar task; (3) use Battista (1999) to compare students' opportunity to develop an understanding of volume in traditional instruction versus inquiry-based classrooms; (4) use the ideas in Bright (1976) to consider the role that estimation played in Ms. Upshaw's lesson and plays in problem-solving more generally; or (5) use one of the tasks featured in Coburn and Shulte (1986) or in Geddes and colleagues (1994) as the basis for a lesson in your own classroom. Then, collect student work on the task and compare the thinking and volume sense of your students with those of the students in "The Case of Nancy Upshaw."

Battista, M., & Clements, D. (1996). Students' understanding of 3-D rectangular arrays of cubes. *Journal for Research in Mathematics Education, 27,* 258–292.

This research article discusses students' solution strategies and errors in perceiving, enumerating, and constructing 3-D arrays of cubes. Various tasks as well as detailed student responses are provided. Figure 4 (p. 263) categorizes the strategies employed by students when solving the tasks.

Battista, M. T. (1998). How many blocks? *Mathematics Teaching in the Middle School, 3,* 404–411.

This article discusses students' difficulties with spatial structuring by exploring student thinking and strategies on a volume task in which students are asked to predict how many cubes will fit into various rectangular prisms. The author provides suggestions for supporting the development of structural reasoning. The role of student predictions and student-generated procedures in developing structural reasoning is particularly interesting and useful in looking at Ms. Upshaw's class.

Battista, M. (1999). Fifth-graders enumeration of cubes in 3-D arrays: Conceptual progress in an inquiry-based classroom. *Journal for Research in Mathematics Education, 30,* 417–448.

This research article examines student thinking and common errors regarding volumes of cubic arrays. The article focuses on three case studies of pairs of 5th-grade students. Each pair is asked to predict and verify how many cubes fit in a given box, given a pattern picture, box picture, combination of the two, or with given dimensions. The role of sociocultural issues such as collaboration, communication, goal-setting, and gender differences is discussed.

Bright, G. W. (1976). Estimation as part of learning to measure. In D. Nelson (Ed.), *Measurement in school mathematics* (pp. 87–105). Reston, VA: National Council of Teachers of Mathematics.

This chapter provides a concise explanation of what it means to measure as well as the foundations of estimation in measurement. The chapter discusses eight different kinds of estimation and offers advice for teaching and assessing estimation in the context of measurement.

Coburn, T. G., & Shulte, A. P. (1986). Estimation in measurement. In H. Schoen (Ed.), *Estimation and mental computation* (pp. 195–203). Reston, VA: National Council of Teachers of Mathematics.

This chapter revisits ideas in Bright (1976). The authors provide several tasks and activities that can be used to teach estimation in measurement, including tasks involving volume and capacity, that teachers might use in their own classrooms.

Geddes, D., Berkman, R., Fearon, I., Fishenfeld, M., Forlano, C., Fuys, D. J., Goldstein, J., & Welchman, R. (1994). *Cur-*

riculum and evaluation standards for school mathematics ad-
denda series, grades 5–8: Measurement in the middle grades.
Reston, VA: National Council of Teachers of Mathematics.
   This book contains a variety of tasks and activities
designed to engage students with exploring measurement ideas. One activity related to "The Case of Nancy
Upshaw" is Activity 15, Volume (pp. 49–51), in which
students investigate filling boxes (rectangular prisms)
and other kinds of spaces with various solid shapes,
including cubes and spheres.

Part II

FACILITATING LEARNING FROM CASES

In Part II of this book (Chapters 6–10), we turn our attention to providing support for case facilitators. Chapter 6 introduces this part of the book and describes how to facilitate learning from the cases. Chapters 7 through 10 provide support materials intended to assist facilitators in utilizing the cases and related materials provided in Chapters 2 through 5, respectively. The intended audience for Part II is those readers who will be facilitating discussions around the cases and related materials found in Part I. These facilitators may include any professionals who contribute to improving the quality of mathematics teaching and learning through their work in diverse settings: schools (e.g., teacher leaders, coaches, mentors, administrators); school district offices (e.g., curriculum coordinators, staff developers); regional intermediate units and state agencies; or colleges and universities (e.g., instructors of mathematics or methods courses).

6

Using Cases to Support Learning About Teaching

The cases found in Part I of this book embody a vision of mathematics teaching and learning that is very different from how most teachers have learned mathematics and learned to teach mathematics. The vision calls for students who can think and reason about challenging and complex problems that give rise to significant mathematical understandings. It also calls for teachers who can appropriately scaffold and support students' learning by creating environments that foster communication, inquiry, and investigation. It is now widely accepted that meeting these goals and standards will require a great deal of learning on the part of teachers.

The kind of learning that is required of teachers has been described as transformative (i.e., sweeping changes in deeply held beliefs, knowledge, and habits of practice) as opposed to additive (the addition of new skills to an existing repertoire) (Thompson & Zeuli, 1999). Teachers of mathematics cannot successfully develop their students' thinking, reasoning, and communication skills simply by adopting a new curriculum or by using more hands-on materials. Rather they must thoroughly overhaul their thinking about what it means to know and understand mathematics and how they can best support their students as they struggle to learn deeper and more complex mathematics.

One approach to helping teachers transform their practice involves situating the professional education of teachers "in practice" (Smith, 2001). In a seminal chapter on this topic Ball and Cohen (1999) argue that "teachers' everyday work could become a source for constructive professional development" (p. 6) through the development of a curriculum for professional learning that is grounded in the tasks, questions, and problems of practice. They propose that teachers' instructional practice be seen both as a site for professional learning and as a stimulus for developing inquiry into

practice from which many teachers could learn. To accomplish this goal, they argue that records of authentic practice—curriculum materials, narrative or video summaries of teachers planning for and/or engaging in instruction, samples of student work—should become the core of professional education, providing a focus for sustained teacher inquiry and investigation.

This book represents such an approach to teacher education. The materials and activities in Part I encourage teachers and other readers to construct knowledge central to teaching by engaging in activities that are built around artifacts of classroom practice. The narrative cases provide the opportunity to analyze how teacher and student interactions in the classroom influence what students learn. The instructional tasks that appear in the Opening Activity of each chapter (which are drawn from actual classroom practice) invite teachers and other readers to explore important mathematical ideas. Finally, activities such as the comparison of the cases and/or instructional tasks with a teacher's own practice or with other curricular materials provide yet more opportunities for teachers or other readers to learn about practice from the actual work of practice.

WHY CASES?

Similar to many other teacher educators, we have been drawn to cases because they capture the complexity and situatedness of instructional practice. Unlike theories, propositions, principles, or other abstractions, the particularities of cases vividly convey the profusion of events, actions, and thought that comprise the moment-by-moment lived experience of a classroom lesson. Told through the voice of the classroom teacher, our cases offer the additional advantage of allowing the reader to listen in as the teacher in the case struggles with the multitude of decisions and dilemmas that make up the lived experience of the middle school mathematics classroom.

Cases are also an effective medium for capturing the *interdependence* of teachers' knowledge of mathematics, pedagogy, and students. By exposing how these different kinds of knowledge are accessed and used in the decisions that teachers make, cases portray how teachers simultaneously think about and pull from mathematical knowledge, pedagogical expertise, and knowledge of how students learn mathematics, in order to reach an instructional goal.

LEARNING FROM CASES

In order to learn from cases, readers must do more than simply read them. We have found it useful to distinguish between two classes of activities in which participants engage in order to learn from cases: analysis and generalization. Analysis involves the careful examination of a case teacher's decisions and interactions with students in light of the goals that the teacher wishes to accomplish. Generalization involves viewing the particularities of case-based episodes as instantiations of a broader set of ideas about mathematics, about teaching, and about learning. Each of these is discussed in more detail in the following sections.

Analysis

Analyzing the instructional practice in a case involves the interpretation of teacher thinking and action in the context of the overall lesson. For example, a case facilitator might want participants to analyze how a teacher drew students' attention to the mathematical ideas that constituted his or her goals for the lesson. This would involve paying attention to the teaching moves that built upon certain student responses (and not others) and instances in which the teacher took a more directive role. Near the end of "The Case of Keith Campbell" (Chapter 4), for example, the teacher focuses his students' attention on the chart that students have jointly constructed showing the dimensions of different configurations of prisms they have assembled, along with their surface areas and volumes. By encouraging students to reflect on this information, Mr. Campbell develops his students' realization that the more cube-like the configuration, the smaller its surface area will be (even though the volume remains constant). Analyzing

Keith Campbell's moves in the final minutes of the lesson involves not only noting what he did and how, but also interpreting why he did it with respect to his goals for the lesson.

Because they appear as narratives in a print form, the cases in this book represent a controlled way for readers to learn these skills of lesson analysis. Unlike observations of real teaching, readers can stop the action at any moment to ponder the implications of a particular decision. They can even revisit a particular part of the lesson in order to check the facts and deepen their analysis. And, finally, narrative cases allow the reader to more easily keep the entire lesson in view while interpreting the teacher's action at a given point in the lesson.

Generalization

The ultimate goal of reading and analyzing cases is for readers to recognize specific situations in the cases as instances of something larger and more generalizable. For readers to be able to move from a specific instance of a phenomenon to a more general understanding, they need multiple opportunities to consider an idea, to make comparisons across situations, and ultimately to examine their own ideas, beliefs, and, if they currently are teaching, their own instructional practice.

Our goal for all readers is that, through reading and discussing cases, they will connect the events depicted in cases to an increasingly elaborated knowledge base of mathematics, teaching, and learning, and, when applicable, to their own practice. For example, consider "The Case of Barbara Crafton." The manner in which Mrs. Crafton conducts the discourse in her classroom can be seen as an instantiation of a larger, more generalizable idea: the use of mathematical argumentation as a method for encouraging students to make and justify claims and to hold others accountable for the claims that they make. By elevating the case discussion to the ideas associated with mathematical argumentation as a form of knowledge production and verification, participants have the opportunity to view Barbara Crafton's lesson in more general and potentially more transferable terms.

For classroom teachers specifically, extracting general principles from the specific instances in a case is necessary for them to begin to formulate, *in their own classrooms*, ways of acting and interacting that are thoughtful, principled, sharable, and effective (Shulman, 1996). In order to achieve this goal, teachers must learn to connect the specifics of deeply contextualized, case-based moments to a broader set of ideas about mathematics, teaching, and learning. Generalizing allows teachers to view the specific incidents within the cases as instantiations of larger patterns and principles—patterns and principles that will have applicability to their own practice as well.

To foster the development of this kind of skill, our cases are situated within a larger, more general set of mathematical and pedagogical ideas that we intend for current or future teachers to understand and to utilize in making sense of new situations that they will encounter in their own practice. Toward this end, well-conducted case discussions are crucial because they highlight the question, "What is this a case of?" thus stimulating learners "to move up and down, back and forth, between the memorable particularities of cases and powerful generalizations and simplifications of principles and theories" (Shulman, 1996, p. 201).

WHAT CAN BE LEARNED FROM OUR CASES

In addition to learning the skills of analyzing and generalizing, there is also specific mathematical content that teachers can learn through engagement with our cases. As noted in Chapter 1, the cases were designed to instantiate a broader set of ideas about geometry and measurement and about ways in which teachers may support or inhibit students' learning in the context of cognitively challenging mathematical tasks. Each of these is discussed briefly in the following section.

Geometry and Measurement

Geometry and measurement are important content strands in the middle school curriculum that span several important topics, including perimeter, area, surface area, and volume (NCTM, 2000). These topics, however, often are taught as a set of formulas to be memorized and applied with little attention to concepts underlying them (Kamii & Clark, 1997). As a result, students have difficulty constructing figures when given the perimeter or area (Chappell & Thompson, 1999) and they frequently confuse perimeter and area (Bright & Hoeffner, 1993; Chappell & Thompson, 1999) as well as surface area and volume (Martin & Strutchens, 2000). In addition, middle school students seem unaware that area can vary for rectangles of a fixed perimeter and experience great difficulty in explaining how two different rectangles can have the same area but different perimeters (Chappell & Thompson, 1999).

Research suggests that preservice and inservice middle school teachers also have limited knowledge of geometry and measurement (Fuys, Geddes, & Tischler,

1988; Hershkowitz & Vinner, 1984; Mayberry, 1983; Swafford, Jones, & Thornton, 1997). Although nearly 75% of 8th-grade teachers report that they consider themselves to be very well prepared to teach measurement, only 35 to 43% indicate that they have received training in this area through courses, workshops, or seminars (Grouws, Smith, & Sztajn, 2004). This inconsistency raises questions regarding teachers' opportunities to develop a conceptual understanding of key issues related to geometry and measurement.

Situations aimed at encouraging teachers and other readers to revisit and question their own understanding of geometry and measurement have been purposefully built into the cases in this volume. We have embedded multiple opportunities for readers to actively analyze problem situations that involve perimeter, area, surface area, and volume. These include cognitively challenging problems that encourage (or require) readers to reach beyond standard algorithms and to reason based on a more conceptual approach to area and volume. In addition, readers are asked to investigate and to generalize how attributes, dimensions, and units are related. Readers are expected to develop deep understandings of geometry and measurement by repeatedly encountering these situations in our cases in different contexts and in slightly different forms.

Ways of Supporting and Inhibiting Student Learning

After years of focusing on the mastery of nonambiguous, procedurally oriented skills—skills that are easy to mimic and apply successfully without much thought—many students find high-level tasks intimidating and anxiety provoking. As increasing numbers of middle schools have taken up the challenge of using more ambitious tasks, it has become clear that many teachers need assistance in learning how to support their students' capacities to engage with and successfully complete these tasks. Those who are most effective are able to both retain high-level expectations for how students should tackle such tasks and provide the right kind and amount of assistance to allow the students to succeed. Other, less effective teachers either supply too much assistance, essentially taking the difficult pieces of thinking away from the students and doing it for them, or fail to provide enough direction and assistance, allowing students to flounder in unsystematic and nonproductive ways.

Situations aimed at encouraging teachers and other readers to identify and understand ways of supporting students' learning of complex mathematical ideas have been purposefully built into the cases. We have embedded multiple opportunities for readers to notice and analyze how student thinking can be supported during a lesson. These include situations in which the teachers in the cases keep expectations high by pressing students to explain and justify their thinking and reasoning; situations in which the case teachers assist students as they try to use and make connections between different ways of representing the same relationship; and situations in which the case teachers provide students with sufficient time and resources to wrestle with and make sense of emerging mathematical ideas. As with the mathematical ideas, readers can develop deeper understandings of ways of supporting student thinking by repeatedly encountering these ideas in our cases in different contexts and in slightly different forms.

PREPARING FOR AND FACILITATING CASE DISCUSSIONS

Although we recognize that individual readers may elect to use the cases on their own (and Part I is written to allow them to do so), we feel that engaging readers as a group around the central ideas of the cases has even greater potential to lead to robust learning and improved practice. The success of group sessions, however, is directly dependent on the skill and preparedness of the facilitator. In this section, we describe how facilitators can prepare for and carry out effective learning experiences using our cases.

Preparing for Case Discussions

Similar to the wisdom of teachers preparing for lessons by anticipating how their students will approach planned instructional tasks, it is a good idea for facilitators to prepare for case discussions by reading and thinking about the case from the perspective of the learners. We encourage facilitators to begin their preparations by first completing the problems presented in the Opening Activity and then reading the case. By keeping in mind how the specific group with whom they will be working might approach the Opening Activity and the case, the facilitator often can predict what issues will arise and prepare for how to deal with them.

The next preparation step is to study the facilitation materials that have been prepared for each case (found in Chapters 7–10). These materials have been designed specifically to help facilitators assist readers as they in-

teract with the case materials. As the facilitation chapters were being written, we were keenly aware of the fact that the cases would be used in a variety of settings and with a variety of individuals (i.e., with teachers at different points in their careers, with future teachers of mathematics, with school administrators, or with other individuals interested in mathematics teaching and learning). Moreover, we expect that facilitators will have a variety of backgrounds and will be pursuing a multitude of important and worthwhile goals. As such, the facilitation chapters do not prescribe certain formats or routes through case discussions. Rather they have been designed to make explicit what is embedded in the cases so that facilitators can make their own decisions regarding how to connect learning opportunities in the cases to the particular group with whom they are working and the goals that they have for their work.

The heart of each facilitation chapter is the "Case Analysis." This section indexes the main ideas embedded in the case; more specifically, it allows the facilitator to prepare for case discussions that connect particular case-based incidents to larger, more generalizable sets of ideas. The "Case Analysis" has two major components. First, the key mathematical ideas are more fully described in an easy-to-access fashion, and the specific places in the case that contain incidents related to each of these ideas are identified. The incidents are identified by their paragraph numbers in the case and by a short explanation of how the incident relates to the mathematical idea. Likewise, the key pedagogical ideas are identified and accompanied by markers of specific places in the case that contain incidents related to those ideas and a brief explanation of how the incident relates to the pedagogical idea.

A complaint sometimes raised about case discussions is that they can be all over the board, with the facilitator appearing to have only loose control over what gets talked about and how. Becoming familiar with the materials in the "Case Analysis" section of the facilitation chapters will enable facilitators to avoid this pitfall and to lead a focused and productive case discussion. By studying both the mathematics and pedagogy sections of the "Case Analysis," facilitators will become familiar with the big ideas of the case and exactly where examples of those ideas are embedded in the case. This knowledge will help them to recognize when readers are grappling with case incidents that have the potential to lead to deeper insights, to encourage readers to consider specific episodes of the case at opportune moments, and to help readers to look across various instances to surface the big ideas.

Other sections of the facilitation chapters will help the facilitator to prepare for activities related to the case discussions. For example, a section entitled "Facilitating the Opening Activity" provides suggestions for orchestrating the mathematical problem-solving session, utilizing a task related to the mathematical task that is featured in the case. In "Facilitating the Case Discussion," suggestions are provided for how to have participants prepare for case discussions and various strategies for conducting the discussion. Finally, in "Extending the Case Experience," we provide facilitators with ideas regarding how they might extend explorations of the mathematical and pedagogical ideas on which the cases are based.

Facilitating Case-Based Experiences

We recommend having participants work on the problems in the Opening Activity prior to reading the case. In our experience, having participants complete and reflect on ways of solving the tasks in the Opening Activity is critical to an informed reading of the case and to a rich and successful case discussion. By grappling with the mathematics in the tasks, participants become familiar and confident with the underlying mathematical ideas in the case and are therefore better prepared to think flexibly about the solution strategies that students produce as the case unfolds.

The role of the facilitator during the Opening Activity is to elicit a variety of solution strategies to the problems and, to the extent possible, help participants to identify how those strategies are both similar to and different from one another. We have found it useful to have participants work on the tasks first individually, then in small groups, and finally to participate in a large-group discussion in which various solution strategies are made public.

We also have found that case discussions are most productive when participants have read the case on their own prior to the session in which the case will be discussed. In this regard, reading the case with a guiding question in mind appears to lead to more active reading of the case and more thoughtful and focused participation in the case discussion. Toward this end, we have provided in the facilitation chapters suggestions for ways to focus participants' initial reading of the case.

Facilitating the case discussion itself is a learned skill. Not unlike classroom teachers, facilitators must listen intently to the participants and learn how to steer the conversation in useful directions. Toward this end, it is important for a facilitator to have specific learning goals in mind for the case discussion. With respect to "The Case of Isabelle Olson," for example, a facilitator may

want participants to learn what effective teachers do to support student learning, especially with ambitious, open-ended tasks. To accomplish this goal, the facilitator might ask participants to break into small groups and create a three-column chart indicating what Ms. Olson's students learned or were in the process of learning, what Ms. Olson did to facilitate or support her students' learning (especially when they were struggling and not making progress on the task), and evidence to support their claims. Afterwards, the facilitator can bring the groups together, post the charts, and ask participants to compare and contrast the ideas in the charts and possibly generate a master chart. Points of disagreement also can become the focus of the discussion, as they are likely to be fruitful topics for further analysis.

Extending Case-Based Experiences

Finally, facilitators sometimes choose to extend the case-based experiences by providing additional opportunities to explore the mathematical and pedagogical ideas on which each case is based. By moving beyond the specifics of a case and task, participants can begin to generalize the ideas and issues raised in the case discussion. Specifically, teachers can begin to examine their own practice in light of new understandings about mathematics, instruction, and student learning. The following activities suggest ways in which facilitators might extend the case experience.

Connecting to teachers' practice. Several suggestions are made for how to draw links to the teacher's own practice in the section (in Chapters 2–5) entitled "Connecting to Your Own Practice." Facilitators may wish to assign one or more of these activities as follow-up assignments for teachers to explore in their own classrooms.

Facilitators also might consider asking teachers to identify an issue that the case raised for them and collect these ideas into a master list of issues with which their particular group of teachers is grappling. Facilitators then could ask teachers to identify one issue that they would like to collectively work on and begin working collaboratively on planning a lesson in which the issue can be addressed. By focusing on an issue, teachers will be able to base the lesson on whatever mathematical content they currently are teaching.

Exploring the mathematical ideas in curricular materials. Facilitators also can have participants examine the manner in which the mathematical ideas portrayed in the case play out in mathematics curricula, by asking them to identify similar tasks in a given curriculum and the kind of thinking required to solve them, how the tasks build on students' prior knowledge, and how the tasks collectively shape students' learning of the mathematical content.

Alternatively, facilitators could ask teachers to compare two different curricula. By comparing and contrasting curricula, participants have the opportunity to see how different texts develop a particular mathematical idea or set of ideas and to analyze the extent to which the texts are designed to engage students in mathematical thinking and reasoning. (When working with preservice teachers, facilitators may want to have the teachers compare the curriculum that is used in the school in which they will be doing their student teaching with one that reflects an alternative view of mathematics teaching and learning.)

In addition, facilitators may want to have participants engage in solving additional mathematical tasks. The tasks identified and described in the section entitled "Exploring Curricular Materials" in Chapters 2 through 5 are mathematically similar to the tasks featured in each case.

Using professional readings to enhance and extend learning. In the section entitled "Connecting to Other Ideas and Issues" in Chapters 2 through 5, several suggestions are made for how to use the resources that are identified and described. Facilitators can assign one or more of the suggested activities and readings as follow-up assignments in order to help participants broaden or deepen their understanding of the teaching of geometry and measurement.

PUTTING THE PIECES TOGETHER

Based on our own experiences in using the cases and the experiences of colleagues, we can recommend their use in preservice mathematics methods and content courses, in professional development efforts for practicing teachers, and in workshops with various school administrators. However, it is important to note that the cases in this volume are not meant to represent a complete curriculum for middle school mathematics teacher education.

Depending on one's circumstances, however, the cases can be used in a variety of ways. For example, facilitators may want to build an entire course around the cases and related activities in this volume or they may want to select one or two specific cases to blend into an already planned teacher education agenda in order to address an identified need. Whatever the situation-of-use, facilitators should find in the facilitation chapters the support that they need to make optimal use of each case.

7

Facilitating Learning from The Case of Barbara Crafton

"The Case of Barbara Crafton" focuses on the work of a 6th-grade teacher and her students during a lesson in which students discuss and present solutions to a homework problem in which they had to determine the area of an irregular shape, first in square centimeters and then in square millimeters. Mrs. Crafton expects that students will disagree about the solution to the problem, and she attempts to use the competing claims to spur a mathematical debate. Students are actively engaged in the lesson as they discuss their solutions in pairs and share their work with the class. Throughout the lesson, Barbara Crafton encourages student-to-student talk and steers the conversation in directions that help achieve her mathematical goals. She intends that the series of lessons in which this task is embedded will help students to generalize the relationship between linear and area ratios when converting between units and, ultimately, when comparing similar figures.

In the following sections, we provide support for case facilitators' use of the materials in Chapter 2, "Reasoning About Units for Linear and Area Measure: The Case of Barbara Crafton." Sample responses for the Opening Activity and for the "Analyzing the Case" activity are provided in Appendix A.

CASE ANALYSIS

In this section, we provide a detailed analysis of each of the mathematical and pedagogical ideas that are found in the case. These analyses may help you in determining which aspects of the case you wish to highlight during the discussion.

Considering the Mathematics in the Case

The task featured in the case is a homework problem that Barbara Crafton assigned during the previous day's lesson. Students are asked to determine the area of an irregular shape, first in square centimeters and then in square millimeters. Finding the area of the shape in square centimeters was relatively easy for most students because it can be accomplished through counting the number of squares and half squares that constitute the shape (each square is 1 square centimeter). However, many students experienced difficulty expressing their answers in square millimeters because they recently had performed conversions between linear centimeters and millimeters. Many students assumed that they should multiply the number of square centimeters by 10 in order to arrive at the answer in square millimeters. To determine the answer in square millimeters (and to be able to explain and justify their solution), students needed to conceptually differentiate linear versus area measurement and to realize that each square centimeter consisted of 100 square millimeters (rather than 10).

In the following paragraphs, we identify several important mathematical ideas that surface in the case, and we provide examples of where these ideas appear in "The Case of Barbara Crafton" in Chapter 2.

Area measurement. The concept of area as a two-dimensional region pervades the homework tasks that are the focus of the lesson in the case. Beginning with the gum wrapper task, which stresses coverage of a region, Mrs. Crafton has implemented a series of lessons that serve to build students' conceptions of area and of linear versus square units. Students in the case determine area by counting square units and by using the standard formula for finding the area of geometric figures.

- Square centimeter pieces, the grid on the homework problems, and Mrs. Crafton's reminders to use *square* units all strengthen students' understanding of area as being measured in square units. (paras. 8, 11, and 14)
- Ellen counts the square units on the grid to determine the area of the irregular figure. (para. 10)
- Michael uses the "length times width" formula to find the area of a portion of the irregular figure. (para. 11)
- Charlene implicitly uses "length times width" to find the area of one square centimeter. (para. 17)
- When "blowing up" a square centimeter, Natalie also uses "length times width" to find the area of a square. (paras. 20–21)

Linear versus area measurement. Students in the case have experience in converting between centimeters and millimeters when dealing with linear measurements. This prior knowledge causes some students to overlook the fact that they are now being asked to convert *square* centimeters to *square* millimeters. Explanations offered by Natalie and Charlene help illuminate the relationship between conversion factors for linear and area attributes. Mrs. Crafton hopes that this series of lessons will lead students to generalize that the area ratio is the square of the linear ratio when converting between units (and also when comparing similar figures).

- Mrs. Crafton anticipates that students will not consider the difference between linear and area measurements when converting from square centimeters to square millimeters. This is confirmed when she notes that many students have reached a solution of 175 square millimeters (rather than 1,750 square millimeters). (paras. 7, 9, 12)
- Larry confuses linear measurements with area measurements while he presents his solution to the class. (para. 14)
- Charlene explicitly uses the term *dimensions* when she challenges Larry's assertion that the total area is 170 square centimeters: "If each centimeter is 10 millimeters, then the dimensions of a 1-centimeter square would be 10 by 10, right?" (para. 17)
- Natalie uses a diagram to illustrate her argument that each square centimeter has the linear dimen-

sions of 10 mm by 10 mm, so its area, by counting or using "Length times Width," would be 100 square millimeters. (para. 21)
- Steve and Dave overgeneralize their memorized rule for converting centimeters to millimeters. Mrs. Crafton comments that they need to connect their thinking to the problem and see that they are dealing with area, not linear, measurement. (paras. 22–23)
- Mrs. Crafton realizes that she needs to provide students with problems that involve nonmetric units in order for students to discover the relationship between the ratios for linear and area measurements when converting between units (and when comparing linear and area measurements in similar figures). (para. 25)

Effect of unit size on area measure. For any given measurement, there is an inverse relation between the size of the measurement unit and the number of units required. That is, the magnitude of an area expressed in smaller units (in this case, square millimeters) is greater than the magnitude of that same area expressed in larger units (square centimeters). This notion is crucial in selecting an appropriate unit of measure and is embedded in both the introductory activity and the homework problem that is discussed during the lesson.

- In an earlier lesson, Mrs. Crafton asked her students to measure a sheet of paper using the outside wrapper from a stick of gum and then a playing card, leading toward the recognition that it took more gum wrappers (precisely four times more) than playing cards to cover the area. (para. 4)
- Mrs. Crafton also notes that the task of the current lesson (converting from measuring an irregular figure in square centimeters to measuring it in square millimeters) embodies the same idea. (para. 5)
- Through this series of lessons, students will be able to determine precisely how many times more of the smaller unit is required to fill an area than of the larger unit by discovering that the area ratio is the square of the linear ratio. (paras. 6–7)

Mathematical conjecture. Mathematical conjecture is an important aspect of creating, validating, and gaining social acceptance of mathematical knowledge. It involves developing a position with respect to a mathematical phenomenon and explicating the reasoning and evidence that support the position. Barbara Crafton provides her students with opportunities to engage in mathematical conjecture throughout the lesson. By setting up a mathematical debate, Mrs. Crafton provides students with an opportunity to take up specific positions and cite evidence to back up their claims.

- Students challenge Larry's claim that the answer is 170 and his justification for this claim. (paras. 15–17)
- After Mrs. Crafton clarifies the poles of the debate, Natalie uses a diagram to support Charlene's claim that the area is 1,750 square millimeters. (paras. 21–23)
- Mrs. Crafton encourages students to challenge Natalie. Then Steve and Dave each make a comment that Mrs. Crafton feels gives voice to the misunderstandings of many students. (para. 22)

Considering How Student Thinking Is Supported

In the case, Barbara Crafton provides opportunities for students to gain experience in mathematical argumentation and justification during a lesson in which she carefully sets up and steers a mathematical debate. Mrs. Crafton is very active in the discussion as she attempts to maintain an environment that allows students to explore, question, and justify mathematics.

In the following paragraphs, we identify several pedagogical moves that Barbara Crafton made that may have influenced her students' opportunities to engage in high-level thinking, reasoning, and communication during the lesson, and we provide examples of where these ideas appear in "The Case of Barbara Crafton" in Chapter 2.

Scaffolding a mathematical debate. Mrs. Crafton intends to use this task to set up a mathematical debate. Her role in orchestrating the discourse involves making decisions about whether or not to pursue particular lines of reasoning as she steers the conversation toward her mathematical goals. Because all student talk does not neatly align with expected or useful responses, Mrs. Crafton must make decisions about what to respond to, what to let go of, and what to put off until later. Mrs. Crafton has prepared her students to participate in a mathematical debate by establishing norms and practices in her classroom that support sharing ideas and taking risks.

- Mrs. Crafton asks questions that prompt students to engage in the debate. (paras. 15, 19, 22)

- Mrs. Crafton decides not to pursue Bonita's comment and Larry's response to it. (para. 16)
- Mrs. Crafton redirects Larry and Charlene's conversation about moving the decimal point by observing, "We still have some discussion here. Charlene is saying that each individual square centimeter is not 10 square millimeters but is 100. Larry and a few others are still saying that each square centimeter is 10." (para. 19)
- Mrs. Crafton asks Natalie to say more about how each square could be both 1 by 1 and 10 by 10, because she thinks this may move the discussion in a productive direction. (para. 20)

Continuing to press students for explanation and meaning. Mrs. Crafton presses students to explain their thinking and to question one another. Students are expected to share their ideas and solution strategies in pairs and in whole-group discussions. Once a solution method has been presented, it is an established routine that students question the presenter or present alternative solution methods.

- Mrs. Crafton often asks students to explain their ideas, sometimes inviting them to the overhead projector to do so. (paras. 10, 14, 20)
- Students in Mrs. Crafton's classroom often question one another. (paras. 15, 16, 17, 22)
- As the pairs discuss the area of the figure in square millimeters, Mrs. Crafton presses students to engage in discussion by asking, "What have you decided?" and "How did you decide?" (para. 12)
- Mrs. Crafton expresses her expectation that students should be asking questions if they got a different answer or thought about the problem differently. (para. 15)

Providing sufficient time to grapple with the task. Mrs. Crafton devotes the majority of the class period to the discussion of one problem (para. 5). She believes this is time well spent, as the discussion should help further her mathematical goals. She also provides time within the lesson for students to discuss the homework problem in pairs before engaging the class in a whole-group debate (para. 12).

Building on students' prior knowledge. Mrs. Crafton believes in the importance of selecting tasks that are challenging, yet build on students' prior knowledge (para. 2). For example, the series of tasks described in paragraphs 4 through 5 build on students' prior knowledge of the metric system and the geometric concepts of linear and area measurement. The tasks are also sequenced in such a way that each problem builds upon previous ones, and each contributes to Mrs. Crafton's mathematical goals. The homework problem Mrs. Crafton assigns at the end of the lesson builds on the ideas generated that day and also serves as a transition to her goals in future lessons (para. 27).

Monitoring students' understanding. Throughout the discussion, Mrs. Crafton never assumes that all students understand. She continually monitors students' understanding by observing students' written and verbal work, specifically asking students if they understand, and calling on students who previously had not grasped a concept.

- Mrs. Crafton scans students' homework papers at the beginning of class. (para. 9)
- Mrs. Crafton observes students as they work in pairs to discuss the number of square millimeters in the shaded region. (para. 12)
- Mrs. Crafton looks around the room, trying to read students' faces after Charlene provides her explanation. (para. 18)
- Following Natalie's demonstration of "blowing up" the square centimeter, Mrs. Crafton checks students' understanding by asking, "How many of you agree with Natalie?" (para. 22)
- Mrs. Crafton monitors Steve's and Dave's understanding during the lesson, and makes a note to check on them in future lessons. (para. 26)
- Near the end of the lesson, Mrs. Crafton once again checks student understanding by asking, "How many of you think the answer is 1,750 square millimeters?" (para. 26)
- Mrs. Crafton calls on Beth, a student who began the class not differentiating between linear and area measurement, to share her solution to the next homework problem. (para. 26)

FACILITATING THE OPENING ACTIVITY

The primary purpose of the Opening Activity is to engage participants with the mathematical ideas that they will encounter when they read the case. The first problem in the Opening Activity (see Figure 2.1) is the same problem that Barbara Crafton and her students discuss during the lesson featured in the case. The second problem in the Opening Activity is identical to the

homework problem that Mrs. Crafton assigns at the end of the lesson. The "Consider" portion of the Opening Activity challenges participants to compare the mathematical ideas in these two problems. By doing so, participants will have the opportunity to explore the relationship between linear and area measurements when converting between units: The ratio of the area measurements will be the square of the ratio between the corresponding linear measurements. This relationship also applies to linear and area measurements in similar figures. In this section, we provide suggestions for using the Opening Activity.

1. Begin by having participants work individually for 5 to 10 minutes, then continue to work on the problems with a partner or a small group. (We have found that beginning with "private think time" ensures that each participant has a chance to grapple with the task prior to engaging in collaborative work.) You may want to provide participants with grid paper (for drawing diagrams) and transparencies of the figure in Problem 1 (for recording their solutions).

2. Assist participants in their work on the task if they appear to be having difficulty. For example:

   - If participants solve Problem 1 by counting the number of shaded squares, you might press them to solve the problem in a different way. For example, you might suggest that they try solving the problem again by breaking the shaded figure into common geometrical figures with which they are familiar (e.g., triangles or rectangles).
   - Watch for a common misconception in Problem 1—applying the linear ratio of 1 cm to 10 mm rather than applying the area ratio of 1 cm^2 to 100 mm^2. If participants reach a solution of 175 mm^2 for the area of the shaded region, they probably are thinking that there are 10 square millimeters in 1 square centimeter. You might pair them with participants who think the area of the shaded region is 1,750 mm and ask the pairs to discuss how they arrived at their solutions and decide if either solution is correct.
   - Encourage participants to explore Problem 2 visually as well as numerically. Drawing a diagram will allow them to visualize the relationship between square feet and square inches and to disprove a common assumption that $1 \text{ ft}^2 = 12 \text{ in}^2$.

3. Orchestrate a whole-group discussion to allow participants to share various solution strategies and approaches. During the discussion you may want to solicit responses that portray general solution strategies that will be found in the case (e.g., arriving at both 175 mm^2 and 1,750 mm^2 for Problem 1; exploring Problem 2 via numeric and visual methods). If you asked the small groups to record their solutions on an overhead transparency earlier, that would facilitate the presentation of solutions during the whole-group discussion. A list of different solution methods that we have seen teachers use to solve these problems can be found in Appendix A. Reviewing this set of solutions may help you prepare for the emergence of methods you might not use yourself in solving the problems.

4. Discuss the "Consider" question in which participants are asked to discuss the similarities in the mathematical ideas underlying Problems 1 and 2. (A list of responses that we have seen teachers provide to the "Consider" question are shown in Appendix A.) During the discussion you may want to press participants to articulate the generalization that Barbara Crafton intended for her students to develop as they progressed through this series of tasks: When linear units of measure have the ratio a:x, their corresponding area units will have the ratio a^2:x^2. This generalization can be illustrated both visually and numerically, and can be applied to linear and area ratios in similar figures as well. You might encourage participants to use the diagrams they created during the small-group and whole-class discussions as a basis from which to generalize that the "area ratio is the square of the linear ratio." If participants also used numeric methods to justify the number of square millimeters in a square centimeter (for example, Problem 1, Solution C, in Appendix A), you might encourage them to use their equations as a basis from which to make the same generalization.

FACILITATING THE CASE DISCUSSION

The case discussion is intended to help participants analyze the mathematical and pedagogical ideas in the case. The "Case Analysis" section should be of assistance in helping you to identify the key ideas in the case and how each idea plays out in the details of the case. Although it is likely that you will begin by having participants examine specific aspects of Barbara Crafton's

teaching practice, you should consider how to connect the specific events that occur in her class to more general ideas about mathematics teaching and learning. In this section we provide suggestions for launching and facilitating the case discussion, and for various follow-up activities that you may wish to pursue.

1. If possible, have participants read and reflect on the case before meeting as a group to discuss the case. As participants read the case, we suggest that you ask them to make note of the pedagogical moves Barbara Crafton made in order to promote discussion in her classroom. (This activity is described in more detail in the section of Chapter 2 entitled "Reading the Case.") This individual activity will help participants think deeply about the pedagogy in the case and help them prepare for the small- and large-group discussions. Alternatively, you may want to select one of the questions found in Chapter 2 (see the section entitled "Extending Your Analysis of the Case") to guide the reading of the case.

2. Begin by having small groups consider how the pedagogical moves Barbara Crafton made to promote discussion may have contributed to students' learning of mathematics. It may be helpful to have small-group members begin by sharing the lists they created during their initial reading of the case. For each item on their lists, participants should indicate how this may have influenced students' learning. In completing this task, participants should be encouraged to cite specific evidence (e.g., paragraph numbers) from the case to support their claims.

3. During the whole-group discussion, you may want to develop a master chart that draws on the work of the individual groups. You might begin building this master chart by asking groups to identify the pedagogical moves in their list that they feel had the greatest impact on student learning and to provide a rationale for their selection. Encourage participants to argue respectfully if they do not agree that an identified move had the greatest impact on students' learning of mathematics. This can lead to a rich evidence-based discussion. (In Appendix A, we have included a chart that was generated by teachers who participated in a discussion of "The Case of Barbara Crafton." We encourage you to develop your own chart prior to reviewing the one provided.)

You may wish to end the discussion by asking participants what lessons could be learned from the case about classroom discourse and argumentation that could be applied to other teaching situations. This will help participants move beyond the particular events that occurred in the case and begin to see them as instantiations of more generalizable ideas about mathematics teaching and learning.

4. If one of your goals is to help participants provide students with opportunities to engage in mathematical argumentation, you might find it beneficial to read O'Connor and Michaels (1996). In this article, the authors introduce a teacher move they call "revoicing," a method used by teachers to socialize mathematical argumentation in the classroom. The authors describe two main functions of revoicing: (1) to reformulate, or rephrase, students' ideas; and (2) to create opportunities for agreement and disagreement. Detailed examples of revoicing are provided, and the article concludes with excerpts from class discussions in which the teachers encourage the students to do the revoicing.

You might want to summarize O'Connor and Michaels (1996) for participants and provide them with examples of the revoicing moves described in the article. You then might ask participants to discuss how revoicing might stimulate mathematical discussion and, if applicable, how they could weave this technique into their own practice.

5. Following the discussion, you may want to have participants reflect individually by writing about some aspect of the case experience. This could involve asking them to consider what Mrs. Crafton had to know and do prior to the lesson in order to anticipate and conduct a discussion in which students engaged in a mathematical debate. Alternatively, you may want to ask participants to consider the value of mathematical argumentation in helping students learn mathematics.

EXTENDING THE CASE EXPERIENCE

If you have additional time, you may want to have participants continue to explore the mathematical and pedagogical ideas on which the case is based. The section "Extending Case-Based Experiences" in Chapter 6 suggests three types of activities you might want to assign for these purposes. Specifically, if you are working with participants who currently are teaching, you may want to provide opportunities for them to consider their own practice in light of the issues that surfaced in reading and discussing "The Case of Barbara Crafton." This will help participants to generalize the issues beyond the specific events of the case.

8

Facilitating Learning from The Case of Isabelle Olson

"The Case of Isabelle Olson" focuses on a 7th-grade teacher and her students at Roosevelt Middle School as they work over 2 days to determine the maximum area of a rectangular rabbit pen (one of whose sides is adjacent to the school building, with the other three sides enclosed with a fixed but unknown amount of fence). Students in Ms. Olson's classroom discover that area can vary for different rectangular pens created from a fixed amount of fence, and they begin to form generalizations about when the maximum area will occur. The problem turns out to be very difficult for Ms. Olson's students. Although they work on the task continuously over the 2-day period, it is only near the end of the second day that students begin to make progress on the mathematical goals of the lesson. Ms. Olson makes it clear to students that she expects that the problem will cause them some frustration, but she provides little guidance on how to proceed. Ms. Olson wants her students to become confident and competent in dealing with ambiguous and challenging situations. She allows students to struggle with the problem, learn from one another, and eventually discover important mathematical ideas through their own efforts.

In the following sections, we provide support for case facilitators' use of the materials in Chapter 3, "Exploring Area and Perimeter: The Case of Isabelle Olson." Sample responses for the Opening Activity and for the "Analyzing the Case" activity are provided in Appendix B.

CASE ANALYSIS

In this section, we provide a detailed analysis of each of the mathematical and pedagogical ideas that are found in "The Case of Isabelle Olson." These analyses may help you in determining which aspects of the case you wish to highlight during the discussion.

Considering the Mathematics in the Case

The problem in the case asks students to determine the dimensions of a rectangular pen that would give the greatest area if one side of the pen is adjacent to the school building and the other three sides are enclosed with a fixed but unknown amount of fence. Ms. Olson has selected this problem because she wants students to create meaning for area and perimeter (para. 7). In particular, she wants students to discover that the maximum area for a given amount of fencing is achieved when the longer side (the one parallel to the school building) is twice the length of the shorter sides. The problem is challenging because students must impose structure on the problem by recognizing that the amount of fencing (which accounts for three sides of the perimeter) is fixed, while the actual dimensions of the pen (and therefore the area) will vary.

In the following paragraphs, we identify several important mathematical ideas that surface in the case, and we provide examples of where these ideas appear in "The Case of Isabelle Olson" in Chapter 3.

Perimeter. In this problem, the perimeter of each rectangular pen is the amount of fencing plus the length of the portion of the school building needed to complete the enclosure. In solving the problem, students work with a fixed amount of fence that will be used to enclose three sides of the pen. So, although the amount of fencing remains constant, the perimeter actually changes based on the portion of the school building used to enclose the pen. However, this point is never explicitly made during the class. For example, in the chart created by Jessica, Jamal, Toby, and Michele (paras. 40–41), it is not clear that the perimeter is not constant for the rectangles they have created (e.g., if the "wall length" of the rectangle is 38 feet, the perimeter is 78 feet; if the "wall length" of the rectangle is 2 feet, the perimeter is 42 feet). In addition, although Tommy's group uses the term *perimeter* on their poster (para. 21), they actually are referring to the amount of fence used, rather than the perimeter.

Area. Throughout the lesson, area is described as the space in the interior of the rabbit pen. The area changes even though the amount of fencing remains constant. Students in the case determine area using the standard formula and by counting the squares in the interior of rectangles created on graph paper or with square tiles. The list that follows provides examples of where area is addressed during the lesson:

- Tommy refers to the area of his pen in terms of "square yards of space." (para. 16)
- Tommy's group "builds" a 100×100 pen and a 125×50 pen in the hallway and counts the linoleum squares to determine the area of the pens and check Michael's calculations. (paras. 30–31)
- Cassandra notes that her group can determine the area of the pens by counting the squares on the inside. (para. 36)

Variations in area for rectangles with fixed perimeters. Among rectangles with a fixed perimeter, a square has the maximum area. In the fencing problem, however, because a portion of the school building is used as one side of the rectangle, the maximum area is obtained when the rectangle has a length (the side parallel to the school building) that is twice its width. As students work on the problem on the first day, Ms. Olson realizes that they do not know that rectangles created from the same amount of fence can have different areas. This misconception limits their ability to engage with the main mathematical ideas of the problem, since they do not see the need to test different configurations of rectangles and generate evidence. As Ms. Olson presses students to prove to her that they have identified the pen with the largest possible area, students eventually become successful in doing so. The list that follows provides examples of students' explorations of the relationship between area and perimeter:

- Ms. Olson presses several groups to convince her that the rectangle they have created will have the

most area for that specific amount of fence. (paras. 16, 20, 21)
- Students' comments indicate that they believe that the area remains constant if the amount of fence is the same. For example, students in Tommy's group decide that "it will still be the same area if you keep the same perimeter every time." (para. 21)
- At the end of the first day, Tommy's group realizes that a 100×100 pen and a 125×50 pen both use 300 yards of fence but do not have the same area. At the beginning of the second day, they confirm this observation by creating rectangular pens from square tiles in the hallway and comparing the areas. Ms. Olson requests that they present this finding to the class. (paras. 24, 30–32)
- Other groups begin to create and test different configurations of rectangles for a fixed amount of fence and discover that they have different areas. (paras. 36–37, 38, 40–41)

Representations. In order to make sense of the problem, students use a variety of representations to model and explore the problem's constraints. In particular, students' diagrams and tables prove to be especially helpful. The list that follows provides examples of how students make use of different representations:

- Tommy's group builds rectangles using linoleum squares in the hallway to confirm their calculations. (paras. 30–31)
- Michael draws rectangles on the overhead to show the class that the areas are different. (para. 34)
- Cassandra comments that her group drew the pens on graph paper in order to determine the length of fence and area for each pen. (para. 36)
- Toby's group uses a table to organize their data and look for patterns. (para. 42)

Generalization. Ms. Olson's goal is for students to reach the generalization that for any amount of fence, the maximum area is obtained when the rectangle has a length (the side parallel to the school building) that is twice its width. Students are expected to arrive at this conclusion by examining rectangles created with a specific amount of fence, looking for patterns within each case, and then testing their conjectures across cases. By the end of the second class, some students have started to notice patterns in their data for a specific amount of fence and are considering the need to test other cases. The list that follows provides examples of how generalization is addressed during the lesson:

- Liz explains that in her group's trials with 20 feet of fence the "biggest area" was always the rectangle with a width that was half its length. Ms. Olson indicates that this is interesting and they should see if it holds for other lengths of fence. (para. 38)
- Toby comments that he and his group were going to try other lengths of fence and see if they notice any patterns. Jamal adds that they know they can stop building their table once the area reaches a maximum and beginning to decrease. (para. 41)

Considering How Student Thinking Is Supported

Isabelle Olson expects that the problem will cause her students discomfort (i.e., disequilibrium) since it is the most open-ended task she has ever given them. In Ms. Olson's view, it is only when students struggle that they learn, and she feels that this short-term discomfort is needed in order to achieve her long-term goals. Her "no pain, no gain" attitude strengthens her resolve to let students struggle with the problem and develop mathematical ideas through their own exploration. However, by the end of the first day, Ms. Olson's students have made little progress on the problem. It is only during the second day that students begin to advance toward the mathematical and problem-solving goals of the task.

In the following paragraphs, we identify several pedagogical moves that Isabelle Olson made that may have influenced her students' opportunities to engage in high-level thinking, reasoning, and communication during the lesson, and we provide examples of where these ideas appear in "The Case of Isabelle Olson" in Chapter 3.

Building on students' prior knowledge and experiences. Although she recognizes that the rabbit pen problem will be challenging for her students, Ms. Olson believes their prior experiences (as 6th-graders and as her students) will help them engage with the problem. Her intention in presenting this problem is to have students apply their problem-solving skills to an under-specified, ill-structured situation. The list that follows provides examples of how this lesson builds on students' prior knowledge and experiences:

- Ms. Olson's students' experiences in 6th grade have prepared them to solve challenging problems in her classroom. She hopes to provide them with additional experience that will prepare them for algebra as 8th-graders. (para. 5)

- Ms. Olson's students have had experience in exploring challenging problems and facing disequilibrium in her classroom. She notes that this is the most open-ended task she has ever given to this group of students. (paras. 6, 8)
- Ms. Olson's students' experience with coming to a generalization by looking at specific examples, making conjectures, and trying additional cases should be helpful in their work on this problem. (para. 12)

However, Ms. Olson is not aware that her students lack some crucial mathematical knowledge needed to solve the problem. Students do not know that different rectangles created from a fixed amount of fence will have different areas. This misconception prevents students from exploring the problem as intended because they do not see the need to test different rectangles and generate evidence. The list that follows provides examples of comments made by Ms. Olson and her students that suggest that the lesson does not build on students' prior mathematical knowledge:

- Tommy's group is convinced that all rectangles created from 300 yards of fence will have the same area. (para. 21)
- During her reflection at the end of the first day, Ms. Olson comments that she was surprised that students did not know that two figures could have the same perimeter but different areas. (para. 26)
- On the second day, Tanya and Michael share their thinking with the class and admit that initially they did not believe that pens with the same amount of fence could have different areas. Cassandra's and Marcus's comments following the presentation by Tommy's group indicate that they did not expect the area to vary. (paras. 33, 36, 38)

Continuing to press students for justification, explanation, and meaning. As students construct rabbit pens during the first day of the lesson, Ms. Olson presses them to justify their thinking by repeatedly asking them how they know that their enclosure has the most area. Ms. Olson also consistently asks students to explain their strategies, diagrams, and calculations as she checks on each group's progress. The list that follows provides examples of when and how Ms. Olson presses her students for explanation:

- Ms. Olson often asks students how they know that the pen they built gives the rabbits the most room for that amount of fence. When students do not provide adequate justification, she requests that they provide evidence to convince her that their rabbit pen has the maximum area. (paras. 16, 21)

- As Ms. Olson visits each group, she asks students to explain their strategies. Once an explanation has been given, Ms. Olson continues to ask questions to clarify why students took a particular step or performed a particular calculation. (paras. 17, 36–37, 38, 40–41)

Holding students accountable for high-level products and processes. At the beginning of the lesson, Ms. Olson indicates that she expects each group to create a poster that shows "the claim they were making about the dimensions of the pen that would give the most room and showed, in some systematic fashion, the evidence that supported their claim" (para. 12). During the second day, Ms. Olson frequently asks students what they plan to do next and makes suggestions that remind students of her expectations. The list that follows provides examples of how Ms. Olson holds students accountable for high-level work:

- Ms. Olson begins the lesson on the first day by clearly stating her expectations. (paras. 12–13)
- Ms. Olson holds Tommy's group accountable for their work by stopping by to check on their progress. (para. 21)
- Ms. Olson tells Tommy's group that they need to prove to her their claim that no matter how the pen is shaped, the area will be the same if the amount of fence is kept the same. (para. 21)
- At the end of each class, Ms. Olson assigns students the task of returning the next day with ideas on how their group should proceed. (paras. 25, 43)
- Ms. Olson encourages students to continue their explorations, often repeating the need to test conjectures, organize data, and provide evidence of their claims. (paras. 21, 37, 38, 41)

Having capable students model high-level performance. Ms. Olson decides to begin work on the second day by having students meet with their groups to discuss what they might do next. She listens in on the groups' conversations and selects Tanya and Michael to share their realization that two different pens constructed from the same amount of fence can have different areas (paras. 33–34). Having Tanya and Michael model high-level performance appears to have helped other students make progress on the task (paras. 36–38).

Supporting students' learning through questioning. Ms. Olson believes that a certain amount of discomfort and struggle are well worth the effort in doing mathematics. She supports students as they work on the task by keeping her questions and suggestions open-ended, not giving in to students' requests for more specific information, and continuing to require that students provide evidence to test their conjectures. The list that follows provides examples of how Ms. Olson supports students' learning through questioning:

- As students demonstrate initial confusion with the task, Ms. Olson provides only general suggestions and asks very open-ended questions that are intended to help students focus on the important features of the problem. (para. 14)
- When students do not appear to be making progress on the task, Ms. Olson begins asking task-specific questions to guide students in more a productive direction. For example, she asks Tommy's group how they know that their pen built from 300 yards of fence with an area of 10,000 square yards is the largest amount of room possible. (para. 16)

FACILITATING THE OPENING ACTIVITY

The primary purpose of the Opening Activity is to engage participants with the mathematical ideas that they will encounter when they read the case. The problem that is found in the Opening Activity (see Figure 3.1) is similar to the problem Ms. Olson's students solve in the case. The problem is intended to highlight the notion that area can vary for rectangles created from a fixed amount of fence and that the maximum area for a given amount of fence is achieved when the longer side (the one parallel to the back of your house) is twice the length of the shorter sides. The problem is challenging because participants must impose structure upon it—that is, like Ms. Olson's students, they need to identify which aspects of the problem are and are not important. In addition, this problem is likely to be quite different from other problems that participants have solved because it contains no numeric values. The "Consider" portion of the Opening Activity challenges participants to think deeply about the relationship between perimeter and area. In this section, we provide suggestions for using the Opening Activity.

1. Begin by having participants work individually on the problem for 5 to 10 minutes and then to continue to work on the task with a partner or

small group. (We have found that beginning with "private think time" ensures that each participant has a chance to grapple with the task prior to engaging in collaborative work.) You may want to encourage participants to model the rectangular pens by either drawing the pens on graph paper or building the pens with square tiles. You may want to provide each pair or small group with grid paper (for drawing models of the rabbit pens); square tiles (for building models of the rabbit pens); and a sheet of newsprint (for sharing their data during the whole-group discussion). Participants who have experience with technological tools such as spreadsheets, graphing calculators, or *The Geometer's Sketchpad* (Jackiw, 1995) may find them helpful in completing this task.

2. Assist participants in their work on the task if they appear to be having difficulty. Consider the following suggestions.

   - If some participants have difficulty getting started, you might suggest that they choose a specific amount of fence to begin working with (e.g., the original version of the problem [para. 8] asks students to create a pen using 24 feet of fence, then to test other lengths and look for patterns).
   - If participants believe that all rectangular pens created with the same amount of fencing have the same area, you may want to ask them to compare the areas of different rectangular pens visually (on graph paper or using square tiles) as well as numerically (using the area formula).
   - If participants have difficulty generating different rectangles for a fixed amount of fence, you might want to select one of the rectangular pens they have created and ask, "What would happen if you increased the width of the pen by one foot?" If each side (width) of the pen is increased by one foot, then the side parallel to the back of the house (length) would decrease by two feet. Systematically increasing (or decreasing) the width by one while decreasing (or increasing) the length by two would allow participants to generate all of the rectangular pens (with whole number dimensions) that can be created from a fixed amount of fence.
   - If participants do not appear to be using a systematic approach, you may want to ask how they can convince you that there are no other pens that could be created from that amount of

fence. This may help participants see the need to organize their data.

3. Orchestrate a whole-group discussion to allow participants to share various solution strategies and approaches. During the discussion you may want to:

   - Elicit different strategies for determining the rectangular pen that has the largest area. You may want to select several groups to present their data (for different amounts of fence). If you asked the small groups to record their data on newsprint earlier, that would facilitate these presentations. Participants will be able to look for patterns and test conjectures across several different examples. If the idea of creating a table as a way of keeping track of the different rectangular pens and their respective dimensions, areas, and perimeters has not been suggested, you may want to suggest this as a way of organizing the data.
   - Elicit participants' ideas and observations about the rectangular pens that have the maximum area for each amount of fence. You may want to ask, "How is the length related to the width?" or, "Could you determine the length if you knew the width?" in order to guide participants toward generalizing that maximum area is obtained when the length is twice the width. (A list of different strategies and observations we have seen teachers use to solve this problem can be found in Appendix B. This may help you prepare for the emergence of methods you might not use yourself in solving the problem.)
   - Elicit different ways of describing the generalization, especially those that participants might expect their students to use (such as explanations tied to a specific number, verbal descriptions, or symbolic representations using letters or phrases). You also may want to ask participants how they might prove this generalization and how they might expect their students to prove it. (See Appendix B for generalizations made by teachers and for proofs based on algebra and calculus.)
   - If any participants solved the task using algebra or calculus, you may want to ask them to present their solutions last to serve as proof of the observations and generalizations identified during the discussion.
   - If participants used only lengths of fencing that were divisible by 4 (and therefore resulted in

pens with whole-number dimensions), you might ask them to consider the dimensions of a pen that is constructed from 30 feet of fencing. In order to identify the pen built from 30 feet of fence that yields the maximum area, participants would need to consider pens that do not have whole-number dimensions.

- Ask participants to discuss any difficulties they experienced in solving the task and to brainstorm ways in which they could provide support to students who encountered similar difficulties.

4. Discuss the "Consider" questions. Encourage participants to provide examples or counter-examples to support their responses and conclusions. Answering the questions might require participants to engage in some additional explorations. For example:

- You may want to encourage participants to use graph paper to show that rectangles can have the same perimeter but different areas. Ask participants to draw more than one rectangle with a perimeter of 24 units, and then compare the areas of the different rectangles that they have drawn (any rectangle in which $L + W = 12$ will have a perimeter of 24 units). This work can be used to conclude that you cannot determine the area of a rectangle by knowing only its perimeter.

- You might also want to encourage participants to use graph paper to show that rectangles can have the same area but different perimeters. Ask participants to draw more than one rectangle with an area of 12 square units, and then compare the perimeters of the different rectangles that they have drawn (any rectangle in which $L \times W = 12$ will have an area of 12 square units). This work can be used to conclude that you cannot determine the perimeter of a rectangle by knowing only its area.

- You may want to ask participants whether their ideas hold only for rectangles or if they can be generalized to other figures as well (e.g., two circles with the same circumference would have the same area; two triangles with the same perimeter could have different areas).

FACILITATING THE CASE DISCUSSION

The case discussion is intended to help participants analyze the mathematical and pedagogical ideas in the case. The "Case Analysis" section should be of assistance in helping you to identify the key ideas in the case and how each idea plays out in the details of the case. Although it is likely that you will begin by having participants examine specific aspects of Isabelle Olson's teaching practice, you should consider how to connect the specific events that occur in her class to more general ideas about mathematics teaching and learning. In this section we provide suggestions for launching and facilitating the case discussion, and for various follow-up activities that you may wish to pursue.

1. If possible, have participants read and reflect on the case before meeting as a group to discuss the case. As participants read the case, we suggest that you ask them to make note of the pedagogical moves Isabelle Olson made during the lesson. (This activity is described in more detail in the section of Chapter 3 entitled "Reading the Case.") This individual activity will help participants think deeply about the pedagogy in the case and help them prepare for the small- and large-group discussions. Alternatively, you may want to select one of the questions found in Chapter 3 (see the section entitled "Extending Your Analysis of the Case") to guide the reading of the case.

2. Begin by having small groups consider how the pedagogical moves made by Ms. Olson throughout the lesson served to support and/or inhibit students' opportunities to engage with the mathematical ideas in the task. Exploring the effects of Ms. Olson's pedagogical moves on student learning will help participants consider how their own actions affect their students' opportunities to do mathematics. It may be helpful to have small-group members begin by sharing the lists they created during their initial reading of the case, and then as a group discuss whether each move served to support or inhibit students' opportunities to engage with the mathematical ideas in the problem. We suggest that you also ask participants to consider *why* the pedagogical moves they have identified are important in terms of students' opportunities to learn. In completing this task, participants should be encouraged to cite specific evidence (i.e., paragraph numbers) from the case to support their claims.

3. Once the small groups have completed their work, you may want to begin the whole-group discussion by first asking participants to identify

the teaching move that they think had the greatest impact on students' learning. Encourage participants to argue respectfully if they do not agree that an identified move had the greatest impact on students' learning. The key in the discussion is to connect teacher actions (either implicit or explicit) with student learning opportunities. For each move identified, participants should indicate whether the move supported or inhibited students' learning and provide evidence from the case that makes salient why the move was important. (See Appendix B for a chart that was created by a group of teachers with whom we worked.)

Conclude the discussion by asking participants to consider what lessons can be learned from "The Case of Isabelle Olson" about the use of open-ended problems that can be applied to teaching more broadly. This raises the discussion from the particulars of what Isabelle Olson did in the case to a more general discussion of the potential impact of the decisions made by a teacher before, during, and after instruction on students' opportunities to learn and understand mathematics.

4. Following the discussion, you may want to have participants reflect individually by writing about some aspect of the case experience. This could involve asking them to consider what Ms. Olson might do the next day to summarize her mathematical and problem-solving goals. You also might ask participants to consider what Ms. Olson might look for as evidence of student learning as she assesses the groups' posters.

EXTENDING THE CASE EXPERIENCE

If you have additional time, you may want to have participants continue to explore the mathematical and pedagogical ideas on which the case is based. The section "Extending Case-Based Experiences" in Chapter 6 suggests three types of activities you might want to assign for these purposes. Specifically, if you are working with participants who currently are teaching, you may want to provide opportunities for them to consider their own practice in light of the issues that surfaced in reading and discussing "The Case of Isabelle Olson." This will help participants to generalize the issues beyond the specific events of the case.

9

Facilitating Learning from The Case of Keith Campbell

"The Case of Keith Campbell" focuses on a 7th-grade teacher and his students at Franklin Middle School. Mr. Campbell is an experienced teacher who is attempting to facilitate inquiry, communication, and high-level thinking after years of telling students exactly what to do and how to do it. Some aspects of Mr. Campbell's teaching still reflect a directive style, but his transition toward a more open-ended approach is evident in the classroom activities that he selected for this lesson.

The case portrays one day of an extended investigation of surface area and volume of rectangular prisms set in the context of packaging "moon gems." In the lesson, Keith Campbell's students determine the possible surface areas for different configurations of rectangular prisms with volumes of 8 through 12 cubic units. Mr. Campbell intends for students to discover the formula for volume of a rectangular prism and to identify the characteristics of a rectangular prism that appear to maximize or minimize surface area.

In the following sections, we provide support for case facilitators' use of the materials in Chapter 4, "Exploring Volume and Surface Area: The Case of Keith Campbell." Sample responses for the Opening Activity and for the "Analyzing the Case" activity are provided in Appendix C.

CASE ANALYSIS

In this section, we provide a detailed analysis of each of the mathematical and pedagogical ideas that are found in "The Case of Keith Campbell." These analyses may help you in determining which aspects of the case to highlight during the discussion.

Considering the Mathematics in the Case

The Moon Gems Task asks students to create different rectangular prisms consisting of a fixed number of cubes (8 and 12) and to determine the surface area for each of these prisms. For several days prior to the lesson in the case, students have been designing covers for moon-gem packages (rectangular prisms) consisting of 1 to 6 cubes. These earlier explorations helped students to develop a conceptual understanding of surface area and volume and to discover the foundational mathematical ideas featured in the lesson in the case.

The mathematical ideas in the case develop as Keith Campbell's students create rectangular prisms with stacking cubes, draw 2-D representations of prisms, and record numeric data pertaining to the dimensions, surface area, and volume of the prisms. Students are not directed to apply a predetermined formula or procedure, and instead generate a variety of ideas that utilize their understanding of surface area and volume. After students investigate the task in pairs, data are organized into a class chart that provides the basis for a whole-class discussion. By looking for patterns and relationships in the chart and in the characteristics of the different rectangular prisms, students are able to develop the formula for volume of a rectangular prism and to form generalizations about the maximum/minimum values of surface area for rectangular prisms of a fixed volume.

In the following paragraphs, we identify several important mathematical ideas that surface in the case, and we identify specific locations where these ideas appear in "The Case of Keith Campbell" in Chapter 4.

Surface area of rectangular prisms. Surface area is the total area of all the surfaces of a 3-D object. In a rectangular prism, surface area is the sum of the areas of its six rectangular faces and is computed by the formula SA = 2LW + 2LH + 2WH (where L, W, and H represent the length, width, and height of the rectangular prism, respectively). In the case, students encounter a concrete representation of surface area as the number of square units of special paper required to wrap a moon-gem package. The context and the manipulatives allow students to conceptualize and illustrate surface area as a 2-D covering of a 3-D rectangular prism and offer a concrete representation of square units.

- In previous lessons, students created nets or covers for 1 to 3 cubes. (para. 6)
- Sheila describes the process underlying the surface area formula, using cubes and a diagram to model the prism. (paras. 14–15 and Figure 4.4)
- Antonio offers a diagram that illustrates surface area as a 2-D covering of a 3-D rectangular prism. (paras. 17–18 and Figure 4.5)
- Students are asked to try to develop the formula for surface area as a homework problem. (para. 38)

Volume of rectangular prisms. Volume is the amount of space, or the capacity, of a three-dimensional object. In a rectangular prism, volume is the number of cubic units required to fill up the space inside of the prism and is computed by the formula V = L × W × H (where L, W, and H represent the length, width, and height of the rectangular prism, respectively). In the case, students encounter a concrete representation of volume as the number of cubic moon gems being packaged or covered in arrangements shaped as rectangular prisms. Students construct rectangular prisms of different volumes and different rectangular prisms of the same volume. The context and the manipulatives allow students to conceptualize volume of a rectangular prism and offer a concrete representation of cubic units.

- In the lesson, each "moon gem" (1-inch cube) corresponds to one unit of volume in the packages (rectangular prisms) being covered. (para. 4)
- One of Mr. Campbell's main goals for the lesson is for students to discover a formula for the volume of a rectangular prism. (paras. 4 and 11)
- Antonio and Erica describe the process underlying the formula for volume, which leads Tyrone to verbalize a formula and then represent it symbolically as FE × SE × H. (paras. 29–30)

Comparing the surface area of rectangular prisms of a fixed volume. Different rectangular prisms with the same volume can have different surface areas. For rectangular prisms of a fixed volume, surface area decreases as the prisms become more cube-like and increases as the prisms become more elongated. The surface area of a rectangular prism is minimized when the prism is shaped as a cube. The lesson portrayed in the case was intended to help students form generalizations about the shapes of the rectangular prisms for each fixed volume that had the maximum and minimum values of surface area.

- Mr. Campbell's comments and the list of observations indicate that in the lesson prior to the case, students discovered that rectangular prisms of the same volume can have different shapes and that these different shapes result in different surface areas. (para. 7)
- One of Mr. Campbell's main goals was for students to realize that for different rectangular prisms with the same volume, elongated prisms have a greater surface area than more compact prisms. (para. 11)
- Latisha overlooks volume to conclude that two rectangular prisms with the same surface area must be the same prism. (para. 27)
- Students compare the characteristics of rectangular prisms of a constant volume that seem to have the maximum and minimum values of surface area. (paras. 35–37)

Connections between representations. Connecting various mathematical representations helps students to make sense of mathematical ideas and to communicate their ideas to others. Students in the case use stacking cubes and 2-D drawings to generate information about rectangular prisms that is recorded in a list of observations and in a table of data. Students frequently explore and connect concrete, pictorial, verbal, and tabular representations and can be seen to employ different representations for different purposes (e.g., the chart facilitates identifying numeric patterns in the data; the drawings make it possible for students to identify which characteristics of the prisms seem to contribute to the maximum and minimum values of surface area).

- Mr. Campbell provides an opportunity for Antonio and others to use Antonio's diagram to construct a formula, and to consider the connection between the formula and Rochelle's observation. (paras. 18–19)

- Angelique's observation (paras. 22) and students' comparisons of prisms with maximum and minimum values of surface area (paras. 35–37) rely on relating numeric data in the chart to a concrete or pictorial representation of the rectangular prism.
- Antonio uses blocks and Erica uses data from the chart (Tables 4.2 and 4.3) to create and verify a verbal formula for volume, which Tyrone then is able to express symbolically. (paras. 28–30)

Generalizations. Exploring patterns and forming generalizations allow students to strengthen their mathematical reasoning skills. In the case, students identify patterns in numeric data and use these observations to make generalizations and to develop formulas. Students also generalize the characteristics of the rectangular prisms that always seem to have the greatest or least surface area for a fixed volume.

- Antonio and other students develop the formula based on Antonio's diagram. (paras. 18–19)
- Tyrone also uses the verbal generalizations of other students to generate a formula for volume. (para. 30)
- Students generalize that for different rectangular prisms with the same volume, elongated prisms always seem to have the greatest surface area and more compact prisms always seem to have the least surface area. (paras. 35–37)

Prime and composite numbers. When only whole numbers are used for dimensions, the dimensions of a rectangular prism are always factors of the numeric value of its volume, V. If V is a prime number, then the dimensions and the configuration of the rectangular prism are uniquely determined, whereas if V is a composite number, several differently shaped rectangular prisms can be made. This idea arises in the case as students consider whether they have found all of the rectangular prisms that can be created from a fixed number of cubes and how to use the factors to determine the dimensions of the rectangular prisms.

- In describing how to compute volume, Antonio observes that the dimensions are "three numbers that multiply to 12." (para. 28)
- Sheila's description of how to tell if you have all of the possible rectangular prisms for a constant volume also relies on relating the factors of 12 to the dimensions of the rectangular prism. (para. 33)

Considering How the Teacher Supports Student Thinking

After years of teaching by telling, Keith Campbell is attempting to provide opportunities for his students to develop an understanding of mathematical ideas through exploring and discussing mathematical ideas with their classmates. In the case, Mr. Campbell allows students to work together and use a variety of representations to make sense of surface area and volume, to develop the formula for volume of a rectangular prism, and to make generalizations about the shape of rectangular prisms that maximize or minimize surface area for a fixed volume. These aspects of Keith Campbell's teaching reflect an open-ended approach to facilitating student learning, although other aspects of Keith Campbell's pedagogy remain more teacher-directed.

In the following paragraphs, we identify several pedagogical moves that Keith Campbell made that supported or inhibited his students' opportunities to engage in high-level thinking, reasoning, and communication during the lesson, and we identify specific instances where these moves can be seen in "The Case of Keith Campbell" in Chapter 4.

Continuing to press students for explanation and meaning. Mr. Campbell frequently presses students to think harder about proposed ideas. He often requests that students provide more thorough explanations of their solution strategies or clarify ideas presented by others.

- Mr. Campbell presses students to develop the "4 × GEMS + 2" formula and to use Antonio's drawing to justify why this formula "will always work." (paras. 18–19)
- Mr. Campbell asks students to "explain it to us again" (para. 29) and to "describe more precisely what it is that we are multiplying together to get the volume." (para. 30)
- Mr. Campbell asks Cameron to "explain what volume is without using moon gems." (para. 32)
- Mr. Campbell presses for a more precise description of prisms that appear to have the least surface area. (para. 36)

Keith Campbell does, however, maintain the mathematical authority in the classroom by validating students' ideas and solutions himself rather than requesting verification from other students. Also, most of the classroom discourse is filtered through Mr. Campbell, with the exception of the exchange between Maria and Jamal (para. 16).

- Rather than consulting the opinions of his students, Mr. Campbell confirms that Jamal has used a "good approach" (para. 16) and that Antonio has made a "great observation." (para. 18)
- Mr. Campbell validates Angelique's idea for determining whether two prisms are the same or different rather than allowing the class to determine whether her idea is valid. (para. 22)
- Mr. Campbell responds to Latisha's question himself rather than redirecting it to the class. (para. 27)
- Mr. Campbell affirms Tyrone's formula for volume rather than asking for verification from the rest of the class. (para. 31)

Modeling of high-level performance. Mr. Campbell creates opportunities for students to model high-level thinking. He provides class time for students to explain their strategies, to present diagrams, and to contribute important ideas to the class discussion. He also notes examples of high-level performance during pairwork that he wants to incorporate into the whole-class discussion.

- Mr. Campbell asks Sheila to repeat her method of totaling the surface area since it relates directly to the surface area formula. (para. 15)
- Several students are given the opportunity to model high-level performance, such as Antonio, Angelique and Erica. (paras. 18, 22, and 29, respectively)

Providing scaffolding for students' learning. Mr. Campbell provides support for his students to engage with the Moon Gems Task at a high level. He frequently asks questions or offers suggestions intended to guide students' thinking toward the goals of the lesson. He incorporates a data table that facilitates students' discovery of patterns and relationships. Mr. Campbell also utilizes students' journals throughout the whole-class discussion to review and extend previous observations and to re-examine unanswered questions.

- Mr. Campbell incorporates a table to organize data and to aid in determining patterns and relationships. (Table 4.1)
- Several students refer to the table to support their ideas, such as Angelique, Rochelle, Latisha and Erica. (paras. 22, 25, 27, and 29, respectively)

- Mr. Campbell asks questions that help students to form a generalization based on Antonio's diagram and formula. (paras. 18–19)
- Mr. Campbell attempts to guide Rochelle and Brian's thinking during pairwork by suggesting that they look for similarities between rectangular prisms that "cost the most" or "cost the least." (para. 25)
- Class observations and questions are publicly displayed on a side chalkboard as well as in students' individual notebooks. Mr. Campbell and his students revisit this list throughout the lesson. (paras. 10, 22, 32, and 34)

On a few occasions, Mr. Campbell asks questions intended to elicit a specific response that he wishes to incorporate into the discussion, rather than asking questions that guide students' thinking toward the mathematical goals of the lesson.

- Mr. Campbell interjects the term *factors* into Sheila's explanation and asks for a choral response to elicit the term *prime numbers.* (paras. 33 and 34)
- Mr. Campbell leads students to offer the term "cubes." (para. 37)

Drawing conceptual connections. Mr. Campbell frequently provides opportunities for students to draw connections between the concepts of surface area and volume and the formulas used to measure these attributes. As his students develop common formulas through their own explorations, they gain an understanding of how and why the formulas work.

- Mr. Campbell calls students' attention to Sheila's system for finding surface area. (para. 15)
- Mr. Campbell guides the discussion as the class develops the formula for volume. (paras. 29–31)
- Mr. Campbell and Cameron discuss what volume is versus how to find volume. (para. 32)

Using a task that builds upon students' prior knowledge. Previous lessons in Mr. Campbell's classroom, as well as students' experiences in earlier grades, provided learning opportunities that enabled students to engage with the Moon Gems Task. Working with stacking cubes and the moon-gems context in earlier lessons allowed students to develop an understanding of surface area and volume and to discover ideas that would be foundational to Mr. Campbell's goals for this lesson.

- Mr. Campbell discusses students' experiences with surface area and volume in prior grades. (para. 4)
- Creating nets or covers for rectangular prisms consisting of smaller numbers of cubes would help students to conceptualize surface area and square units. (para. 6)
- Students previously had discovered that rectangular prisms with volumes of 4 and 6 cubic units could have different dimensions, different shapes, and different surface areas. (para. 7)
- The lesson in the case builds directly on students' homework assignment from the previous lesson. (para. 13) Similarly, the homework assigned following the lesson in the case serves to extend ideas generated during the lesson. (para. 38)
- Mr. Campbell takes advantage of opportunities to revisit misconceptions generated in previous lessons. (paras. 21 and 22)

FACILITATING THE OPENING ACTIVITY

The primary purpose of the Opening Activity is to engage participants with the mathematical ideas that they will encounter when they read "The Case of Keith Campbell." Similar to the task used by Keith Campbell, the task in the Opening Activity (see Figure 4.1) asks participants to create different rectangular prisms consisting of 8, 9, 10, 11, and 12 cubes and to record the dimensions, surface area, and volume for each of these prisms. The activity is intended to enrich participants' understanding of surface area and volume by giving meaning to the units and formulas used to measure surface area and volume and by highlighting the notion that surface area can vary for rectangular prisms of a fixed volume. This activity challenges participants to think about the concepts of surface area and volume in ways that go beyond memorizing and applying common formulas. In this section, we provide suggestions for using the Opening Activity.

1. Begin by having participants work individually on the problem for 5 to 10 minutes and then have them continue to work on the task with a partner or small group. (We have found that beginning with "private think time" ensures that each participant has a chance to grapple with the task prior to engaging in collaborative work.) You should provide each pair or small group with the following materials: 24 small cubes (to build the rectangular prisms), and a sheet of newsprint and marker (to make a poster of one of their solutions to present during the whole-group discussion).

2. Assist participants if they appear to be having difficulty with the "Solve" portion of the Opening Activity. For example:

- If some participants have difficulty getting started, ask one or two successful pairs or groups to present one of the rectangular prisms they created with 8 cubes and to explain how they determined the dimensions, surface area, and volume. This might help to clarify or refresh important ideas about these attributes, and it will make the demonstrated strategies available for participants to use in creating other rectangular prisms.
- If some participants move directly to creating a data table rather than building prisms with cubes or drawing diagrams, you may want to ask them to consider ways in which the manipulatives and diagrams might benefit students' understanding of surface area and volume.
- Participants may think that they *need* formulas to determine the surface area and volume of the prisms. You might find it helpful to explicitly relate the cubes to cubic units for measuring volume, and the square faces of the cubes to square units for measuring surface area. Stress that participants should be using methods that they can explain, understand, and make sense of every step of the way.
- If some participants are only able to complete the task by applying memorized formulas, suggest that they approach the task from the viewpoint of a student who does not have access to these formulas. Participants who demonstrate facility with (or reliance on) common formulas also could be asked to use diagrams or models to explain why these formulas work, or to develop other formulas for the surface area of rectangular prisms with special shapes (e.g., the surface area of an $n \times n \times n$ cube is $6n^2$ and the surface area of an $n \times 1 \times 1$ prism is $4n + 2$).
- Watch for participants to attempt to use incorrect formulas for volume. Some commonly misapplied formulas include $V = L \times W$, $V = B \times H$ (where one of the dimensions is used for B, rather than the area of the base), and

$V = 2L + 2W$. Participants also might encounter difficulty in substituting values into formulas and in evaluating formulas once these numbers have mechanically been plugged in.

- Watch for a common misconception—some participants may draw a rectangle to represent a rectangular prism, especially if the prism has a width of 1 (since the area and volume would both have the same numeric value). This could indicate (or create) confusion between area and volume or about the units used to measure these attributes, as often seen in middle school students. Asking participants to compare diagrams similar to the two diagrams produced in the case by Sheila (Figure 4.4) might help participants realize that drawing a rectangle does not communicate the width of the rectangular prism and misrepresents the units for surface area and volume.

3. Orchestrate a whole-group discussion in which participants present the different rectangular prisms they created for each fixed number of cubes and share strategies for determining the dimensions, surface area, and volume of the rectangular prisms. During the discussion you may want to:

- Have each pair or group present a different rectangular prism to the whole group using the newsprint. (You may want to assign each pair or group a specific prism, or a specific volume, to present based on your observations during group-work, and you may want to have the pairs or groups create and post their newsprint posters prior to the whole-group discussion.) Display all of the posters throughout the discussion to help participants consider whether all possible prisms are listed for each fixed volume and to notice characteristics of a prism that influence surface area. If creating a data table has not been suggested in the discussion, ask participants to consider how the information might be organized in a way that would be helpful in thinking about the "Consider" portion of the Opening Activity. (Tables 4.1, 4.2, and 4.3 provide data for rectangular prisms consisting of 1–12 cubes. Also, Appendix C contains a set of solutions generated by teachers who completed the Opening Activity as part of a professional development experience that focused on "The Case of Keith Campbell." This may help you prepare for the emergence of

methods you might not use yourself in solving the problem.)

- Solicit strategies that utilize different representations, since different representations can help to illuminate different aspects of the exploration. For example, the cubes offer a concrete model of surface area and volume and of the units used to measure these attributes; a diagram with a 3-D appearance preserves the shape of the prism for considering maximum/minimum surface area; a diagram such as a net clearly portrays surface area; and organizing data into a table facilitates the discovery of numeric relationships and the development of formulas.

- Solicit different ways that groups approached creating the rectangular prisms (such as determining the dimensions first, building layers, or randomly arranging the cubes). The first two approaches might help others to make sense of the common formula for volume of a rectangular prism.

- Solicit responses that use different strategies to determine surface area (e.g., counting the square units on each face of the prism; finding the area of each face of the prism and adding these values together or developing a shortcut based on this approach; using a diagram such as a net; or applying a formula). Looking at nonalgorithmic strategies based on finding and adding the area of the faces of the prism might help participants make sense of the common formula for surface area of a rectangular prism.

4. Discuss the "Consider" portion of the Opening Activity. (Examples of teacher-generated responses to the "Consider" questions appear in Appendix C.) During the discussion, you may want to:

- Encourage participants to justify their responses to Question 1. Participants often consider prisms with the same dimensions but a different orientation to be different prisms, such as counting $6 \times 2 \times 1$ as a long, flat prism and $2 \times 1 \times 6$ as a tall, skinny prism. (Keith Campbell and his students discuss the issue of orientation in the case, in paras. 21–22.) This type of response could provide the basis for a discussion of how to determine whether two prisms are mathematically different compared with being different for practical purposes.

- For Question 2, focus on making sense of the common formulas for finding the surface area and volume of a rectangular prism. (Note that participants may find it easier to make sense of the formula for volume of a rectangular prism than for surface area.) Participants typically can describe a general procedure for determining surface area, but they encounter difficulty in expressing the procedure as a formula using L, W, and H. (You may want to explore the issue of generalization and using letters as variables in more depth than discussed here, depending on your goals.) You may want to make explicit connections between the procedures participants used to determine surface area and how these procedures are stated concisely in the common formula.

- In responding to Question 3, participants may easily recognize that the more elongated prisms consistently have the maximum surface area and that the more compact prisms consistently have the least surface area. But since there is only one cube in the list (the $2 \times 2 \times 2$), the notion that a cube minimizes surface area for a given volume may not arise spontaneously through the discussion. You might be able to use participants' comments to get at this generalization directly. Alternatively, you may need to ask participants whether their responses would have been different if the dimensions did not have to be whole numbers. This also will make explicit that there are other possible rectangular prisms for a fixed volume if the dimensions are not limited to whole numbers.

FACILITATING THE CASE DISCUSSION

The case discussion is intended to help participants analyze the mathematical and pedagogical ideas in "The Case of Keith Campbell." The "Case Analysis" section should be of assistance in helping you to identify the key ideas in the case and how each idea plays out in the details of the case. Although it is likely that you will begin by having participants examine specific aspects of Keith Campbell's teaching practice, you should consider how to connect the specific events that occur in his class to more general ideas about mathematics teaching and learning. In this section we provide suggestions for launching and facilitating the case discus-

sion, and for various follow-up activities that you may wish to pursue.

1. If possible, have participants read and reflect on the case before meeting as a group to discuss the case. As participants read the case, we suggest that you ask them to identify the mathematical ideas that students appear to be learning during the lesson depicted in "The Case of Keith Campbell." (This activity is described in more detail in the section of Chapter 4 entitled "Reading the Case.") This individual activity will help participants think deeply about students' opportunities to learn mathematics in "The Case of Keith Campbell" and will help them prepare for the small- and large-group discussions. Alternatively, you may want to select one of the questions found in Chapter 4 (see the section entitled "Extending Your Analysis of the Case") to guide the reading of the case.

2. In small groups, have participants discuss the mathematical ideas learned by students that they identified when they read the case. For each mathematical idea identified, participants should indicate the pedagogical move(s) Mr. Campbell made that appeared to support (or inhibit) his students' learning and provide evidence (i.e., paragraph numbers) from the case to support their claims. It might be helpful to have groups organize their work into a two-column chart—one column for mathematical ideas the other for Mr. Campbell's pedagogical moves.

3. Once the small groups have completed their work, you should create a master chart that draws on the work of the individual groups. One way to facilitate the development of a master chart is to first ask the groups to share what they think Mr. Campbell's students learned or were in the process of learning. Then you may want to choose a subset of these mathematical ideas as the focus of a discussion on what Mr. Campbell did to support or inhibit his students' learning and provide evidence from the case that supports the claims. The key in the discussion is to connect teacher actions (either implicit or explicit) with student learning opportunities. (The "Case Analysis" section earlier in this chapter, as well as a chart produced by a group of teachers who engaged in this activity, found in Appendix C, may be helpful in identifying passages in "The

Case of Keith Campbell" where student learning occurs and how it is supported or inhibited by Keith Campbell.)

Conclude the discussion by asking participants to consider what lessons could be learned from "The Case of Keith Campbell" about the use of different representations of a concept or idea that apply to teaching more broadly. The goal here is to help participants generalize the pedagogy used by Keith Campbell to mathematics teaching beyond the specific lesson that is the focus of the current analysis.

4. Following the discussion, you may want to have participants reflect individually by writing about some aspect of the case experience. This could involve having participants consider what Mr. Campbell should do the next day to guide students to develop the formula for surface area

and to provide closure for the entire Moon Gems Task.

EXTENDING THE CASE EXPERIENCE

If you have additional time, you may want to have participants continue to explore the mathematical and pedagogical ideas on which the case is based. The section "Extending Case-Based Experiences" in Chapter 6 suggests three types of activities you might want to assign for these purposes. Specifically, if you are working with participants who currently are teaching, you may want to provide opportunities for them to consider their own practice in light of the issues that surfaced in reading and discussing "The Case of Keith Campbell." This will help teachers to generalize the issues beyond the specific events of the case.

10

Facilitating Learning from The Case of Nancy Upshaw

The case of Nancy Upshaw focuses on a 7th-grade teacher and her students at El Toro Middle School. Ms. Upshaw is an experienced mathematics and science teacher who is always looking for ways to involve her students in inquiry-oriented mathematical tasks that, at the same time, provide opportunities to reinforce students' basic skills in the context of working on good problem-solving activities.

In the lesson portrayed in the case, Ms. Upshaw's students are in the process of working on the Large Numbers Lab activities. This set of lab activities was intended to provide students with the opportunity to explore the relative sizes of large numbers through concrete investigations involving measurement, estimation, and computation of volume. Students work together in small groups to make predictions and estimates, as well as to devise strategies for measuring volume. The groups make varying levels of progress during the lesson, but most of the small groups engage in rich mathematical discussions of their reasoning and strategies for solving the task. At the end of the lesson, Ms. Upshaw involves students in a discussion of their strategies and observations about the lab activities.

In the following sections, we provide support for case facilitators' use of the materials in Chapter 5, "Estimating and Calculating Volume: The Case of Nancy Upshaw." Sample responses for the Opening Activity and for the "Analyzing the Case" activity are provided in Appendix D.

CASE ANALYSIS

In this section, we provide a detailed analysis of each of the mathematical and pedagogical ideas that are found in "The Case of Nancy Upshaw." These analyses

may help the case facilitator determine which aspects of the case to highlight during the case discussion.

Considering the Mathematics in the Case

The mathematics in "The Case of Nancy Upshaw" unfolds as Ms. Upshaw and her students work on the Large Numbers Lab activities. The Large Numbers Lab activities are designed to give students an opportunity to increase their understanding of large numbers such as 1,000 and 1,000,000 in the context of volume measurement, thus also increasing their understanding of what it means to measure volume. Students must make reasonable predictions and compare these predictions with actual measurements. In order to be successful with the tasks, students must draw on and determine how best to use a variety of resources at their disposal, including their peers; various measurement tools; and their prior knowledge and experiences in determining length, area, and volume. The complexity of the tasks is derived from the fact that students are not given a clear pathway for solving the problems and must draw on their conceptual understanding of volume measurement in order to devise a solution strategy.

In the following paragraphs, we identify several important mathematical ideas that surface in the case, and we provide examples of where these ideas appear in "The Case of Nancy Upshaw" in Chapter 5.

Volume of a rectangular prism. A good understanding of the volume of a rectangular prism involves being able to see the spatial structure underlying the formula—that is, the connection between filling up space with layers of objects and the formula Length × Width × Height (Battista, 1998). The Large Numbers Lab activities provide students with the opportunity to make this connection by visualizing the layers of blocks or balls that will fill the room. Students also are able to visualize cubic units as they manipulate the blocks and consider how much space will not be filled by the soccer balls.

- Ms. Upshaw discusses how the lab activity helps build students' volume sense. (para. 8)
- Ms. Upshaw uses the idea of layers to help Jorge and Roberto get back on track, and several other students also use a layering approach to solve the lab activities. (paras. 13–14, 19–20, 30)
- Students also use the Length × Width × Height formula throughout the lab activities. (paras. 15, 16, 18, 20)
- José and Lucia argue about the possible dimensions of a box that is 8 cubic meters in volume. (para. 15)
- Ms. Upshaw asks Mariola to explain her observation in the chart. Mariola's response clearly articulates the connection between the layering approach and the formula for volume of a rectangular prism. (para. 30)

Effect of unit size on volume measure. When a fixed volume is measured, using a smaller unit results in a larger magnitude for the volume measure and using a larger unit yields a smaller magnitude for the volume measure. That is, it takes more objects of a smaller size or unit to fill up the same amount of space than of a larger size or unit. Students address this idea in the lab activities by comparing the number of blocks versus soccer balls that are necessary to fill the classroom.

- Roberto observes that when larger units are used, they take up more space so you need less of them to fill the space. (para. 25)
- The homework question is intended to extend students' understanding of the relationship between the object's size and the number of objects that will fit in the room. (para. 30)

Unit conversions. The Large Numbers Lab activities require students to convert between nonstandard units (soccer balls and big blocks) and metric units (centimeters or meters). In determining the volume of a box that would hold exactly 1,000 blocks or balls, students must give a solution in metric units. To determine how many blocks/balls will fill the classroom, students can choose to measure the blocks or balls in metric units or to determine how many blocks or balls fit into one meter (or into one dimension of the classroom). Another type of unit conversion embedded in the task involves convert-ing within different units of the metric system for linear and volume measurements.

- Rolando's, Andres's, and Tomás's groups use an approach in which the metric measurement of each dimension is converted to the nonstandard unit of soccer balls (e.g., Rolando's group determines how many balls will fit along each dimension of the classroom). (paras. 10, 18, and 19–20, respectively)
- Jorge asks why the dimensions of the big block have to be expressed as 20 centimeters rather than as 10 small cubes. His group determines the volume in cubic centimeters. Roberto later suggests that another strategy would be to find out how many blocks are in each dimension, then find the volume in terms of the number of blocks. (paras. 14 and 18, respectively)
- Many students measured the edge-length of a block or the diameter of a ball and used these metric measurements to reason through the problems. (paras. 14 and 19)
- Roberto says that they also could have used "times 100 for each dimension" (i.e., converted cubic meters to cubic centimeters). (para. 16)
- Ms. Upshaw comments that several groups used the strategy of finding the volume of the room and dividing by the volume of 1 block (both in metric units). She then elicits a strategy based on determining how many blocks would fit along each dimension. (paras. 26–27)

Prediction and estimation. Students often rely solely on counting strategies or formulas to determine measurement attributes of geometric figures. However, opportunities to make predictions and estimations help to develop students' intuition or sense of measurement attributes. In the Large Numbers Lab activities, students' ability to predict and estimate the number of blocks/balls needed to fill the classroom draws on their understanding of how to arrange the objects to fill up the classroom space and on their understanding of large numbers. Students also estimate measurements and computations, and engage in rounding or approximating both metric units and nonstandard units of blocks/balls.

- Students are asked to make a prediction at the outset of each section of the lab about how many objects would fill up the room. (Figure 5.2)
- Ms. Upshaw mentions that strengthening students' skills at estimating volume is a subgoal of the

lesson. (para. 8) This is one of the reasons that she does not make calculators available. (para. 9)

- Rolando's group explicitly makes use of how the objects would be arranged in layers to reason through their estimate of how many objects would fill the classroom. (para. 10)
- Jimmy's group rounds the dimensions of the room to whole numbers. (para. 16)
- Tomás's group estimates the metric measurement of the diameter of the ball. Ms. Upshaw comments that she is glad that they are concerned with accuracy and acceptable error in measuring since she previously had addressed these issues. (para. 19)

Relative size of large numbers. The Large Numbers Lab activities allow students to get a better sense of large numbers by visualizing 1,000 objects arranged in a rectangular array (in the context of measuring volume). Toward the end of the lesson when the prediction chart is compared with the actual results of the labs, there is evidence that some students gained a better sense of how many objects would fill the room, as well as the relative size of 1,000, and larger numbers.

- Ms. Upshaw mentions that developing a sense of large numbers is a goal of the unit in which this lesson is embedded. (para. 7)
- The choices for estimating the number of blocks and balls that will fill the room are powers of 10, intended to give students a feel for these important benchmarks in developing large-number sense. (Figure 5.2)
- Jimmy comments that more blocks would fit into the room than he had guessed. (para. 25)
- In discussing their predictions, students have the opportunity to compare the relative magnitude of 1,000, 10,000, and 1,000,000. (para. 25)

Computation. Students should be given the opportunity to practice computations in the context of solving meaningful problems (NCTM, 2000). Ms. Upshaw intends to use the Large Numbers Lab activities to provide her students with practice in arithmetic computations. Students in the case appear to do some calculations mentally and some with paper and pencil.

- Ms. Upshaw comments that she intends to use these activities as an opportunity for students to practice basic skills. She intentionally does not make calculators available and also encourages students to keep a written record of their work. (para. 9)

- Students in the case use paper and pencil calculations in solving the Large Numbers Lab activities. (paras. 15, 17, 20, 21)
- Students in the case also perform some calculations mentally. (paras. 14 and 16)

Considering How Student Thinking Is Supported

Nancy Upshaw engages her students in the Large Numbers Lab activities in order to improve their number sense, their estimation skills, and their understanding of how volume is measured as well as to provide an opportunity to practice computation skills in a problem-solving context. As students work in groups, Ms. Upshaw encourages them to record their thought processes and calculations and to be able to explain their reasoning as they solve the tasks. Students also are afforded the opportunity to abstract some ideas about volume measurement at the end of the lesson when Ms. Upshaw engages them in a discussion of the similarities and differences between the two lab activities and the strategies they used to determine solutions to these activities.

In the following paragraphs, we identify several pedagogical moves that Nancy Upshaw made that may have influenced her students' opportunities to engage in thinking, reasoning, and communication during the lesson, and we provide examples of where these ideas appear in "The Case of Nancy Upshaw" in Chapter 5.

Using a task that builds on students' prior knowledge. Throughout the case, students draw on their previous experiences with linear, area, and volume measurement in order to engage in the Large Numbers Lab activities.

- Students are familiar with the concept of volume from previous experience with measuring volume by counting cubes. Ms. Upshaw comments that this lesson will reinforce their notions of 3-D units and allow them to gain insight into the formula for volume of a rectangular prism. (para. 8)
- The Large Numbers Lab activities assume proficiency with linear and area measurement, which Ms. Upshaw comments that students have had plenty of experience with in 5th and 6th grades. (para. 8)
- Students often rely on a layering approach rather than on the formula provided on their information sheet, which indicates that they had a way of thinking about measuring volume that did not rely

on substituting numbers into a formula and also could be used to make sense of volume formulas in general (e.g., area of the base × the height). (paras. 13–14, 19–20, 30)

- Tran shows his group how the Balls section of the lab is similar to an area problem they solved in a previous lesson. (para. 23)
- The homework assignment provides students with an additional opportunity to reflect on a key mathematical idea in the task—the relationship between the size of a unit and the volume measure obtained. (para. 30)

Consistently pressing students for explanation and meaning. As she visits the small groups, Ms. Upshaw consistently asks students to explain the processes they are using and why they chose these procedures.

- Ms. Upshaw asks Jorge to explain what his group is doing and probes his explanation further. She later revisits the group and presses Jimmy to explain the group's reasoning. (paras. 13–14, 16–17)
- Ms. Upshaw asks Tomás and Rigo to explain their methods for the 1,000 Balls section of the lab in detail. (paras. 19–20)
- Ms. Upshaw asks Roberto why his observation is important. (para. 25)
- Ms. Upshaw asks Mariola to elaborate further on her observation about building layers. (para. 30)

Encouraging written records of students' work and thought processes. Ms. Upshaw encourages students to record all of their work, including sketches, verbal explanations, and calculations. Students often refer to written records of their work when explaining their reasoning to Ms. Upshaw and to one another. Ms. Upshaw publicly records students' predictions about the number of blocks that will fill the room and uses this chart as a common object of reflection for the class to consider the relative size of large numbers. Ms. Upshaw also uses the list of students' observations about the similarities and differences between the measurement processes used in the two lab activities as an opportunity to connect the layering approach to the volume formula.

- Ms. Upshaw notes the importance of recording work, especially when dealing with a complex task. (para. 9)
- Ms. Upshaw reminds students to record their predictions for the two lab activities. Students later

reflect on these predictions in comparing the relative size of large numbers. (paras. 12, 24–25)
- Ms. Upshaw encourages Mariola's group to make a sketch and be sure to label it correctly. (para. 14)
- Students often refer to written records of their work when explaining their reasoning to Ms. Upshaw and to one another. (paras. 15, 17, 19, 21)
- Ms. Upshaw records student observations on a class chart at the overhead. She then has students reflect on their recorded observations about the similarities and differences between the measurement processes used in the two sections of the lab. (paras. 29–30)

Encouraging communication. Ms. Upshaw also makes significant efforts to avoid telling students how to proceed. She consistently directs individual student questions back to the groups for consideration. Ms. Upshaw also provides opportunities for students to communicate about mathematics in both small- and large-group settings.

- Students are working on the Large Numbers Lab in groups of four or five. (para. 6)
- Jorge asks whether it matters what units one uses to represent the volume, and Ms. Upshaw redirects the question back to the group without providing an answer. (para. 14)
- Ms. Upshaw provides an opportunity for the less-verbal members of the group to do the explaining. (para. 16)
- Ms. Upshaw presses Rolando's group to tell her what they know about the problem and provides them with ample time to respond. (para. 21)
- Ms. Upshaw encourages the groups to pursue their own ideas about how to determine the amount of space filled up by the balls. (paras. 22–23)
- Ms. Upshaw provides an opportunity for students to present their strategies and engage in a whole-group discussion. (paras. 26–27)

Drawing conceptual connections. Ms. Upshaw encourages students to make connections between the different types of strategies that different groups of students used to solve the problems and between the use of a specific strategy with the blocks versus the balls. Ms. Upshaw also helps students to make connections between the layering approach and the formula for volume of a rectangular prism.

- Ms. Upshaw wants to provide students with an insight into the relationships underlying the

formula for volume of a rectangular prism.
(paras. 8 and 30)
- Ms. Upshaw wants students to see the commonalities across both lab activities (blocks and balls). (para. 27)
- Ms. Upshaw wants students to make connections between different strategies for solving the lab activities. She has students present the two main types of strategies used for determining how many blocks would fill the room and later prompts students to discuss why different strategies result in different answers. (paras. 26–28)

FACILITATING THE OPENING ACTIVITY

The primary purpose of the Opening Activity (see Figure 5.1) is to engage participants with the mathematical ideas they will encounter when they read "The Case of Nancy Upshaw." The task in the Opening Activity is similar to the Large Numbers Lab activities solved by students in the case. Participants are asked to make a prediction about how many blocks and balls would be needed to fill the room; determine as accurately as possible how many blocks and balls would be needed to fill the room; and be able to explain more than one method for doing so. The activity is intended to enrich participants' understanding of different methods for determining the volume as well as how different methods are related to one another mathematically. In this section, we provide the case facilitator with suggestions for using the Opening Activity.

1. Begin by having participants make predictions about the number of blocks and balls needed to fill the room. You may want to record these predictions on a chart at the front of the room. If you feel participants might be apprehensive about giving their predictions publicly, you can ask them to write their predictions on Post-it notes privately and then post them on newsprint at the front of the room as participants begin solving the task.

2. Have participants work individually on solving the task for 5 to 10 minutes and then continue to work on the task in small groups. (We have found that beginning with "private think time" ensures that each participant has a chance to grapple with the task prior to engaging in collaborative work.) The following materials are required for the Opening Activity: 2-cm blocks and tennis balls (for modeling the task of filling up the room), and various

measuring tools such as rulers, meter sticks, and/or tape measures (for measuring the room, the blocks, or the balls). We suggest providing approximately 100 blocks and 5–10 tennis balls per group. Note that tennis balls are about 6.5 cm in diameter and about 3,800 will fit into one cubic meter. You also may want to provide participants with chart paper or transparencies (for recording their solutions).

3. Assist participants in their work on the task if they appear to be having difficulty. For example:

- If your session is taking place in a room with an unusual shape or floor plan, some participants may struggle with how to define the space they are filling up. You may want to discuss this with the whole group and agree on what to do with features such as difficult corners or pillars in the middle of the room.
- If a group is having trouble getting started, you might ask them to think about how they would go about filling a smaller space (i.e., a large box). You also might ask them whether they can think of any way the measurement tools they have might be helpful. Alternatively, you could ask one group that seems to have made progress to share how they got started, keeping in mind that everyone should try to find more than one approach.
- If some participants solve the task by applying memorized formulas, encourage them to find an alternative method that might be used by someone who is not familiar with the formulas. Perhaps suggesting that they visualize how the blocks or balls would be arranged to fill up the room might lead them to reason through a layering approach or to create a diagram. You also may want to encourage them to use the manipulatives and/or the context of the problem to justify why the formulas work.
- Each group should be challenged to find and explain more than one way of solving the task. If participants have difficulty finding more than one solution method, you might have groups who used different methods describe only the first step of their strategy to the whole group, or you could pair groups who used different strategies together and have them compare the similarities and differences between the two approaches. (Samples of solutions for the Opening Activity produced by teachers are

provided in Appendix D. These solutions may help you prepare for the emergence of methods you might not use yourself in solving the problems.)

4. Orchestrate a whole-group discussion to allow participants to share various solution strategies and approaches. During the discussion you may want to:

   • Have several participants explain their solutions and strategies, and provide opportunities for other participants to ask questions or request clarification of the mathematical ideas and strategies presented by their peers. You may find it helpful to display all work (including diagrams, explanations, and computations) on newsprint or a chalkboard so that several different solution methods may be examined at the same time.

   • When you have at least three or four different methods available, you may want to address the "Consider" questions in the Opening Activity, which ask participants to reflect on the similarities and differences in working with blocks versus balls and among the given solution methods. Look for connections between methods used for blocks and balls; between different ways of determining volume; between choice of metric units or nonstandard units, and so on. (See Appendix D for samples of different approaches that have been used by teachers and some similarities, differences, and connections that can be made among them.)

   • Challenge participants to focus on similarities and differences in mathematical reasoning (e.g., use of standard versus nonstandard measurement units; allowing partial versus whole blocks or balls; when and how they converted between linear and cubic units) rather than only on surface features (e.g., type of measurement tool used, order in which dimensions were measured, order in which certain numbers were computed, and so forth).

   • You may want to address the issue of how the different objects fill up the space of the room. Participants might suggest that the balls could be nested in alternating layers. This would allow more layers of balls to fit into the room than if the layers are centrally aligned (as assumed in all of the solutions provided in Appendix D). Another issue is whether blocks or balls can be partitioned in order to completely fill up the space in the room. Note that most solution methods assume that partial blocks or balls are permissible, with the exception of solutions that round each dimension to a whole number of blocks/balls.

   • You may want to close the discussion by asking participants to identify the mathematical ideas or concepts that *could be learned* from engaging in the Opening Activity. (The "Considering the Mathematics in the Case" portion of the "Case Analysis" section, found earlier in this chapter, also may be helpful in preparing for this discussion.)

FACILITATING THE CASE DISCUSSION

The case discussion is intended to help participants analyze the mathematical and pedagogical ideas in "The Case of Nancy Upshaw." The "Case Analysis" section should be of assistance in helping you to identify the key ideas in the case and how each idea plays out in the details of the case. In this section we provide the case facilitator with suggestions for launching and facilitating the discussion of "The Case of Nancy Upshaw," and for various follow-up activities that might be pursued.

1. If possible, have participants read and reflect on the case before meeting as a group to discuss the case. As participants read the case, we suggest that you ask them to consider what Nancy Upshaw's students are doing to make sense of, and ultimately to complete the activities in the Large Numbers Lab. (This activity is described in more detail in the section of Chapter 5 entitled "Reading the Case.") This individual activity will help participants focus on students' learning in "The Case of Nancy Upshaw" and will help them prepare for the small- and large-group discussions. Alternatively, you may want to select one of the questions found in Chapter 5 (see the section entitled "Extending Your Analysis of the Case") to guide the reading of the case.

2. In small groups, ask participants to consider the list of observations regarding students' sense-making and problem-solving activities that they created while reading the case. For each student action identified, ask participants to indicate *what* Ms. Upshaw did (or appeared to do) to support the students' efforts at sense-making and

problem-solving and *why* this action served to support their efforts. Encourage participants to cite specific evidence from the case (i.e., paragraph numbers) to support their claims. You may find it helpful to have each small group create a three-column chart that includes what students were doing, what Nancy Upshaw was doing, and why the teacher's actions supported student learning.

3. Once the small groups have completed their work, you should create a master chart that draws on the work of the individual groups. One way to facilitate the development of a master chart is to first ask the groups to share what they think Ms. Upshaw's students were doing to make sense of and complete the activities in the Large Numbers Lab. Then you may want to choose a subset of these ideas as the focus of a discussion on what Ms. Upshaw did to support her students' efforts at sense-making and problem-solving, and why her actions were supportive. (The "Case Analysis" section earlier in this chapter, as well as a chart produced by a group of teachers who engaged in this activity, found in Appendix D, may be helpful in identifying passages in "The Case of Nancy Upshaw" where students are making sense of and solving the problems and how their work is supported by Ms. Upshaw.)

Conclude the discussion by asking participants to consider what lessons could be learned from "The Case of Nancy Upshaw" about the use of mathematical tasks that serve to both reinforce basic skills and provide opportunities for problem-solving that apply to teaching more broadly. The goal here is to help participants generalize the pedagogy used by Nancy Upshaw to mathematics teaching beyond the specific lesson that is the focus of the current analysis.

4. Following the discussion, you may want to have participants reflect individually by writing about some aspect of the case experience. This could involve having participants consider the following questions: What was Ms. Upshaw's role during the whole-group discussion? How did Nancy Upshaw use the information she gained during groupwork as a tool for facilitating the whole-group discussion? What evidence of student understanding is present in the whole-group discussion?

EXTENDING THE CASE EXPERIENCE

If you have additional time, you may want to have participants continue to explore the mathematical and pedagogical ideas on which the case is based. The section "Extending Case-Based Experiences" in Chapter 6 suggests three types of activities you might want to assign for these purposes. Specifically, if you are working with participants who currently are teaching, you may want to provide opportunities for them to consider their own practice in light of the issues that surfaced in reading and discussing "The Case of Nancy Upshaw." This will help teachers to generalize the issues beyond the specific events of the case.

Appendix A

Sample Responses to The Case of Barbara Crafton

Appendix A contains sample responses for the Opening Activity and for the professional learning task posed in the "Analyzing the Case" section in Chapter 2. Appendix A might be used by those engaging in the activities described in Chapter 2, especially those who are independently reading and studying "The Case of Barbara Crafton," as a way of considering alternative solutions and responses and comparing them with their own. Case facilitators might use Appendix A to gain a sense of the solutions and responses that might be generated by participants during their work on the Opening Activity or during the case discussion.

TEACHER-GENERATED SOLUTIONS TO THE OPENING ACTIVITY

Teachers who participated in a professional development experience that focused on "The Case of Barbara Crafton" generated the solutions presented in this section.

Problem 1

Solving Problem 1 involves two parts: (A) finding the area of the figure in square centimeters, and (B) converting the area to square millimeters.

Part A: Finding the area in square centimeters. Participants might approach Part A by counting the number of shaded squares and adding half squares together to create whole squares when possible, as Ellen demonstrated (para. 10). Teachers also might determine the number of square centimeters in the shaded region by using the diagram in additional ways, as shown in the following solutions.

SOLUTION A. Teachers might determine the number of shaded squares by determining the number of unshaded squares, 22.5, and subtracting that from the total number of squares in the grid, which is 40. This strategy will give the number of shaded squares, which is 17.5.

SOLUTION B. Teachers also might break the shaded region into shapes with which they are more familiar, as shown in Figure A.1 (similar to Michael's strategy in the case [para. 11]).

The area of the shaded figure is equal to: Area of triangle A + Area of rectangle B + Area of triangle C + Area of rectangle D. Using the formulas for finding the area of a triangle ($\frac{1}{2}BH$) and a rectangle (L × W), the area of the shaded figure is equal to: $\frac{1}{2}(3 \times 3) + (2 \times 3) + \frac{1}{2}(2 \times 2) + (1 \times 5) = 17.5$ cm^2.

FIGURE A.1. A Strategy for Solving Problem 1 That Relies on Breaking the Shaded Region into Familiar Shapes

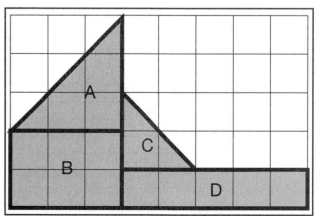

Part B: Converting the area to square millimeters. Teachers often approach Part B by multiplying their answer to Part A, 17.5, by 100 to determine the number of square millimeters in the shaded region. When pressed to explain *why* this calculation converts square centimeters into square millimeters, teachers may use a diagram similar to the one used by Natalie in the case (para. 20) to justify why this calculation works. Teachers also might justify this calculation numerically, as shown in the solution that follows.

Solution C. The following calculations prove that one square centimeter equals 100 square millimeters:

$$1 \text{ cm} = 10 \text{ mm}$$

$$(1 \text{ cm})^2 = (10 \text{ mm})^2$$

$$(1 \text{ cm}) \times (1 \text{ cm}) = (10 \text{ mm}) \times (10 \text{ mm})$$

$$1 \text{ cm}^2 = 100 \text{ mm}^2$$

Problem 2

Participants might determine the number of square inches in a square foot either numerically (as shown in Solutions A and B) or visually (as shown in Solution C).

Solution A. A square foot can be expressed as 1 foot by 1 foot. Since there are 12 inches in 1 foot, a square foot also can be expressed as 12 inches by 12 inches, or 144 square inches.

Solution B. The following calculations prove that 1 square foot equals 144 square inches:

$$1 \text{ ft} = 12 \text{ in}$$

$$(1 \text{ ft})^2 = (12 \text{ in})^2$$

$$(1 \text{ ft}) \times (1 \text{ ft}) = (12 \text{ in}) \times (12 \text{ in})$$

$$1 \text{ ft}^2 = 144 \text{ in}^2$$

Solution C. The diagram shown in Figure A.2 shows that there are 144 square inches in 1 square foot.

"Consider" Question

Participants may make the following observations about Problems 1 and 2:

- Both problems involve converting between different units of area.

FIGURE A.2. A Visual Strategy to Problem 2 That Shows the Number of Square Inches in a Square Foot

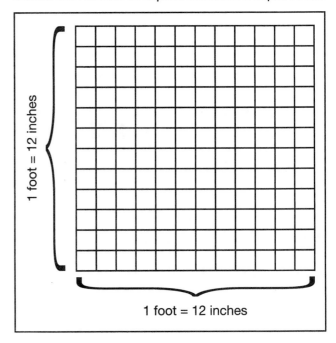

- For both problems, knowing the conversion factor between the linear units of measure allows one to determine the conversion factor between the units of area measure.
- Centimeters and millimeters are related by a 1:10 ratio, while square centimeters and square millimeters are related by a 1:100 ratio. Feet and inches have a 1:12 ratio, while square feet and square inches have a 1:144 ratio.
- The area ratio is the square of the linear ratio.
- If two linear units of measure are related by a ratio of a:x, then their corresponding area units are related by a ratio of a^2:x^2.

TEACHER-GENERATED RESPONSES TO THE "ANALYZING THE CASE" ACTIVITY

The chart shown in Table A.1 was generated by teachers who participated in a discussion of "The Case of Barbara Crafton." The teachers were responding to the activity featured in the "Analyzing the Case" section of Chapter 2 in which they analyzed the pedagogical moves made by Barbara Crafton.

TABLE A.1. Teacher-Generated List of the Pedagogical Moves Barbara Crafton Made in Order to Promote Discussion

Pedagogical Move Made by Barbara Crafton	How This Move Influenced Student Learning
Plans to set up a mathematics argument and let the students play it out. (para. 9)	Provides students with opportunities to participate in a discussion in which they need to use mathematical evidence to support their ideas.
Decides to begin the discussion by establishing what the class agrees upon. (para. 10)	Begins the debate by giving all students a common entry point. Also, establishing something that everyone agrees upon allows students to refer to this idea as needed.
Decides that students should have some time to think about and practice defending their solutions to the second part of the problem. Asks students to work in pairs and to discuss the area of the figure in square millimeters. (para. 12)	Allows students to practice mathematical argumentation by working with a partner before participating in a debate with the whole class.
During the pairwork, Mrs. Crafton tries to encourage conversation by continually asking, "What have you decided?" and "How did you decide?" (para. 12)	Helps students communicate their thinking and models the kind of communication they will need to use during the whole-class discussion.
Begins the whole-class discussion with Larry, even though his answer of 170 square millimeters is incorrect. (para. 14)	Begins with a controversial statement so students will be compelled to disagree.
After Larry shares his solution of 170 square millimeters, Mrs. Crafton asks the class, "Anybody have a question about that?" and "Did everybody get 170 square millimeters for their answer?" When few students respond to these queries, Mrs. Crafton poses the following questions to the class: "How many of you got 170 square millimeters? How many of you got something else? If you got something else, I don't understand why your hand isn't in the air asking him how he got what he did." (para. 15)	Reminds students that it is their job to question one another. Also, these questions provide students who hold opposing viewpoints several opportunities to disagree.
Lets Bonita's comment and Larry's response to it slide and hopes that the next comment is more on track. (para. 16)	Focuses discussion on the mathematics in question.
Redefines the poles of the debate by commenting, "We still have some discussion here. Charlene is saying that each individual square centimeter is not 10 square millimeters but 100. Larry and a few others are still saying that each square centimeter is 10." (para. 19)	Refocuses the discussion and highlights the two answers that are on the table—one that is correct and one that represents a common misconception.
When Natalie comments that "things are 1 by 1 and 10 by 10 . . . so, you multiply by 100 instead of 10," Mrs. Crafton asks her to come up to the overhead projector to show the class what she means. (para. 20)	Although it is abstract, Natalie's comment indicates that she has a conceptual understanding of the mathematics underlying the disagreement. By going to the overhead, Natalie has an opportunity to explain her thinking more concretely with a diagram, and thus helps advance Mrs. Crafton's mathematical goal for the lesson.
Asks, "How many of you agree with Natalie? Because if you don't, we need to go further. How many of you do not agree with that? How many of you still think it's 175? It's okay to think differently. I think we need more discussion here." (para. 22)	Monitors all students' understanding and concludes that not everyone is convinced.
Reinforces Natalie's explanation by saying, "So, Natalie is saying that you need to move the decimal point two powers of 10 when you're working with area measurement." (para. 24)	Rephrasing Natalie's statement communicates to students that her idea is an important one. Also, rephrasing her statement gives students another opportunity to hear it.
At the end of the lesson, assigns homework problems that involve nonmetric units of measurement. (para. 27)	The homework problems lay the groundwork for the next day's discussion, in which Mrs. Crafton hopes students will observe the $1:x$ relationship between linear units and the $1:x^2$ relationship between corresponding area units.

Appendix B

Sample Responses to The Case of Isabelle Olson

Appendix B contains sample responses for the Opening Activity and for the professional learning task posed in the "Analyzing the Case" section in Chapter 3. Appendix B might be used by those engaging in the activities described in Chapter 3, especially those who are independently reading and studying "The Case of Isabelle Olson," as a way of considering alternative solutions and responses and comparing them with their own. Case facilitators might use Appendix B to gain a sense of the solutions and responses that might be generated by participants during their work on the Opening Activity or during the case discussion.

TEACHER-GENERATED SOLUTIONS TO THE OPENING ACTIVITY

Teachers who participated in a professional development experience that focused on "The Case of Isabelle Olson" generated the solutions presented in this section. Teachers typically solve the problem using one of two general approaches: (1) numeric approaches in which the generalization is derived from considering all possible rectangular pens that can be constructed from fixed amounts of fence; or (2) algebraic approaches that focus on generating an equation. To explore the "Consider" questions, teachers typically expand on the work they produced to solve the problem.

Numeric Approaches

Teachers often approach the task by drawing or building all of the rectangular pens that can be created from a fixed amount of fence, calculating the area of

each pen, and identifying the pen that yields the greatest area (as Marcus's group did on the second day, in para. 38). Teachers might calculate the area of each pen by using the area formula or by counting square units (if they drew the pens on graph paper or built the pens with square tiles).

Alternatively (or in combination with drawing or building the pens), teachers might use a table to organize the dimensions and areas of all possible pens that can be built from a fixed amount of fence (similar to the table created by Jessica's group, in paras. 40–41).

Once teachers have generated data for one or several specific amounts of fence, they can begin to look for patterns and make observations about the pens that have the maximum area. Using the pens that can be built from 24 feet of fencing (shown in Figure B.1) as an example, possible observations include:

- The area values occur twice, except for the maximum area value, which occurs only once.
- The area increases until it reaches a maximum and then begins to decrease.
- For the pen that provides the maximum area, the length is equal to half the total amount of fence.
- For the pen that provides the maximum area, the width of the pen is equal to half the length of the pen.
- For the pen that provides the maximum area, the width of the pen is equal to one-fourth the total amount of fence.
- If the widths and/or the lengths are listed in numeric order, the dimensions listed in the middle row will yield the fence with the most area.

FIGURE B.1. The Relationship Between the Width, Length, and Area of the Pen When the Total Amount of Fence Is 24 Feet

Width	Length	Area
0	24	0
1	22	22
2	20	40
3	18	54
4	16	64
5	14	70
6	**12**	**72**
7	10	70
8	8	64
9	6	54
10	4	40
11	2	22
12	0	0

Based on these observations, teachers might express a generalization in one of the following ways:

- explanations tied to a specific number (e.g., "for 24 feet of fence, the longer side would be 12 feet and the shorter sides would be 6 feet")
- verbal descriptions that refer to an unknown number (e.g., "the longer side is half the amount of fence," or "the width is half the length")
- symbolic representations using letters or phrases (e.g., when L = 2W; when Length = Half the total amount of fence; when Width = [Total amount of fence] ÷ 4)

Algebraic Approaches

Teachers may approach the problem by creating equations that represent the relationship between the length of the shorter side of the pen and the area. Teachers might draw a diagram such as the one shown in Figure B.2 to help them create an equation.

FIGURE B.2. Model of the Rabbit Pen Situation

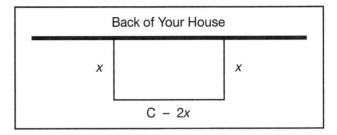

If the shorter sides are each called x, then the length of the longer side is equal to the total length of the fence (which we will call C) minus the lengths of the shorter sides, or $C - 2x$. Therefore, the area of the pen could be determined by using the area formula, Width × Length, or $x(C - 2x) = Cx - 2x^2$.

At this point, teachers could either choose a value for C or allow C to remain unknown. Each of these methods is described in more detail in the following paragraphs.

Choosing a value for C. If teachers choose a value for C, they may then use their area equation to generate a table and/or create a graph. For example, if teachers assume the total length of fence is fixed at 12 feet, the equation becomes: Area $= x(12 - 2x) = 12x - 2x^2$, which yields the table of values and the graph shown in Figure B.3.

Once this process has been repeated for other fixed lengths of fence (as described in "Numeric Approaches"), teachers can look across cases and make observations about when the maximum area seems to occur. (Note that graphing calculators can facilitate the process of examining other lengths of fence.)

Allowing C to remain unknown. Particularly if you are working with secondary teachers, you might observe one or both of the strategies described in the following paragraphs. The first strategy makes use of information that teachers may recall (or want to look up) about parabolas and their vertices; the second strategy is a maximization approach based on calculus.

SOLUTION A. If teachers allow C to remain unknown, they might rewrite their equation for area as follows:

$$\text{Area} = x(C - 2x) = Cx - 2x^2 = -2x^2 + Cx + 0$$

This is the standard equation for a parabola ($y = ax^2 + bx + c$). Teachers might then recall (or want to look up)

FIGURE B.3. The Relationship Between the Width and Area of the Pen When the Total Amount of Fence Is 12 Feet

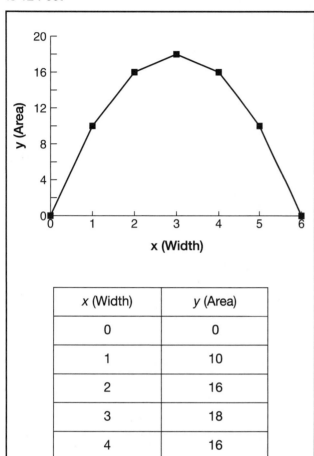

x (Width)	y (Area)
0	0
1	10
2	16
3	18
4	16
5	10
6	0

the following information and use it to determine the dimensions of the pen that yields the maximum area (they also might sketch a graph similar to the one shown in Figure B.4):

- Since the leading coefficient is −2, the parabola opens down. This would indicate that the maximum value for area would occur at the vertex of the parabola.
- The parabola intersects the x-axis at $x = 0$ and $x = {}^C/_2$. Parabolas are symmetrical, so the vertex occurs at $x = {}^C/_4$.
- The vertex also can be found from the formula $x = {}^b/_{-2a}$. In this case, $x = {}^C/_{(-2)(-2)} = {}^C/_4$.

FIGURE B.4. The Relationship Between Width and Area When the Total Amount of Fence Is C

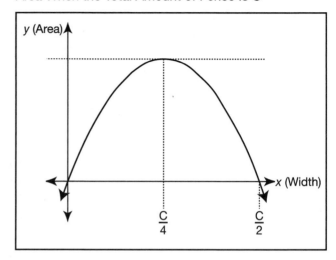

Therefore, the maximum area occurs when Width = ${}^C/_4$ = (Total length of fence) ÷ 4.

The length can be determined by substituting $x = {}^C/_4$ into the equation for Length:

$$\text{Length} = C - 2({}^C/_4) = C - {}^C/_2 = {}^C/_2 = \text{(Total length of fence)} \div 2$$

In other words, the maximum area occurs when the length is twice as long as the width (i.e., ${}^C/_2$ is twice as long as ${}^C/_4$).

SOLUTION B. If the teachers with whom you are working allow C to remain unknown and are familiar with calculus, they might solve the problem using the following approach:

- $y = x(C - 2x) = Cx - 2x^2$ (where y is the area and x is the width)
- Taking the first derivative: ${}^{dy}/_{dx} = C - 4x$
- A maximum or a minimum will occur when ${}^{dy}/_{dx} = 0$, or when $x = {}^C/_4$.
- This indicates that the maximum value for the area occurs when the width, x, is equal to the total amount of fence, C, divided by 4. (One way to determine that this is a maximum value is by graphing the equation.)
- The length can be determined by substituting $x = {}^C/_4$ into the equation for Length:

$$\text{Length} = C - 2x = C - 2({}^C/_4) = C - ({}^C/_2) = {}^C/_2 = \text{(Total length of fence)} \div 2$$

Both Solutions A and B serve as proof of many of the observations listed under "Numeric Approaches" that the maximum value of area occurs when:

- the width (the smaller side of the pen) is ¼ of the total length of fence
- the length (the longer side, parallel to the back of your house) is ½ of the total length of fence
- the length is twice the width (or conversely, the width is half the length)

Exploring the "Consider" Questions

Teachers can use the same general strategies they used to solve the problem as a starting point in exploring the "Consider" questions, taking into consideration that the "Consider" questions involve a fixed perimeter rather than a fixed amount of fence.

Questions 1 and 2. For Questions 1 and 2, teachers might draw rectangles or create a table to demonstrate that: two rectangles can have the same perimeter but different areas (i.e., consider a rectangle that is 1×4 units compared to one that is 2×3 units), and two rectangles can have the same area but different perimeters (i.e., the rectangles shown in Figure B.5 all have an area of 16 square units but have different perimeters).

Questions 3 and 4. Teachers typically use the diagrams they produced to explore the first and second "Consider" questions to argue that the perimeter cannot be determined if the area is known nor can the area be determined if the perimeter is known.

Alternatively, secondary teachers might explore these questions using an algebraic approach. For example, for Question 4 (Can the area be determined if the perimeter is known?), teachers might assign a value for the perimeter and then try to determine the area, as described in the following strategy:

- Let Perimeter = 20.
- Perimeter = 2L + 2W, so 20 = 2L + 2W, or 10 = L + W
- Area = L × W.
- Solving for L in the Perimeter equation, L = 10 – W. By substitution, Area = (10 – W) × W = 10W – W².

Thus, both W and L cannot be determined (teachers may have noticed by observing that there are three unknowns [Area, L, and W] and only two equations, that this is not possible, even before they tried solving the equations).

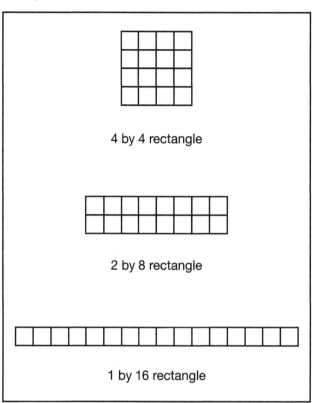

FIGURE B.5. Three Rectangles That Have an Area of 16 Square Units but Different Perimeters

4 by 4 rectangle

2 by 8 rectangle

1 by 16 rectangle

Finally, teachers might notice that although fixing the area does not uniquely determine the perimeter or the dimensions, and fixing the perimeter does not uniquely determine the area or the dimensions, fixing *both* the perimeter and area does uniquely determine the dimensions. A proof follows:

Assume that two rectangles with different dimensions (l_1, w_1) and (l_2, w_2) have the same perimeter, P, and the same area, A. Then:

$$\text{(1)} \quad 2l_1 + 2w_1 = P$$
$$2l_2 + 2w_2 = P$$

and

$$\text{(2)} \quad l_1 \times w_1 = A$$
$$l_2 \times w_2 = A$$

Set each set of equations equal:

$$\text{(1)} \quad 2l_1 + 2w_1 = 2l_2 + 2w_2$$

and

$$\text{(2)} \quad l_1 \times w_1 = l_2 \times w_2$$

Solve one of the equations for one variable. For example:

$$(1) \quad 2l_1 + 2w_1 = 2l_2 + 2w_2$$
$$l_1 + w_1 = l_2 + w_2$$
$$w_1 = l_2 + w_2 - l_1$$

Substitute into the other equation:

$$(2) \quad l_1 \times w_1 = l_2 \times w_2$$
$$l_1 \times (l_2 + w_2 - l_1) = l_2 \times w_2$$

Simplify:

$$(3) \quad l_1 l_2 + l_1 w_2 - l_1{}^2 = l_2 w_2$$
$$l_1 l_2 + l_1 w_2 - l_1{}^2 - l_2 w_2 = 0$$
$$l_2(l_1 - w_2) - l_1(l_1 - w_2) = 0$$
$$l_2(l_1 - w_2) = l_1(l_1 - w_2)$$
$$l_2 = l_1$$

This is a contradiction, since l_1 and l_2 are supposed to be different. If l_1 and l_2 are equal, it easily can be proven that w_1 and w_2 are equal as well, and there exists only one unique set of dimensions for a rectangle whose perimeter and area are fixed.

TEACHER-GENERATED RESPONSES TO THE "ANALYZING THE CASE" ACTIVITY

The chart shown in Table B.1 was generated by teachers who participated in a professional development experience that focused on "The Case of Isabelle Olson." The teachers were responding to the activity featured in the "Analyzing the Case" section in Chapter 3, in which they were asked to determine how the pedagogical moves made by Ms. Olson supported and/or inhibited students' opportunities to engage with the mathematical ideas in the task.

TABLE B.1. Teacher-Generated Table That Identifies Supporting and Inhibiting Moves Made by Isabelle Olson

Pedagogical Move	Whether Move Served to Support or Inhibit Learning	Importance of Pedagogical Move in Terms of Students' Opportunities to Learn
Alters the problem to be more open-ended and challenging. (paras. 8–10)	Support/Inhibit	Increases the complexity and ambiguity of the task.
Allows sufficient time for students to explore the problem. (paras. 11, 12, 13, and 41–43)	Support	Students have the opportunity to fully explore the problem themselves before Tanya and Michael share their group's thinking.
Allows students to work in groups. (para. 12)	Support	Makes the task more accessible than working alone; students can learn from and build upon one another's ideas as they work together to solve difficult problems.
Indicates that she expects the groups to provide evidence of their claims and to produce a final poster displaying their results. (para. 12)	Support	Students are aware of what they will be held accountable for.
Problem builds on students' prior experience (with the handshake problem). (para. 12)	Support	Students have resources and knowledge to draw upon in solving the problem.
Gives students a word to describe their frustration—"disequilibrium." (para. 13)	Support	By doing so, she acknowledges that the work she asks them to do is challenging.
Presents the problem in a very open manner. Provides encouragement to students. Indicates that this task will be difficult. (para. 13)	Support	Does not proceduralize the task by providing an example or suggesting a strategy. Sets high expectations by implying "this is tough, but with some hard work, you can do it!"
Has materials available for students to use. (para. 13)	Support	Students can use these materials to create alternative solution strategies.
Lets students wrestle with the problem. (paras. 14, 16, 18–19, and 35)	Support	Helps students achieve her goal of exploring and imposing structure upon ill-defined problems.
Keeps her responses and questions to students very open-ended and general. Does not give in to students' requests for more specific information/ guidance on the task. (para. 14)	Support	Does not take away the challenge of the task. However, her responses might have been too general to lead students to engage with the task as intended.
Decides to change her questioning strategy. Begins asking questions that address the task directly, such as, "How do you know that this is the largest amount of room possible with 300 yards of fence?" and "Does the building have to be 50 yards?" She comments that students seem to need this "push." (paras. 16, 18, and 19)	Support	Students need task-specific guidance at this point in order to make progress on the task. Ms. Olson's earlier, more open-ended questions and suggestions do not appear to be helping students to make progress on the task.
Considers whether to provide students with a fixed amount of fence, and decides against it. (para. 19)	Support	Maintains the challenge of the task—giving a fixed amount of fence would remove some of the ambiguity that Ms. Olson wanted students to struggle with.
Becomes directive with Tommy's group and tells them to test different rectangles for 300 yards of fence. (para. 21)	Support	Holds them accountable for providing evidence; moves them into a space where they could make progress on the task.
Asks students to justify their solutions. (para. 21)	Support	Students are forced to develop conjectures and conclusions based on mathematical evidence.
Realizes that her students do not know that two figures can have the same perimeter but different areas. (para. 26)	Inhibit	This limits students' ability to engage with the problem, and forces her to re-evaluate her plan to accommodate her students' knowledge.
Plans to begin work on the second day by having students meet with their groups, then share ideas on how to proceed. Has identified students to share important information about the problem. (para. 28)	Support	Gives students authority in mathematics; allows students to model high-level thinking.
Asks Tommy's group to present their finding that different rectangles created from the same amount of fence can have different areas. Not knowing this restricted students' progress on Day 1. (para. 32)	Support	Students do not have the background knowledge necessary to explore the mathematical ideas in the task. Letting students share this finding rather than telling them herself again allows students to have mathematical authority and to share high-level mathematical thinking.
Ends the whole-group discussion and sends students back to working with their groups, now armed with new information. (para. 35)	Support	Allows students to test the ideas that were presented and to discover an important mathematical relationship for themselves.
In her interactions with the groups, poses questions that indicate her continued expectations. (paras. 37–38, and 40–41)	Support	Continues to hold high expectations throughout the task; reminds students of what they are accountable for.

Appendix C

Sample Responses to The Case of Keith Campbell

Appendix C contains sample responses for the Opening Activity and for the professional learning task posed in the "Analyzing the Case" section in Chapter 4. Appendix C might be used by those engaging in the activities described in Chapter 4, especially those who are independently reading and studying "The Case of Keith Campbell," as a way of considering alternative solutions and responses and comparing them with their own. Case facilitators might use Appendix C to gain a sense of the solutions and responses that might be generated by participants during their work on the Opening Activity or during the case discussion.

TEACHER-GENERATED SOLUTIONS TO THE OPENING ACTIVITY

In response to the "Solve" component of the Opening Activity, participants generally construct rectangular prisms by randomly arranging the cubes, by building layers, or by determining appropriate dimensions. Participants may create diagrams similar to those used by Keith Campbell's students in the case, such as Sheila's diagram with a 3-D appearance (Figure 4.4b) or Antonio's diagram portraying the faces of the prism as individual rectangles (Figure 4.5).

To determine volume, participants may apply the formula for volume of a rectangular prism, or they simply may relate cubic units to the number of cubes used to create the prism. To determine surface area, participants may create diagrams or may use the actual rectangular prisms to count, compute, or verify the area of each of the faces. Some strategies for determining surface area include

- counting the square units on the outside of the rectangular prism.
- using the common formula for finding the surface area of a rectangular prism: $SA = 2LW + 2LH + 2WH$.
- finding the areas of each of the faces of the prism and adding these values together, as described in the case by Sheila (para. 15). This method often resembles the common formula for finding the surface area of a rectangular prism.
- determining that the surface area of rectangular prisms that have identical sides (e.g., a cube) can be found by multiplying the number of squares on one side by the number of sides.

Tables 4.2 and 4.3 in Chapter 4 provide the dimensions, surface area, and volume for prisms that can be created from 8 through 12 cubes.

Responses to the "Consider" Component of the Opening Activity

To determine whether they have constructed all of the rectangular prisms for a fixed number of cubes, participants may respond to Question 1 by

- referring directly to their attempts to create different rectangular prisms with cubes (e.g., stating that "there are no other ways to arrange the cubes to make a complete rectangular prism").
- making reference to the factors of the numerical value of the volume, such as, "We used all of the factors of 12," or "we found all possible unique combinations of the factors of 12."

- providing detailed descriptions, such as, "You must choose the dimensions from the factors of 12 so that $L \times W \times H = 12$," or "we first used all of the factor-pairs and a height of 1. That gave us (12, 1, 1), (6, 2, 1), and (3, 4, 1). Then we tried to keep a product of 12 and let the height equal 2. The only way to do this is (3, 2, 2)."

For Question 2, participants may make sense of the volume formula in a number of ways, such as

- describing the prism as having "layers"—taking the numbers of cubes in one layer and multiplying by the number of layers. This approach views the formula as Volume = (number of cubes in one layer) times (number of layers), or symbolically as V = $(L \times W) \times H$.
- similarly, describing the prism as the area of the base "carving out space up to the given height." Expressing the formula as Volume = (area of base) times (height) provides a way of making sense of the volume of prisms and cylinders in general.
- noticing from the data table that multiplying the dimensions together gives the numeric value of the volume, represented symbolically as V = $L \times W \times H$.

Participants generally make sense of the surface area formula by relating it to the strategy of finding the areas of each of the faces of the prism and adding these values together, as described in the case by Sheila (para. 15) or as illustrated in Antonio's diagram (Figure 4.5).

Participants may respond to Question 3 by

- comparing the number of square units exposed on the rectangular prisms, and commenting that the prisms with maximum surface area have "more sides exposed on the outside" and "more sides facing out to be counted," as compared with prisms with minimum surface area having "more sides hidden" and "more sides facing in and not counted."
- comparing the shape of the prisms and describing prisms with maximum surface area as "more elongated" and "long and thin," as compared with prisms with minimum surface area as being "more compact."
- comparing the numeric values of the dimensions, and referring to the dimensions of prisms with maximum surface area as having "one dimension at an extreme" or "N $\times$ 1 $\times$ 1 where N is the volume." Prisms with minimum surface area are observed to "have dimensions closer together numerically."

TEACHER-GENERATED RESPONSES TO THE "ANALYZING THE CASE" ACTIVITY

The chart shown in Table C.1 was generated by teachers who participated in a professional development experience that focused on "The Case of Keith Campbell." The teachers were responding to the activity featured in the "Analyzing the Case" section of Chapter 4 in which they were asked to determine: What mathematics did Keith Campbell's students learn or were in the process of learning? What pedagogical moves did Keith Campbell make that supported or inhibited his students' learning? What evidence from the case supports your claims?

TABLE C.1. Teacher-Generated List of the Mathematics Learned by Keith Campbell's Students and the Pedagogical Moves Made by Keith Campbell That Supported or Inhibited Their Learning

Mathematical Ideas That Students Were Learning	Pedagogical Moves Made by Keith Campbell That Supported or Inhibited Students' Learning
Surface area of rectangular prisms	*Support:* Used a series of tasks that provided students with visual representations of surface area and that allowed students to build up increasingly more complex ideas about surface area. (paras. 4, 6–7, 9, and 11)
	Support: Asked Sheila to repeat her method of adding up the areas of the faces of the prism to determine the surface area. (para. 15)
	Support: Asked Antonio to explain how he determined the surface area and to share his diagram with the class. Asked questions that allowed other students to use Antonio's diagram to reason about the surface area of other rectangular prisms. (para. 18)
	Support: Provided a homework assignment that supported students' abilities to develop the formula for the surface area of a rectangular prism. (para. 38)
	Inhibit: Did not press or ask "why" questions as students explained how they determined surface area. (paras. 15–18)
	Inhibit: Did not ask students to respond to the ideas of their classmates. Instead, often validated students' approaches and ideas himself, such as with Jamal and Antonio. (paras. 16 and 18)
Volume of rectangular prisms	*Support:* Used a series of tasks that provided students with visual representations of volume and that allowed students to build up increasingly more complex ideas about volume. (paras. 4, 6–7, 9, and 11)
	Support: Asked students to "explain it to us again" and to "describe more precisely what it is that we are multiplying together to get the volume." (paras. 29 and 30)
	Support: Asked Cameron to "explain what volume is without using the moon gems." (para. 32)
	Support: Allowed students to share their ideas about volume and the formula for finding the volume of a rectangular prism with the rest of the class, such as Antonio and Sheila. (paras. 28 and 33)
	Inhibit: Affirmed Tyrone's formula for volume rather than asking for verification from the rest of the class. (para. 31)
Comparing the surface area of rectangular prisms of a fixed volume	*Support:* Provided opportunities for students to discover that rectangular prisms of the same volume can have different shapes and that these different shapes result in different surface areas. (paras. 7 and 11)
	Support: Suggested that Rochelle and Brian see if they can find anything in common about the gem packages that cost the most or the ones that cost the least. Selected Rochelle and Brian to share their ideas during the whole-group discussion (paras. 25 and 35)
	Support: Asked questions that provided students with opportunities to compare the characteristics of rectangular prisms of a constant volume that seem to have the maximum and minimum values of surface area. (paras. 35–37)
	Inhibit: Led students to offer the term "cubes." (para. 37)
Generalizations	*Support:* Pressed students to develop the "4 × GEMS + 2" formula and to use Antonio's drawing to justify why this formula "will always work." (paras. 18–19)
	Support: Asked questions that prompted students to generalize that for different rectangular prisms with the same volume, elongated prisms always seem to have the greatest surface area and more compact prisms always seem to have the least surface area. (paras. 35–37)
	Inhibit: Allowed several examples to serve as proof, such as when Antonio claimed, "We proved it by building it" and when Erica said that "it works for every one we have listed in our chart." (paras. 28 and 29)
Connections between representations	*Support:* Provided an opportunity for Antonio and others to use Antonio's diagram to construct a formula and to consider the connection between the formula and Rochelle's observation. (para. 19)
	Support: Pressed students to make comparisons of prisms with maximum/minimum values of surface area that rely on relating numeric data in the chart to a concrete or pictorial representation of the rectangular prism. (paras. 35–37)
	Support: Asked questions that allowed students to develop a formula for finding volume based on their work with blocks and data from the chart. (Tables 4.2 and 4.3, paras. 28–30)

Appendix D

Sample Responses to The Case of Nancy Upshaw

Appendix D contains sample responses for the Opening Activity and for the professional learning task posed in the "Analyzing the Case" section in Chapter 5. Appendix D might be used by those engaging in the activities described in Chapter 5, especially those who are independently reading and studying "The Case of Nancy Upshaw," as a way of considering alternative solutions and responses and comparing them with their own. Case facilitators might use Appendix D to gain a sense of the solutions and responses that might be generated by participants during their work on the Opening Activity or during the case discussion.

TEACHER-GENERATED SOLUTIONS TO THE OPENING ACTIVITY

Teachers who participated in a professional development experience that focused on "The Case of Nancy Upshaw" generated the solutions presented in this section. Teachers typically begin to solve the problems by determining some combination of the following calculations or measurements: dimensions of the room in meters or centimeters, volume of the room in cubic meters or cubic centimeters, the number of objects in 1 cubic meter, the number of objects that fit along a dimension of the room, and the volume of the objects being used to fill the room. The following four methods describe various combinations of these activities.

Method 1

- Determine the volume of the room in cubic meters or cubic centimeters.

- Determine the volume of 1,000 blocks or tennis balls in cubic meters or cubic centimeters (the measurement units must be consistent with the units used to express the volume of the room).
- Divide the volume of the room by the volume of one block or ball to determine how many blocks/balls will fill the room.

Note that this method assumes that portions of blocks/balls can be utilized to *completely* fill the space in the room. This method is used by Mariola's group in the case (para. 16).

Method 2

- Measure the dimensions of the room in meters or centimeters.
- Measure the dimensions of the block or the diameter of the ball.
- Determine how many blocks/balls will fit along each dimension of the room.
- Multiply the number of blocks/balls in each dimension to determine the number of blocks/balls that will fill the room (i.e., determine the volume of the room using "blocks" or "balls" as the unit).

This method is similar to the strategy used by Tomás's group in the case (para. 20). Method 2 requires a decision on whether to round the dimensions so that only whole blocks/balls are counted or whether portions of blocks/balls are allowed to fit along each dimension as well. Note that in Method 2, space would be left between each layer of balls, producing quite different results than Method 1.

Method 3

- Determine how many blocks/balls are needed to create a layer that covers the floor.
- Determine how many layers would be needed to reach the ceiling.
- Multiply the number of blocks/balls in each layer by the number of layers to determine how many blocks/balls would be needed to fill the room.

This method is similar to the strategy used by Rolando's group in the case (para. 10) and might be a viable strategy for finding the volume of irregularly shaped rooms. Note that Method 3 also leaves spaces between each layer of balls.

Method 4

- Determine the number of blocks or balls in 1 cubic meter.
- Determine volume of the room in cubic meters.
- Multiply number of blocks/balls in each cubic meter by the number of cubic meters in the room.

This method is similar to the strategy used by Andres's group in the case (para. 18). Depending on how the number of blocks or balls in 1 cubic meter is determined, this method can assume that portions of blocks or balls completely fill a cubic meter or that they leave spaces (especially between the layers of balls). If a cubic meter is divided by the volume of 1 ball or block, the result would provide how many balls/blocks completely fill up a cubic meter. If the number of blocks or balls in each dimension is determined, the balls would leave spaces between layers and the number of blocks in each dimension might be rounded to allow only whole blocks. This method also would work well for irregularly shaped rooms, especially if the room is considered as being "chunked" into different segments.

Some issues that arise in solving the Opening Activity include:

- What to do with portions of units (i.e., whether to round dimensions to whole numbers; whether to round the volume to a whole number; whether to allow only whole blocks and balls along each dimension). The heart of the issue is practicality (could a block or ball be split?) versus filling the entire space.

- Using consistent measurement units and performing conversions between meters and centimeters (which are related by a factor of 100) or between cubic meters and cubic centimeters (which are related by a factor of 1,000,000).
- Whether the balls are layered or "nested." If the balls are considered as layered, the empty space could be calculated by determining the volume of the balls and subtracting it from the volume of the room. Pursuing the difference between layering and nesting would be feasible using Method 4, in which a smaller cubic unit than the entire room could be used for comparison purposes.
- Whether the results are high or low estimates, and why. This question is influenced by rounding, by allowing portions versus whole blocks/balls, and by layering versus nesting.

Responses to the "Consider" Questions

In general, any method that would be used to determine the number of blocks that fill the room also could be used to determine how many balls would fill the room (ignoring the "nesting" issue). Specifically, Methods 1–4 compare with one another in the following ways:

- Method 1 differs from Methods 2 and 3 in that it uses standard measurement units until the last step rather than using the block or ball as the unit of measure. Method 1 determines the total volume of the room in cubic meters, then divides by the volume of one block or ball. Methods 2 and 3 determine the number of blocks or balls in each dimension or layer (respectively) and then compute the volume of the room in blocks or balls.
- Method 1 is very similar to Method 4 for rectangular rooms. Method 4 determines the number of blocks in a smaller cubic unit, then scales up to the number of cubic units in the room.
- Methods 2 and 3 are very similar for rectangular rooms in which the number of blocks or balls in one layer can be determined by multiplying Length × Width. Method 3 might be very different for irregularly shaped rooms in which the floor would need to be partitioned into sections in order to determine the number of blocks/balls in each layer.
- The calculations for each method are equivalent, just performed in a different order. For a rectangular room, each method can be simplified to the expression:

$$\frac{L \text{ of the room} \times H \text{ of the room} \times W \text{ of the room}}{L \text{ of 1 block/ball} \times H \text{ of 1 block/ball} \times W \text{ of 1 block/ball}}$$

In response to the question regarding how the change in the diameter of one ball would change the number of balls that would fit in the room, teachers often think about this in one of two ways:

- If the room was filled with balls with a diameter twice the size of those used in the lab activity, only half as many balls would fit along each dimension. So, if the number of original balls in each dimension is $a \times b \times c$, then the number of double-diameter balls in each dimension is $\frac{a}{2} \times \frac{b}{2} \times \frac{c}{2} = \frac{1}{8} (a \times b \times c)$. Hence, it would take one-eighth as many double-diameter balls to fill the room as original-size balls. (So if the diameter of the ball was ½ the diameter of the original ball then it would take twice as many balls to fit along each dimension. So then the number of balls in each dimension is $2a \times 2b \times 2c = 8 (a \times b \times c)$. So it would take eight times as many half-diameter balls to fill the room as original-size balls.)

- A ball with a diameter twice the size of the original ball would have a volume eight times as large as the original ball, so it would take one-eighth as many of the larger balls to fill the room. (So a ball with a diameter half the size of the original ball would have a volume one-eighth as large as the original ball, so it would take eight times as many of the smaller balls to fill the room.)

TEACHER-GENERATED RESPONSES TO THE "ANALYZING THE CASE" ACTIVITY

The chart shown in Table D.1 was generated by teachers who participated in a professional development experience that focused on "The Case of Nancy Upshaw." The teachers were responding to the activity featured in the "Analyzing the Case" section of Chapter 5 in which they were asked to determine: What did Nancy Upshaw's students do to make sense of and complete the lab activities? What did Ms. Upshaw do to support her students in making sense of and solving the problems? Why did Ms. Upshaw's actions support her students' learning?

TABLE D.1. Teacher-Generated List of the Ways in Which Nancy Upshaw Supported Her Students' Efforts to Make Sense of Mathematics

What Students Did to Make Sense of and Complete the Lab Activities	What Nancy Upshaw Did to Support Students' Sense-Making Efforts	Why Ms. Upshaw's Actions Supported Students' Learning
Students draw sketches and diagrams. (paras. 15, 18, 19, and 21)	Encouraged students to use diagrams. (paras. 14 and 23)	Diagrams and sketches support students in making sense of problem situations and communicating their mathematical thinking to one another.
Students build models. (paras. 12–13)	Provides materials such as 2-centimeter cubes. (para. 5)	Students create a visual representation of a 1,000-cube block, which is the unit of volume for the 1,000 Cubes activity.
Students work in groups. (para. 14–16, 21–22)	Provides opportunities for students to work in groups. (para 6)	Students work together to make sense of the tasks, supplement each others' ideas, or justify their own ideas.
Students in Mariola's group talk and argue with one another about building a 1,000-cube block. (para. 14)	Asks questions to help the group realize their own misconception. Redirects Jorge's question about whether the 1,000-cube block is 10 cubes long or 20 centimeters long back to the group and walks away. (paras. 13–14)	Provides students with a new avenue for pursuing the problem without telling them how to do it.
Students draw on intuitive notions that you need more of a smaller thing to fill up a space. (paras. 15 and 25)	Selects two objects to "fill the room" that are different sizes. (para. 5)	Students are able to explain why it takes more cubes (the smaller object) than soccer balls (the larger object) to fill the room.
Mariola's group seeks advice and council from Ms. Upshaw. (paras. 16–17)	Asks questions to assess how the group is thinking and provides them with feedback that they are "on the right track." (paras. 16–17)	Ms. Upshaw can assess whether the group has recovered from their earlier misconception. Her feedback encourages the group to continue to make progress on the problem.
Tran relates the 1,000 Balls problem to a warm-up exercise completed the previous week. (para. 23)	Has provided students with previous opportunities to solve problems that relate to the Large Numbers Lab activities. (paras. 8 and 23)	Connecting to prior knowledge and experiences helps Tran's group to explore the 1,000 Balls problem.
Some students use a layering approach to solve the lab activities. (para. 13–14, 19–20, and 32) Other students use "Length × Width × Height." (paras. 15, 16, 18, and 20)	Leaves task open for students to enter and solve using their own strategies. Does not suggest a pathway for students to follow. (para. 12)	Students must think, reason, and make sense of the problem situation. Students have an opportunity to make sense of volume and how volume is measured.
Some students use metric units (paras. 14 and 19), while others use the block or the ball as the unit of measure (paras. 10, 18, and 19–20).	Allows students to pursue their own choice of measurement units for solving the tasks. During the whole-group discussion, she selects groups that used both metric and non-standard units and asks students to consider why different groups came up with different answers. (paras. 26–28)	Students can consider the similarities and differences between different strategies.
Students explain their strategies and share their ideas during a whole-group discussion. (paras. 26–32)	Provides time for a whole-group discussion in which students share strategies and ideas. (paras. 26–32)	Students can hear how others solved the problem and Ms. Upshaw can ask questions that advance students understanding of the mathematical ideas and that foster connections between the different strategies.
Students will explore the homework problem, in which they are asked to predict the number of balls that will fit in the classroom if they use soccer balls of varying sizes. (para. 30)	Provides students with additional opportunities to consider how the volume of the room changes as the unit with which they are measuring changes. (paras. 11 and 30)	Helps students achieve one of the goals she set for the lesson, to consider what would happen if the size of the unit of measure changes.

References

Ball, D. L., & Cohen, D. K. (1999). Developing practice, developing practitioners: Toward a practice-based theory of professional development. In L. Darling-Hammond & G. Sykes (Eds.), *Teaching as the learning profession: Handbook of policy and practice* (pp. 3–32). San Francisco: Jossey-Bass.

Battista, M. T. (1998). How many blocks? *Mathematics Teaching in the Middle School, 3*, 404–411.

Battista, M. (1999). Fifth-graders' enumeration of cubes in 3-D arrays: Conceptual progress in an inquiry-based classroom. *Journal for Research in Mathematics Education, 30*, 417–448.

Battista, M. T. (2003). Understanding students' thinking about area and volume measurement. In D. H. Clements & G. Bright (Eds.), *Learning and teaching measurement* (2003 Yearbook of the National Council of Teachers of Mathematics) (pp. 122–142). Reston, VA: National Council of Teachers of Mathematics.

Battista, M., & Clements, D. (1996). Students' understanding of 3-D rectangular arrays of cubes. *Journal for Research in Mathematics Education, 27*, 258–292.

Ben-Chaim, D., Lappan, G., & Houang, T. (1985). Visualizing rectangular solids made of small cubes: Analyzing and effecting student performance. *Educational Studies in Mathematics, 16*, 389–409.

Billstein, R., & Williamson, J. (1999a). *Middle grades math thematics: Book 1.* Evanston, IL: McDougal Littell.

Billstein, R., & Williamson, J. (1999b). *Middle grades math thematics: Book 2.* Evanston, IL: McDougal Littell.

Boston, M., & Smith, M. S. (2003). Providing opportunities for students and teachers to "measure up." In D. H. Clements & G. W. Bright (Eds.), *Learning and teaching measurement* (2003 yearbook of the National Council of Teachers of Mathematics) (pp. 209–220). Reston, VA: National Council of Teachers of Mathematics.

Bright, G. W. (1976). Estimation as part of learning to measure. In D. Nelson (Ed.), *Measurement in school mathematics* (pp. 87–105). Reston, VA: National Council of Teachers of Mathematics.

Bright, G. W., & Hoeffner, K. (1993). Measurement, probability, statistics, and graphing. In D. Owens (Ed.), *Research ideas for the classroom: Middle grades mathematics* (pp. 78–98). New York: Macmillan.

Chappell, M. (2001). Geometry in the middle grades: From its past to its present. *Mathematics Teaching in the Middle School, 6*, 516–519.

Chappell, M. F., & Thompson, D. R. (1999). Perimeter or area? Which measure is it? *Mathematics Teaching in the Middle School, 5*, 20–23.

Coburn, T. G., & Shulte, A. P. (1986). Estimation in measurement. In H. Schoen (Ed.), *Estimation and mental computation* (pp. 195–203). Reston, VA: National Council of Teachers of Mathematics.

Del Grande, J., & Morrow, L. J. (1993). *Curriculum and evaluation standards for school mathematics addenda series, grades 5–8: Geometry and spatial sense in the middle grades.* Reston, VA: National Council of Teachers of Mathematics.

Education Development Center, Inc. (1998a). *MathScape: Family portraits: Comparing function families* (Student guide). Mountain View, CA: Creative Publications.

Education Development Center, Inc. (1998b). *MathScape: Measuring and scaling* (Student guide). Mountain View, CA: Creative Publications.

Education Development Center, Inc. (1998c). *MathScape: Shapes and space: Thinking three-dimensionally* (Student guide). Mountain View, CA: Creative Publications.

Foreman, L. C., & Bennett, A. B., Jr. (1996). *Visual mathematics: Course II, Lessons 1–10.* Salem, OR: The Math Learning Center.

Fuys, D., Geddes, D., & Tischler, R. (1988). The van Hiele model of thinking in geometry among adolescents. *Journal for research in mathematics education monograph series (Vol. 3)*. Reston, VA: National Council of Teachers of Mathematics.

Geddes, D., Berkman, R., Fearon, I., Fishenfeld, M., Forlano, C., Fuys, D. J., Goldstein, J. & Welchman, R. (1994). *Curriculum and evaluation standards for school mathematics addenda series, grades 5–8: Measurement in the middle grades.* Reston, VA: National Council of Teachers of Mathematics.

Grouws, D. A., Smith, M. S., & Sztajn, P. (2004). The preparation and teaching practices of United States mathematics teachers: Grades 4 and 8. In P. Kloosterman & F. K. Lestor, Jr. (Eds.), *Results and interpretations of the 1990–2000 mathematics assessments of the National Assessment of Educational Progress* (pp. 221–267). Reston, VA: National Council of Teachers of Mathematics.

Henningsen, M., & Stein, M. K. (1997). Mathematical tasks and student cognition: Classroom-based factors that support and inhibit high-level mathematical thinking and reasoning. *Journal for Research in Mathematics Education, 29,* 524–549.

Hersberger, J., & Frederick, B. (1995). Flower beds and landscape consultants: Making connections in middle school mathematics. *Mathematics Teaching in the Middle School, 1,* 364–367.

Hershkowitz, R., & Vinner, S. (1984). Children's concepts in elementary geometry: A reflection of teachers' concepts? In B. Southwell, R. Eyland, M. Cooper, J. Conroy, & K. Collis (Eds.), *Proceedings of the eighth international conference for the Psychology of Mathematics Education* (pp. 63–69). Darlinghurst, Australia: Mathematical Association of New South Wales.

Hirstein, J. J., Lamb, C. E., & Osborne, A. (1978). Student misconceptions about area measure. *Arithmetic Teacher, 6,* 10–16.

Jackiw, N. (1995). *The geometer's sketchpad.* Berkeley: Key Curriculum Press.

Jones, G. A., Thornton, C. A., McGehe, C. A., & Colba, D. (1995). Rich problems—big payoffs. *Mathematics Teaching in the Middle School, 1,* 520–525.

Kamii, C., & Clark, F. B. (1997). Measurement of length: The need for a better approach to teaching. *School Science and Mathematics, 97,* 116–121, 299–300.

Kenney, P. A., & Lindquist, M. M. (2000). Students' performance on thematically related NAEP tasks. In E. A. Silver & P. A. Kenney (Eds.), *Results from the seventh mathematics assessment of the National Assessment of Educational Progress* (pp. 343–376). Reston, VA: National Council of Teachers of Mathematics.

Lampert, M., Rittenhouse, P., & Crumbaugh, C. (1996). Agreeing to disagree: Developing sociable mathematical discourse. In D. R. Olson & N. Torrance (Eds.), *The handbook of education and human development: New models of learning, teaching, and schooling* (pp. 731–764). Cambridge, MA: Blackwell.

Lappan, G., Fey, J. T., Fitzgerald, W. M., Friel, S. N., & Phillips, E. D. (1998a). *Covering and surrounding: Two-dimensional measurement.* Menlo Park, CA: Dale Seymour.

Lappan, G., Fey, J. T., Fitzgerald, W. M., Friel, S. N., & Phillips, E. D. (1998b). *Data around us: Number sense.* Menlo Park, CA: Dale Seymour.

Lappan, G., Fey, J. T., Fitzgerald, W. M., Friel, S. N., & Phillips, E. D. (1998c). *Filling and wrapping: Three-dimensional measurement.* Menlo Park, CA: Dale Seymour.

Lappan, G., Fey, J. T., Fitzgerald, W. M., Friel, S. N., & Phillips, E. D. (1998d). *Looking for Pythagoras: The Pythagorean theorem.* Menlo Park, CA: Dale Seymour.

Martin, W. G., & Strutchens, M. E. (2000). Geometry and measurement. In E. A. Silver & P. A. Kenney (Eds.), *Results from the seventh mathematics assessment of the National Assessment of Educational Progress* (pp. 193–234). Reston, VA: National Council of Teachers of Mathematics.

The Mathematics in Context Development Team. (1998a). Mathematics in context: Get the most out of it (Student guide). In National Center for Research in Mathematical Sciences Education & Freudenthal Institute (Eds.), *Mathematics in context.* Chicago: Encyclopedia Britannica.

The Mathematics in Context Development Team. (1998b). Mathematics in context: Power of ten (Student guide). In National Center for Research in Mathematical Sciences Education & Freudenthal Institute (Eds.), *Mathematics in context.* Chicago: Encyclopaedia Britannica.

The Mathematics in Context Development Team. (1998c). Mathematics in context: Reallotment (Student guide). In National Center for Research in Mathematical Sciences Education & Freudenthal Institute (Eds.), *Mathematics in context.* Chicago: Encyclopaedia Britannica.

Mayberry, J. (1983). The van Hiele levels of geometric thought in undergraduate preservice teachers. *Journal for Research in Mathematics Education, 14,* 58–69.

National Council of Teachers of Mathematics. (2000). *Principles and standards for school mathematics.* Reston, VA: Author.

O'Connor, M. C., & Michaels, S. (1996). Shifting participant frameworks: Orchestrating thinking practices in group discussions. In D. Hicks (Ed.), *Discourse, learning, and schooling* (pp. 63–103). New York: Cambridge University Press.

Pennsylvania Department of Education. (1999). Academic standards for mathematics. Pennsylvania Code 22, Chapter 4. Available at: *http://www.pde.pa.state.us/stateboard*

Pugalee, D. K., Frykholm, J., Johnson, A., Slovin, H., & Preston, R. (2002). *Principles and standards for school mathematics navigations series: Navigating through geometry in grades 6–8.* Reston, VA: National Council of Teachers of Mathematics.

Resnick, L. (1987). *Education and learning to think.* Washington, DC: National Academy Press.

Rittenhouse, P. S. (1998). The teacher's role in mathematical conversation: Stepping in and stepping out. In M. Lampert & M. L. Blunk (Eds.), *Talking mathematics in school: Studies of teaching and learning* (pp. 163–189). New York: Cambridge University Press.

Schifter, D., Bastable, V., Russell, S. J., & Woleck, K. R. (2002). *Measuring space in one, two, and three dimensions casebook.* Parsippany, NJ: Dale Seymour.

Sherin, M. G. (2000). Facilitating meaningful discussion of mathematics. *Mathematics Teaching in the Middle School*, 6, 122–125.

Shroyer, J., & Fitzgerald, W. (1986). *Middle grades mathematics project: Mouse and elephant: Measuring growth.* Menlo Park, CA: Addison-Wesley.

Shulman, L. S. (1996). Just in case: Reflections on learning from experiences. In J. Colbert, K. Trimble, & P. Desberg (Eds.), *The case for education: Contemporary approaches for using case methods* (pp. 197–217). Boston: Allyn & Bacon.

Silver, E. A., Smith, M. S., & Nelson, B. S. (1995). The QUASAR project: Equity concerns meet mathematics education reform in the middle school. In W. G. Secada, E. Fennema, & L. B. Adajian (Eds.), *New directions in equity in mathematics education* (pp. 9–56). New York: Cambridge University Press.

Silver, E. A., & Stein, M. K. (1996). The QUASAR project: The "revolution of the possible" in mathematics instructional reform in urban middle schools. *Urban Education*, 30, 476–521.

Smith, M. S. (2001). *Practice-based professional development for teachers of mathematics.* Reston, VA: National Council of Teachers of Mathematics.

Smith, M. S., & Boston, M. (2003). Making rabbit pens. In G. W. Bright & D. H. Clements (Eds.), *Classroom activities for learning and teaching measurement* (*2003 Yearbook of the National Council of Teachers of Mathematics*) (pp. 47–49). Reston, VA: National Council of Teachers of Mathematics.

Smith, M. S., & Stein, M. K. (1998). Selecting and creating mathematical tasks: From research to practice. *Mathematics Teaching in the Middle School*, 3, 344–350.

Stein, M. K. (2001). Mathematical argumentation: Putting umph into classroom discussions. *Mathematics Teaching in the Middle School*, 7, 110–112.

Stein, M. K., Grover, B. W., & Henningsen, M. (1996). Building student capacity for mathematical thinking and reasoning: An analysis of mathematical tasks used in reform classrooms. *American Educational Research Journal*, 33, 455–488.

Stein, M. K. & Lane, S. (1996). Instructional tasks and the development of student capacity to think and reason: An analysis of the relationship between teaching and learning in a reform mathematics project. *Educational Research and Evaluation*, 2, 50–80.

Stein, M. K., Smith, M. S., Henningsen, M., & Silver, E. A. (2000). *Implementing standards-based mathematics instruction: A casebook for professional development.* New York: Teachers College Press.

Stern, F. (2000). Choosing problems with entry points for all students. *Mathematics Teaching in the Middle School*, 6, 8–11.

Swafford, J. O., Jones, G. A., & Thornton, C. A. (1997). Increased knowledge in geometry and instructional practice. *Journal for Research in Mathematics Education*, 28, 467–483.

Thompson, C. L., & Zeuli, J. S. (1999). The frame and the tapestry: Standards-based reform and professional development. In L. Darling-Hammond & G. Sykes (Eds.), *Teaching as the learning profession: Handbook of policy and practice* (pp. 341–375). San Francisco: Jossey-Bass.

About the Authors

Margaret Schwan Smith holds a joint appointment at the University of Pittsburgh as an Associate Professor in the Department of Instruction and Learning in the School of Education and as a Research Scientist at the Learning Research and Development Center. She has a doctorate in mathematics education and has taught mathematics at the junior high, high school, and college levels. She currently works with preservice elementary, middle, and high school mathematics teachers enrolled in MAT programs at the University of Pittsburgh, with doctoral students in mathematics education who are interested in becoming teacher educators, and with practicing middle and high school mathematics teachers and coaches in several urban school districts including Pittsburgh. Dr. Smith is the co-author of *Implementing Standards-Based Mathematics Instruction: A Casebook for Professional Development* (Teachers College Press, 2000), which grew out of the work of the QUASAR Project. In addition, she has authored a book entitled *Practice-Based Professional Development for Teachers of Mathematics* (NCTM, 2001), which explores a particular type of professional development that connects the ongoing professional development of teachers to the actual work of teaching. Finally, she is director of two current NSF-funded projects: ASTEROID—which is studying what teachers learn from COMET cases and other practice-based professional development experiences; and ESP—which is focused on enhancing the preparation of secondary mathematics teachers.

Edward A. Silver is Professor of Education and Mathematics at the University of Michigan. Prior to joining the UM faculty in Fall 2000, he held a joint appointment at the University of Pittsburgh as a Professor of Cognitive Studies and Mathematics Education in the School of Education and as a Senior Scientist at the Learning Research and Development Center. In the past he has taught mathematics at the middle school, secondary school, and community college levels in New York, and university undergraduate mathematics and graduate-level mathematics education in Illinois and California. At the University of Michigan, he teaches and advises graduate students in mathematics education, conducts research related to the teaching and learning of mathematics, and engages in a variety of professional service activities. He has published widely in books and journals in several areas, including the study of mathematical thinking, especially mathematical problem-solving and problem-posing; the design and analysis of innovative and equitable mathematics instruction for middle school students, with a special emphasis on encouraging student engagement with challenging tasks that call for mathematical reasoning and problem-solving; effective methods of assessing and reporting mathematics achievement; and the professional development of mathematics teachers. He was director of the QUASAR Project, and he also has led a number of other projects in mathematics education. In addition, he was the leader of the grades 6–8 writing group for the NCTM *Principles and Standards for School Mathematics*, a member of the Mathematical Science Education Board of the National Research Council, and editor of the *Journal for Research in Mathematics Education*.

Mary Kay Stein holds a joint appointment at the University of Pittsburgh as an Associate Professor in the Administrative and Policy Department of the School of Education and as a Research Scientist at the Learning Research and Development Center. She has a Ph.D. in educational psychology from the University of Pittsburgh and has been studying the processes of educational reform for the past 18 years. Her areas of expertise are the study of classroom teaching and the investigation of ways in which educational policy, school organization, and context influence the learning of both adults and students in educational systems. Dr. Stein directed the classroom documentation effort of the QUASAR Project (1989–1996) and co-directed two follow-up, NSF-funded projects that created professional development materials for teachers (COMET, 1998–2001) and studied the impact of those materials on teacher learning (ASTEROID, 2001–2003). Dr. Stein also studies the processes of large-scale instructional improvement in districts, having directed studies of New York City's Community School District No. 2 (1996–2001) and the San Diego City Schools (2000–2003). Currently, she is the principal investigator of an NSF-funded, multiyear study investigating district-wide implementation of elementary mathematics curricula (Scaling Up Mathematics: The Interface of Curricula and Human and Social Capital).

Melissa Boston is a research assistant and doctoral student in mathematics education at the University of Pittsburgh. She has taught mathematics in middle school and high school and holds a masters degree in mathematics from the University of Pittsburgh. She also has taught mathematics methods courses for prospective elementary and secondary teachers and has experience working with practicing middle and high-school mathematics teachers. She served as a research assistant on the COMET Project and is the project manager for the NSF-funded ESP Project, which is focused on the preparation of secondary mathematics teachers. Her areas of interest include teacher learning from cases and effective case facilitation.

Marjorie A. Henningsen is an Assistant Professor of Education at the American University of Beirut, Science and Math Education Center, Beirut, Lebanon. She has a B.A. in mathematics and psychology from Benedictine College, and a masters and doctorate in mathematics education from the University of Pittsburgh. She has been designing and conducting professional development for preservice and inservice elementary and middle school mathematics teachers for over a decade in the United States and throughout the Middle East. She spent over 5 years designing and conducting classroom-based research with the QUASAR Project. Dr. Henningsen is currently the co-director of a nationwide project in Lebanon to study teaching and learning in elementary mathematics classrooms.

Index